A TEXT BOOK OF

CONSTRUCTION MANAGEMENT-I

FOR

SEMESTER – V

T.E. DEGREE COURSE IN CIVIL ENGINEERING

AS PER NEW REVISED SYLLABUS OF
NORTH MAHARASHTRA UNIVERSITY, JALGAON.

(EFFECTIVE FROM JUNE 2014)

Mrs. S. V. PATASKAR
M. E. (Civil)
Assistant Prof, Civil Engg. Deptt.
D. Y. Patil College of Engineering,
Akurdi – Pune, 44

N. S. MUJUMDAR
M.E. (Civil)
Formerly Head of Civil Engineering Department
Government College of Engineering
Aurangabad

Price ₹ : 150.00

N2280

CONSTRUCTION MANAGEMENT-I (TE CIVIL SEM. V – NMU) ISBN 978-93-5164-119-3

Second Edition : July 2015
© : Authors

The text of this publication, or any part thereof, should not be reproduced or transmitted in any form or stored in any computer storage system or device for distribution including photocopy, recording, taping or information retrieval system or reproduced on any disc, tape, perforated media or other information storage device etc., without the written permission of Authors with whom the rights are reserved. Breach of this condition is liable for legal action.

Every effort has been made to avoid errors or omissions in this publication. In spite of this, errors may have crept in. Any mistake, error or discrepancy so noted and shall be brought to our notice shall be taken care of in the next edition. It is notified that neither the publisher nor the authors or seller shall be responsible for any damage or loss of action to any one, of any kind, in any manner, therefrom.

Published By :
NIRALI PRAKASHAN
Abhyudaya Pragati, 1312, Shivaji Nagar,
Off J.M. Road, Pune – 411005
Tel - (020) 25512336/37/39, Fax - (020) 25511379
Email : niralipune@pragationline.com

Printed By :
REPRO INDIA LTD Mumbai

☞ DISTRIBUTION CENTRES

PUNE
Nirali Prakashan : 119, Budhwar Peth, Jogeshwari Mandir Lane, Pune 411002, Maharashtra
Tel : (020) 2445 2044, 66022708, Fax : (020) 2445 1538
Email : bookorder@pragationline.com, niralilocal@pragationline.com

Nirali Prakashan : S. No. 28/27, Dhyari, Near Pari Company, Pune 411041
Tel : (020) 24690204 Fax : (020) 24690316
Email : dhyari@pragationline.com, bookorder@pragationline.com

MUMBAI
Nirali Prakashan : 385, S.V.P. Road, Rasdhara Co-op. Hsg. Society Ltd.,
Girgaum, Mumbai 400004, Maharashtra
Tel : (022) 2385 6339 / 2386 9976, Fax : (022) 2386 9976
Email : niralimumbai@pragationline.com

☞ DISTRIBUTION BRANCHES

JALGAON
Nirali Prakashan : 34, V. V. Golani Market, Navi Peth, Jalgaon 425001,
Maharashtra, Tel : (0257) 222 0395, Mob : 94234 91860

KOLHAPUR
Nirali Prakashan : New Mahadvar Road, Kedar Plaza, 1st Floor Opp. IDBI Bank
Kolhapur 416 012, Maharashtra. Mob : 9850046155

NAGPUR
Pratibha Book Distributors : Above Maratha Mandir, Shop No. 3, First Floor,
Rani Jhanshi Square, Sitabuldi, Nagpur 440012, Maharashtra
Tel : (0712) 254 7129

DELHI
Nirali Prakashan : 4593/21, Basement, Aggarwal Lane 15, Ansari Road, Daryaganj
Near Times of India Building, New Delhi 110002
Mob : 08505972553

BENGALURU
Pragati Book House : House No. 1, Sanjeevappa Lane, Avenue Road Cross,
Opp. Rice Church, Bengaluru – 560002.
Tel : (080) 64513344, 64513355,Mob : 9880582331, 9845021552
Email:bharatsavla@yahoo.com

CHENNAI
Pragati Books : 9/1, Montieth Road, Behind Taas Mahal, Egmore,
Chennai 600008 Tamil Nadu, Tel : (044) 6518 3535,
Mob : 94440 01782 / 98450 21552 / 98805 82331,
Email : bharatsavla@yahoo.com

niralipune@pragationline.com | www.pragationline.com
Also find us on www.facebook.com/niralibooks

PREFACE TO THE SECOND EDITION

We are glad and excited to announce that the First Edition of this book received an overwhelming response from the engineering student community, compelling us to release its Second Edition within a very short period of time.

This thoroughly revised Second Edition has been updated with additional matter, many solved papers, including university examination papers and numerous exercises for practice.

Special care has been taken to maintain high degree of accuracy in the theory and numericals throughout the book.

We take this opportunity to express our sincere thanks to Dineshbhai Furia of Nirali Prakashan, a reputed pioneer in the publication field. Our special thanks to Jignesh Furia for their effective cooperation and great care in bringing out this revised edition. We also appreciate the efforts of M. P. Munde and the entire staff of Engineering Books Deptt. of Nirali Prakashan for bringing this book to the students in a timely manner.

We sincerely hope that this "Second Edition" will also be warmly received by all concerned as in the past.

Valuable suggestions from our esteemed readers to improve the book are most welcome and highly appreciated.

Pune —Authors

PREFACE TO THE FIRST EDITION

It gives us an immense pleasure to present this book on **"Construction Management – I"** to the students of third year Degree Civil Engineering of North Maharashtra University, Jalgaon.

With the tremendous growth of construction sector, more and more manpower is required in all branches of Civil Engineering. Truly speaking, large population is a boon to India and not a curse. But one has to remember that we have to take efforts to mould technicians and engineers according to our requirement. More and more practical expertise should be provided to aspiring engineers so that they can stand in large competitions. Management has become a key word which controls the cost, time and monitors quality. With the uniqueness of construction field, study of **Construction Management** and related techniques are very important to Civil Engineers.

Economics is a branch of science which is very much attached to our day to life. It is a very interesting subject. At the same time, basics of Economics are very important to learn. This will help the students to understand how the money flows, what are the effects of one organisation on other. What is line of balance, construction industry and team, network technique, curve and bar chart, cost analysis.

We have made an effort to include the basics of Construction Management in this single book as per the revised syllabus framed by North Maharashtra, Jalgaon. Our primary aim is to develop and present the subject matter in concise and easily understandable manner to meet the requirements.

We gratefully acknowledge this co-operation from Shri Dineshbhai Furia, Shri Jignesh Furia and Shri M.P. Munde and team, namely Mrs. Neeta Kulkarni, Ms. Sarika Shinde, Ms. Rani Zinjade and Mrs. Sarika Wagh etc.

We are also thankful to Branch Manager, **Mr. P. M. More**, Jalgaon office for his valuable help and efforts for promotion of our book.

Suggestions and constructive criticism so also errors, omissions or misprints, if any brought to the notice of the authors will be thankfully acknowledged and shall be incorporated in the forthcoming editions.

Pune **Authors**

SYLLABUS

Unit I : Basics of Construction Management   (07 Hours, 16 Marks)

Construction industry, construction team, Construction activities, classification of construction, stages in construction, Need of management in construction, Job layout and value engineering. Leadership and its quality, Organization, meaning and function, forms of organization - line, line and staff, functional, Type A, Type B and Type C

Unit II : Network Techniques   (10 Hours, 16 Marks)

Network Technique: - History, Advantages, Bar charts, S –Curve etc. various terms used in network technique, activity, event, critical path, duration etc Development of networks, network scheduling, to find various times and float, EST, EFT, TF etc Monitoring of Network, Three phases of network technique. PERT - its concept and PERT Time.

Unit III : Crashing, Updating, Resource Levelling & Line of Balance
        (08 Hours, 16 Marks)

Cost analysis, Cost Curve, Optimization and crashing of networks. Updating of network During monitoring, resource leveling, allocation, leveling and smoothening. Line of balance- Concept and uses. (no problems on crashing of network)

Unit IV : Engineering Economics and Banking   (07 Hours, 16 Marks)

Engineering economics, its definition and importance, demand and supply, factors affecting demand and supply, cost concept. Bank, its type, uses and functions, banking systems, profit and loss account, appreciation and depreciation of money.

Unit V : Excavating and Hauling Equipments   (07 Hours, 16 Marks)

Excavating & Hauling Equipments:-

(a) Power shovels; size, basic parts, selection ,factors affecting output.

(b) Draglines: - types, size, basic parts.

(c) Bulldozers-types, moving earth with bull dozers.

(d) Clamshells – Clamshell buckets.

CONTENTS

Unit I : Basics of Construction Management	1.1-1.28
Unit II : Network Techniques	2.1-2.70
Unit III : Crashing, Updating, Resource Levelling & Line of Balance	3.1-3.38
Unit IV : Engineering Economics and Banking	4.1-4.50
Unit V : Excavating and Hauling Equipments	5.1-5.12
• **University Question Papers (May 2015)**	P.1-P.1

UNIT I

BASICS OF CONSTRUCTION MANAGEMENT

1.1 CONSTRUCTION INDUSTRY

Since, the dawn of civilisation "Food, shelter and clothing" are the three basic requirements of man-kind. Earlier, the "shelter" was limited only to a structure that protected the humans from sun, wind and rain. Later on, with the help of materials like wood, iron, burnt bricks and the inventions like concrete, man built beautiful homes. As the "world of humans" started expanding, he felt the need of means of communications such as roads, bridges, culverts etc. At the same time, the sanitation systems, water supply systems were also developed which were designed scientifically. This can be studied with the help of Mohen-jodaro and Harappa remains. As the needs further increased, railway lines, tunnels, sky scrapers, dams, large irrigation projects, canals, aeroplanes etc. are now part of the modern world. Construction of such large structures developed a new organised industry and "Construction Management" a new branch was evolved which adopts scientific methods of management principles.

Construction projects involve varying manpower and their duration can range from a few weeks to more than five years. Each one of them is 'unique' and 'temporary' in nature.

1.1.1 Importance of Construction Industry

Construction is an integral part of infrastructure such as houses, offices, schools, hospitals, urban infrastructure, highways, ports, railways, airports, power, irrigation, industrial infrastructure and so on. The importance of construction industry can be highlighted with the help of following facts :

- Cost of construction of certain infrastructure contributes 60-80% of the project cost.
- It is the basic input for socio-economic development.
- It generates employment like skilled and unskilled from urban as well as rural areas.
- Construction industry boosts other industries e.g. building material industry, construction equipment manufacturing, production of steel, paints, cement, chemicals, glass etc.
- Construction industry contributes to GDP of a nation.

1.1.2 Indian Construction Industry

Indian construction industry was accorded industrial concern status under the Industrial Development Bank of India. Now, construction industry is the second largest industry, next to agriculture employing more than 40 million personnel comprising both skilled and unskilled workers. The characteristics of Indian construction industry can be given as :

- The factors that favour Indian construction industry are availability of cheap labour, availability of qualified professionals.
- The factors that are against it are low productivity, low ratio of skilled to unskilled workers, high cost of finance, complicated tax structure, etc.

- Large involvement of small contractors who lack financial and technological back-up reduces the productivity of construction.

Indian construction industry will grow with an accelerated rate in near future. Many projects are coming up and Government is keep in developing those some of the upcoming projects in construction industry are given as under

1. Road Sector
Golden quadrangle project, north-south and east-west corridor development, Pradhan Mantri Gram Sadak Yojana, National Highways Development projects etc.

2. Airports and Sea Ports
Multi-model International cargo hub and airport at Nagpur (MIHAN), Vizhinjam International Seaport, Taj International Airport etc.

3. Dams
Icchampally project, Middle Vaitarana dam, Tipaimukh dam, Kishau dam, Kalpasar dam, Hussainsagar lake and catchments improvement project etc.

4. Industrial and Commercial Projects
India International Trade Center, Shendra-Bidkin Industrial Park, Mumbai-Banagalore Economic Corridor, Gujarat International Finance Tec-City, Vadarevu and Nizampatnam Industrial Corridor (VANPIC) etc.

5. Power Projects
Ultra Mega Power Projects (a series of power projects of more than 1,00,000 MW capacity), super thermal power station etc.

6. Other
India tower GIFT diamond tower, Noida Tower, Unified Settlement Planning (USP) etc.

1.2 CONSTRUCTION TEAM

Construction of any structure is a 'project' with definite beginning and end which involves certain duration. Each construction project involves a number of personnel which comprises as a team. Following section describes the position and role of various team members involved.

1. Architect
Architects are responsible in pre-project and project phases. They are acting on clients behalf. In pre-project phase, they are responsible for preparation of drawings and tender documents and contractor selection. In project phase, they are responsible for checking the measurement, certification of bills and over all project management functions.

2. Client (Owner)
Client is the person or an organisation that gives the specifications and manages the facilities or structure after completion. The client is in a position to judge the use of funds to execute the project and they are at his discretion.

Examples of clients are National or State Governments, public corporations, public enterprises, army, co-operative societies. Stock companies, legal entities and individuals.

3. Contractor

Contractors are profit making firms who completes the project on schedule according to the contract-concluded with the client and in accordance with design drawings and specifications.

Some contractors are big firms that executes large-scale projects involving many subcontractors and some specialised contractors.

Some contractors who are developed for some specialised construction technology and receive subcontracted work. Others are small scale firms who develop by mobilising workers at construction sites for labour intensive construction work.

4. Consultant

Consultants are the engineers who works with the client to conclude the contract. He provides technical services on behalf of the client. Consultant plays an important role as an unbiased arbiter in cases of design alterations, cost and schedule changes, etc. The nature of services offered by the consultants varies from project to project.

However, in general, they are responsible for undertaking project feasibility report, preparation of cost estimate, geotechnical investigation, reviewing and co-ordinating engineering drawings, helping client in bidding process and co-ordinating in execution phase of the project.

5. Subcontractor/Supplier/Vendor

In large projects, very often no single contracting company has adequate expertise and/or resources to be able to undertake all the activities on their own. Under such situation, they employ small contractors for certain specialised items of work, for either execution purpose or material procurement purpose or both. These are referred to as subcontractors or vendors and are a very important party in any construction project.

6. Lawyer, Insurer etc.

In many countries, lawyers are part and parcel of a construction project. Lawyers specialised in claims settlements and disputes play an important role in domestic projects undertaken in India as well as international projects.

Some of the construction companies in India do have a separate legal cell comprising lawyers and insurers specialising in construction disputes and claim settlements.

1.3 CLASSIFICATION OF CONSTRUCTION PROJECTS

As per the new industrial policy resolution 1956, the Government has accepted the policy of socialistic pattern of society and accordingly industries were divided into following categories.

Schedule A : These were industries which were to be exclusively under the control and regulation of the Government. Some of them are
1. Arms and Ammunition
2. Atomic Energy
3. Iron and Steel
4. Heavy Machine and Plant
5. Heavy Electrical Plant
6. Minerals
7. Railways and Roads
8. Aircraft and Air Transport
9. Mineral Oils
10. Post and Telegraph
11. Irrigation

Schedule B : These were industries on which there would be Government Control and were to be progressively owned by Government, some of them are
1. Fertilizer
2. Automobiles
3. Synthetic rubber
4. Road and Water Transport
5. Ferrow alloys.

State had more prominent role in the setting up and running of these industries which had to be run on business lines. Rest of the industries were open for private sector.

However, with the industrial revolution and with the pressure from the world community and institutions like World Bank supporting the different state and other project, there has been a revolutionary change in the Government Policy and many fields of industries which were run by the Government have been opened to private sector. In general, the various forms of ownerships are given below
1. Individual Ownership
2. Partnership Firms
3. Joint Stock Companies
4. Co-operative Industries and Enterprises
5. State Ownership Enterprises

The different forms of owner are further subdivided as below

Partnership Firms
  (a) **General Partnership :** Useful for small engineering firms and retail traders.
  (b) **Limited Partnership :** Liability is limited to the extent of investment.

Joint Stock Companies
  They are divided into classes as below
  (a) **Private Limited Joint Stock Company :** Limited to Two to Fifty members.
  (b) **Public Limited Joint Stock Company :** Membership is open to general public.

Co-operative Organisations : Normally, these organisations are such which provide financial assistance to the members. Normally, they are not industrial production organisation. The different types may be as given below

1. Credit Co-operative Societies,
2. Hiring Co-operative Societies,
3. Consumers Co-operative Societies,
4. Marketing Co-operative Societies,
5. Producers' Co-operative Societies,
6. Co-operative Farming Societies etc.

State Enterprises : State Enterprises may be of the following types

1. **Government Departments :** They have exclusive Government monopoly e.g. Railways, Defence production, Building and Communication Department, Irrigation and Power etc.
2. **Public Corporation :** They are created by an appropriate law in the Parliament
   (a) Indian Airlines Corporation
   (b) Damodar Valley Corporation
   (c) Life Insurance Corporation etc.
3. **Government Companies :** These are the companies setup by the Government and have to be run like a business organisation as
   (a) Bharat Heavy Electricals
   (b) Hindustan Machine Tools

In private ownership industries, they can be divided into two main categories. They are

1. Small Scale and Cottage Industries.
2. General Industries or Large Scale Industries which do not come under small scale industries.

This division is based upon the total investment on machines, plant and equipment. If the total investment does not exceed ₹ 20 lakhs irrespective of the number of workers engaged, then the industry could be termed as a Small Scale Industry.

The limit of investment may exceed upto ₹ 25 lakhs in case of an *ancillary units*. Similarly units with investment upto ₹ 5 lakh are called *tiny units*.

Such units enjoy greater concessions. A cottage industry is one which is carried out at the residence of ten workers and is run without the use of hired labour where only the family members work in it. There are no medium size industries defined in Industrial Development and Regulation Act.

Any industry having investment more than ₹ 25 lakhs excluding ancillaries is termed as large scale unit. The Small Scale Industries enjoy different concessions as compared to large scale units. Cottage and Small Scale Industries are very important for our country where there is problem of excess population, general unemployment, seasonal unemployment, disguised unemployment and under-employment.

From this view point the State Governments have given different concessions to industries and projects under small scale industries and such small scale industries are running efficiently in different parts of the country.

1.4 STAGES IN CONSTRUCTION PROJECT

The different steps in any construction project can be summarized as below

1. **Identification Stage**

Identification of product which can satisfy the consumers' requirements and also the manufacturers' requirements. The idea of launching a new product should be well conceived.

2. **Pre-selection Stage**

   (a) **Preliminary Investigation and thorough Study :** Clear and definite shape has to be given to conceived idea. The practicability of the product has to be tested, working model may be framed.

   (b) **Market Survey :** It is very necessary that before the project is launched, a market survey has to be carried out to ascertain the demand for the product. This could be judged in the beginning by introducing the product on small scale and finding out the results about the demand. Possibility of prevailing competition should be given due consideration.

   (c) **Clarity About the Objective :** This should be very clear. The ultimate aim is to sell the goods which are manufactured and to earn the profit.

   Estimation of profit, investment and cost of operation, outline of manufacturing process, description of the project and the probable risk and any other problems arising should be given due consideration in pre-selection stage.

3. **Feasibility Report**

   Thorough analysis has to be made about the proposed project and a feasibility report has to be prepared. This is a self-contained project scheme prepared on the basis of the

   (a) Market analysis
   (b) Technical analysis
   (c) Financial analysis including Break Even Analysis
   (d) Social profitability analysis.

4. **Administrative Work**

This includes obtaining permission from the Government and other authorities regarding starting of the project. A self-contained project report will have to be submitted to the different authorities for the same and after completing the different formalities, permission may be obtained for starting of the new venture.

5. **Production Planning**

   This step will consist of the following

   (a) Product Planning and Process Planning

(b) Plant Layout
(c) Material Management which includes Purchase and Stores Management
(d) Production Planning and Control
(e) Inspection and Quality Control
(f) Marketing
(g) Evaluation of Financial Analysis.

Flow chart of a Simple Production System is given in Fig. 1.1.

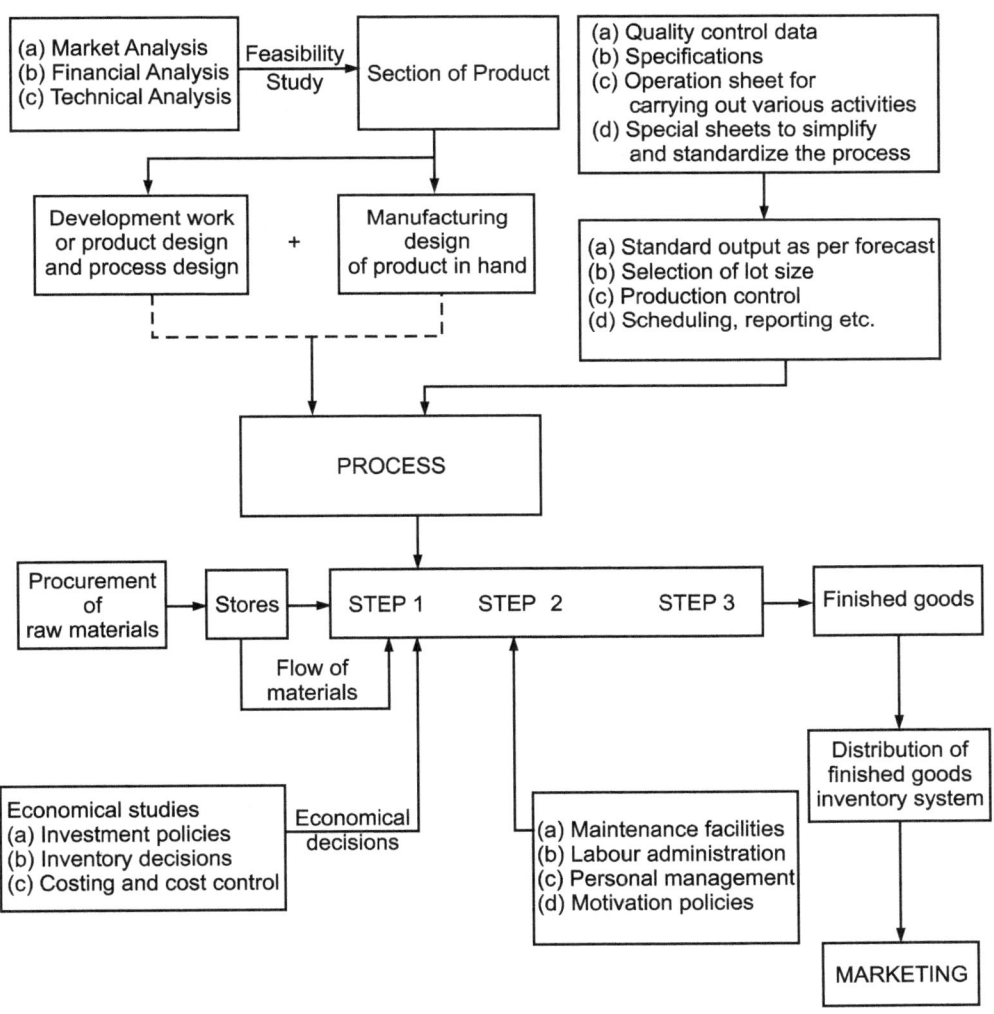

Fig. 1.1 : Flow Chart of a Simple Production System

1.4.1 Project Life Cycle

A project is bounded by various phases from project conception through project execution to project completion.

These phases differ from project to project. Broadly, the phases can be given as project planning, project scheduling and project controlling. Planning and scheduling take place before commencement of the project while controlling is a continuous process after the project starts.

The project life cycle is represented as a line graph with the level of effort (usually measured in manhours) plotted against time. The typical life cycle profile shows the level of effort starting from a low base, building up slowly to a peak, then declining to completion and termination. Following is the project life cycle of a housing project.

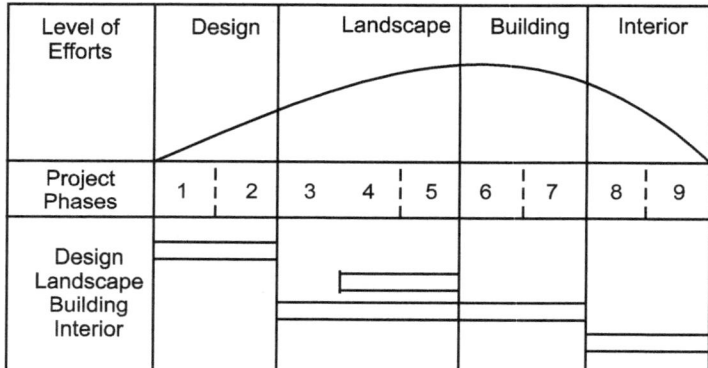

Fig. 1.2 : Project Life Cycle

The housing project is subdivided into four phases as Design, Landscape, Building and Interior. As shown in the above Fig. the level of efforts is maximum in building phase before declining during interior phase.

It is overlapping to some extent with landscape phase. Design phase is slowly gaining momentum as it is the initial phase.

In the above method, we have considered the planned progress of the project. When the project starts, the planned progress can be compared with the actual progress estimating the project slippage (or additional duration required).

The planned life cycle curve can be plotted by taking time on x-axis and percentage progress on y-axis.

While constraints and sequence remain the same, time duration changes depending upon the quantity of work. At point t, the percentage progress is compared with the planned (thick line). Depending upon the amount of work remaining, projected completion of work is calculated. The slippage is found out (e.g. 2 months) as shown in Fig. 1.3.

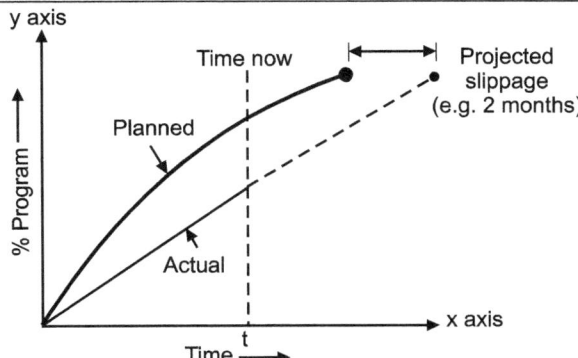

Fig. 1.3 : Planned and Actual Life Cycle Curve

1.4.2 Advantages of Project Life Cycle

1. This curve is used for progress review and control the slippage.
2. On this curve, the project performance is shown very clearly and in a very simple manner.

Following is the Project Life Cycle (PLC) for different parameters on site.

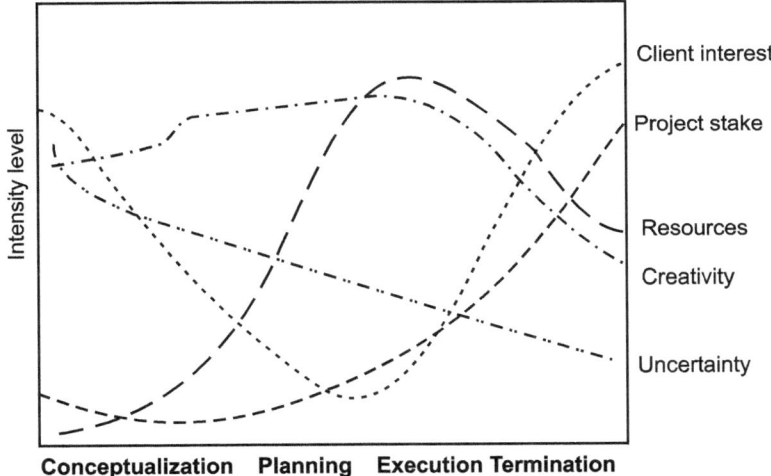

Fig. 1.4 : Project Life Cycle Depending upon Various Parameters

Project Life Cycle for Resources is discussed earlier. From client's point of view, he is keen at the conceptualization and termination stage. He is least bothered about how the execution is taking place. Project stake goes on increasing as the project approaches completion. The creativity is required at conceptualization, planning and execution stage for minimizing the cost, maximizing quality and benefits. Least creativity is required at termination stage. In the initial phases of project, uncertainty level is high from duration, expenses and resources point of view. In the termination stage, as activities are also less, the uncertainty is very low.

1.5 NEED OF MANAGEMENT IN CONSTRUCTION

If the construction products such as buildings, roads, dams etc. are compared with the products of other industries, it can be seen that productivity of construction industry is low but the products have very long life and very high cost. To elaborate this, let us take an example of construction of a residential building with 25 flats which will be constructed within one year. Hence, the rate of production becomes 25 flats every year. The cost of each flat will vary depending upon the area and the amenities provided. On an average, let us consider the cost per flat as Rs. 50 lacs. The life of the building is long and varies from 30 years to more than 50 years. All the management techniques can be applied to construction projects if we see them from this perspective. Hence, management in construction industry is very important to make it as an organised sector aiming to improve its productivity and contributing more and more in National Development.

We will study the basics of management and its principles in the following sections

1.5.1 Management

Management in reality is both art as well as science. It is oldest of Art because it was practiced even in the olden days and it is as old as human civilization and human history. Management is youngest of science as it is still under the stage of development. As the environment of business becomes more dynamic, competition increases, business grows in size, area and volume and the science of management will also change in leaps and bounds. The art of management and the science of management are complementary to each other. Management was developed as a practical art but importance of science of management has increased only recently. Science of management is well developed though not as perfect as physics or chemistry because science of management deals with human beings. Thus, it is a social science and it inexact and suffers from certain limitations.

Management : As an Art

Management is an oldest art. The success of management lies in application of its principles and technologies to various aspects and problem in organisation. The basic definition of management proves it by saying that "Management is an Art of getting things done from others".

In an organisation the goals and objectives are to be achieved and for that the manager has to decide the task, plan the future, analyze the situation, co-ordinate resources, control and evaluate the functions. All this needs the fine art of management which comes only after practice and being in constant touch with the situation. Knowledge acquired by the manager is not sufficient but how the art of management is applied by the manager is more important. Thus, it is an art where manager uses all his skill to get result, just like a painter or musician or a sportsman who try to achieve their goals.

Management : As a Science

Management as a science was recognized only in the later part of nineteenth century but since then the progress and advancement has been rapid in this area.

Management is a science because the subject of management has become well organized and a systematic body of knowledge just any other subject of physical science. It can be learnt and taught in well organized manner.

Just like any other subject of science, management also has certain principles which are developed over a period of time through observation and experiments. Physical Science has universal application. Similarly, subject of management has universal applications. They are not restricted or partial for a particular country or organisation. The subject of management has capacity to produce same results irrespective of the development of the country or organisation.

Management : As a Profession

Management satisfies many of the conditions of profession. Management has a well defined body of knowledge. There are many management education bodies who undertake the responsibility to educate young graduates to enable them to take up management as a profession or career. In the modern business world, there has been a great demand for the professional managers.

1.5.2 Importance of Management

Principles of management are been followed by all individuals in very activity. Let him be a simple layman or a CEO. The only difference is "scale of management" which varies for different post. Management is important to every individual and it can be stated as

- Truly speaking, no enterprise can survive without management, even if it possesses huge money, excellent machinery and expert man-power, because without management, it will be all confusion and no body will know what to do and when to do.
- Management which guides and controls the activities of man-power for the optimum utilization of company resources, such that Five M's (Men, Material, Money Machines, Methods).
- Management creates a vital, dynamic and life giving force to the enterprise.
- Management co-ordinates activities of different departments in an enterprise and establishes team-spirit among the persons.
- Management provides new ideas and vision to the organisation to do better.
- Management tackles business problems and provides a tool for the best way of doing things.
- Management only can meet the challenge of change.
- Management provides stability to the enterprise by changing and modifying the resource in accordance with the changing environment of the society.
- Last but not the least, Management helps in saving time and money through proper planning, co-ordinating and forecasting.

1.5.3 Characteristics of Management

Main characteristics of management can be stated as
- Management is goal oriented. It achieves the organisational goals through co-ordination of the efforts of the personnel.
- Management works as catalyst to produce good using labour, materials and capital.
- Management is a distinct process comprising of functions such as planning, organising, staffing, directing and controlling.
- Management represents a system of authority a hierarchy of command and control. Managers at different levels possess varying degrees of authority.
- Management is a unifying force. It integrates human and other resources to achieve the desired objective.
- Management harmonizes the individual's goals with the organisational goals to minimize conflicts in the organisation.
- Management is a multi-disciplinary subject.
- Management is universal in character. The principal and techniques of management are equally applicable in all engineering fields.

1.5.4 Functions of Management

Management has following important functions
1. Forecasting
2. Planning
3. Staffing
4. Organising
5. Directing
6. Co-ordinating
7. Controlling
8. Decision making

1. Forecasting : Forecasting is necessarily preliminary to planning at every state. Forecasting estimates the future scope of work. Forecasting begins with cost of project, finance available, method of payment, profit, rate of interest, government subsidy, environmental concern and future hurdles. Many manufacturing firms produce their material in advance to meet the future demand.

Following are the Important Advantages of Forecasting
- Overproduction and short supply of raw material can be avoided if there is proper production policy.
- Accurate forecasting can reduce the cost of production.
- It gives proper control over inventory.
- It sets the sales target.

- It gives clear idea for future financial requirements in advance.
- It gives an idea about expansion of existing unit.
- It helps to plan the long-term financial requirement and policies.

2. Planning : It is probably the most important function of management. A very extensive and rigorous planning helps us to complete the activities within given time and cost. It is a process by which a manager anticipates the future and discovers alternative courses of action open to him. Planning is a rational, economical, systematic way of making decisions today, which will affect the future. Without proper planning, the activities of enterprises may become confused, haphazard and infective. Prior planning is very essential for utilizing the available facilities (men, material, money, machines and methods etc.) to the best of advantages. Now-a-day's computer and software based on CPM and PERT such as MS- Project and Primavera is used for planning of construction project.

The main functions of the management are to plan and to take correct decisions. This important activity covers the following sub-activities

- To determine the Company's objectives.
- To formulate correct polices.
- To prepare cost and performance standards and includes them in the company's budget.
- To prepare short-range plans and to measure the achievements of the company.

3. Organising : Organising is the process by which the structure and allocation of jobs is determined. Organising involves calculating activities, its grouping, organising people, materials, jobs, time etc. and establishing a framework in which responsibilities are defined and authorities are laid down. There are two types of organisations viz,

- Formal organisation
- Informal organisation

4. Staffing : It is the process by which managers select, train, promote and retire their subordinates. Staffing is a continuous process. It involves the developing and placing of qualified people in the various jobs in the organisation, training of employees and appraising the personnel as per their skills.

5. Directing : It is the process by which actual performance of subordinates is guided towards common goals of the company. Directing involves following function such as

- Leadership
- Communication
- Motivation
- Supervision

(a) Leadership : Leadership is the quality of behaviour of a person, where by they inspire confidence and trust in their subordinates, get maximum co-operation from them and guide their activities in organized effort. Leadership is more important than personal ability and skill.

(b) Communication : Communication is a process by which ideas are transmitted, received and understood by others for the purpose of effecting desired result. Verbal, written order, reports, instruction, slides are the various types of Communication.

(c) Motivation : Motivation means inspiring the subordinates to the work or to achieve company objectives effectively and efficiently.

(d) Supervision : Supervision is an important function of directing which measures whether the work is going on in proper sequence, quantity and quality.

6. Co-ordinating : Co-ordinating means achieving harmony of individual effort towards the accomplishment of company objective. Co-ordination involves making plans that co-ordinate the activities of subordinates, regulate their activities on the job and regulate their communications.

7. Controlling : It is the process which measure current performance and guide it towards some predetermined goal. Controlling is necessary to ensure that orders are not misunderstood, rules are not violated and objectives have not been unknowingly shifted. It also means control of person and other things such as time, quality, speed and project cost etc. It is a continue process which measures the progress of operation.

8. Decision Making : Decision making is the process by which a course of action is consciously chosen from available alternatives for the purpose of achieving desired result. An outstanding quality of a successful manager is his ability to make sound and logical decisions. Following are important decisions, which the manager of an organisation is supposed to take.

- Marketing decision
- Cost price decision
- Capital investment decisions

1.5.5 Managerial Objectives

Managerial Objectives

Managerial objectives may be defined as 'the intended goals which prescribe scope and suggest direction to the efforts of a manager'.

Management objectives should be,
- Clearly defined and communicated,
- Reasonably attainable,
- Based upon the overall organisational goals,
- Containment of expenditure within budget and time.

Managerial objective may be classified as
- General objectives
- Specific objectives

General Objectives
General objectives contains following terms
- Nature of project
- Continuous supply of capital
- Growth of company
- Increase in work
- Economic objective such as profit, Low cost production
- Environmental objective
- Social objective
- Human objective
- Time scale

Specific Objectives
Specific objectives contains following terms :
- Nature of work to be done.
- Types of project to be selected.
- Market standing (local, national, international).
- Product and service diversification if any.

1.6 VALUE ENGINEERING

Value engineering in construction can be defined as an organised effort directed at analysing the designed features, systems, equipment and material selections for the purpose of achieving essential functions at the lowest life cycle cost consistent with required performance, quality, reliability and safety. Value engineering is concerned with maximising value, seeking optimum solutions by removing unnecessary waste and reducing life cycle cost while improving function, quality and sustainability.

Value engineering was developed in second world war by Lawrence Miles as an outcome of the necessity to obtain a replacement material which can perform the same function in case a particular material is unavailable, later on, in 20th century, 'Value Engineering' was applied by many countries.

1.6.1 Aims of Value Engineering

- To solve problems, identify and eliminate unwanted costs while improving the functions and quality.
- To increase value of products.
- Satisfying the products performance at lowest possible cost.
- To reduce life cycle cost.
- To reduce environmental impact.

Value engineering should start at project inception where the benefits can be greatest.

It is also to be remembered that contributions from contractors are also to be welcome as long as the changes required do not affect duration or incur additional costs.

1.6.2 Value Engineering Process

Thus value engineering process involves
- Identifying the main elements of a products, service or project.
- Analyzing the functions of those elements.
- Developing alternative solutions for delivering those functions.
- Assessing the alternative solutions.
- Allocating costs to the alternative solutions.
- Developing in more detail, the alternatives with the highest likelihood of success.

Value engineering process can also achieved by the use of tools called as "Result Accelerators" as below
- Avoiding generalities.
- Getting all available casts.
- Using information from the best source.
- Increasing creativeness and refining the requirements.
- Identifying and overcoming road blocks.
- Using guidance from industry experts.
- Using price key tolerances.
- Using standard products.
- Using specialists processes.

The project manager must take a pro-active role in both giving direction and leadership in the value engineering process, but must also ensure that time and effort is not wasted and does not have a detrimental effect on the program of the project.

1.6.3 Value Techniques

Commonly used value techniques are as under
- **Value Management (VM) :** Which involves all value techniques adopted for any part of project stage.
- **Value Planning (VP) :** Which involves the techniques applied during the planning phases of a project.
- **Value Engineering :** Which involves techniques applied during the design or engineering phases of a project.
- **Value Analysis :** Which involves technique applied to analyse or audit the projects performance.

1.6.4 Value Engineering and Sustainability

Value engineering is concerned with maximising value, not just reducing costs, it seeks optimum solutions to remove unnecessary waste and reduce life cycle costs while improving functions, quality and sustainability.

The sustainability aspect is achieved by addressing the following issues :
- **Material Sustainability Impact :** To use sustainable materials in the whole life cycle to give lesses carbon footprint.
- **Circular Economy Approaches :** To design economically even at deconstruction, disassembly and demolition stages.
- **Low Carbon Solution :** To plan for off site assembly and production if possible.
- Social Impact : e.g. safety, wellness, local, transport and community impact.
- **Shared Economy Approaches :** To share resources, labour, suppliers and deliveries.
- **Linked to Building Information Model (BIM) :** Development to ensure optimum solutions within the BIM model.

1.7 LEADERSHIP

Many of us understand that a "Leader" is somebody whom people follow or somebody who guides or directs others. In simple terms, leader is one who possess leadership qualities and hence more emphasis should be given on "leadership". It can be described as "a process of social influence in which one person can enlist the aid and support of others in the accomplishment of common task."

The British dictionary definition of leadership says, "the position or function of a leader" and "the ability to lead."

Leadership can also be seen as a technique to influence a group of people towards a specific result. As it is mentioned before, leadership is a technique to accomplish the common tasks. The leadership styles differs from person to person. It is to be remembered that all these styles are to be used depending upon the demand of situation.

1.7.1 Qualities of a Leader

Following are the qualities of a successful leader.
- Successful leaders are one who possesses technical competence not only in his specialized field, but to certain extend competence in order related fields.
- A successful leader must have open mindedness while dealing with the subordinates.
- A leader should be able to think rationally and reasonably.
- A leader must be able to express his thoughts and feelings very clearly.
- A leader must always think broadly and in the interest of the group.
- A leader must possess morality and integrity of high order.
- A leader must be emotionally stable.
- He should possess skill in maintaining human relationship and should have insight in human motivation.
- A leader should have good leadership qualities.
- He must be able to influence his team members.
- He must fulfill the aims and targets of the group he works for.

1.7.2 Leadership Styles

A brief description of these styles are given as under

(1) **Autocratic or Authoritarian**
   - In this style, all decisions are taken by the leader which others obeys.
   - This style gives successful results if the leader has strong motivation towards betterment of the group.
   - This is a quick decision-making style as only one person (leader) is involved.

(2) **Participative or Democratic**
   - This leadership style encourages the leader to share the decision making skills with group members by practicing social equality.
   - Though it take more time for decision making, it can lead to progress of all, being participative in nature.
   - This is also called as "shared leadership."

(3) **Laissez-faire or free rain**
   - In this type of leadership style, leader motivates his subordinates to decide their own policies and methods. A free hand is given to them to keep them creative and innovative.

(4) **Task oriented and relationship oriented**
   - Task oriented leadership focuses more on a certain goal or task while relationship oriented leadership focuses more on relationships among the group.
   - Hence task oriented leaders are less concerned about the well being of group members at the time of achieving the goals. On the other hand, relationship oriented leaders and are focussed on developing the team and relationships which may sometimes affect the productivity.

1.8 ORGANISATION

An organisation is a group of person working together to achieve an establishment goal. It is the relationship which exists between people taking part in a group activity. It defines the responsibilities and authority of individuals in relation to men, materials, money and machinery which constitute the resources of an organisation.

An organisation is needed because a manager at any level can effectively manage the functions of only a limited number of persons working directly under him. The setting up of suitable organisation for various civil engineering works is all the more necessary because the construction industry is a competitive field of endeavors which is susceptible to many risks, variable labour conditions and diverse construction problem. The importance of organisation is given below.

1.8.1 Importance of Organisation

- Sound Organisation can contribute greatly to the continuity and success of the enterprise.
- **Facilitates Administration :** A properly designed and balanced organisation facilitates both management and operation of the enterprise; inadequate organisation may not only discourage but actually preclude effective administration.
- **Facilitates Growth and Diversification :** Sound organisation permits organisational elaboration.
- The organisation structure can profoundly affect the people of the enterprise. Proper organisation facilitates the effective use of the manpower.
- **Optimum Use of Resource :** Sound organisation structure permits use of technical and human resources. The organisation can introduce latest technological improvement.
- **Stimulates Creativity :** Sound organisation stimulates independent, creative thinking and initiative by providing well defined areas of work with broad latitude of the development of new and improved ways of doing things.
- A sound organisation leads to specialization.
- A sound organisation minimizes corruption and inefficiencies.
- A sound organisation does not generate confusion
- A sound organisation decrease wastages and expenditure.
- A sound organisation facilitates the training and managerial development of personnel.

1.8.2 Characteristics of Organisation

The Characteristics or essential features of an organisation are given below
- Organisation is a group of people, small or large.
- The group works under an executive leadership.
- Organisation is a tool of management.
- It leads to division of work and responsibilities.
- Organisation defines and fixes the duties and responsibilities of employees.
- Organisation is a step towards the achievement of established goals.
- It establishes a relationship between authority and responsibility and controls the effort of the group.

1.8.3 Principles of Organisation

Common principles of organisation are given below
- Considerable of objective.
- Relationship of basic components of the organisation.
- Principle Balance between responsibility and authority.

- Span of control.
- Dividing and grouping work.
- Effective delegation.
- Principle of Communication.
- Line and staff relationship.
- Balance, stability and flexibility.

1. **Considerable of Objective :** The objectives of the enterprise have an important bearing on the organisation structure, only those objectives should be taken up and accomplished for which there is real need in the organisation such as action may be taken to increase speed, production, quality, profit etc.

2. **Relationship of Basic Components of the Organisation :** Objective as decide above determines the work to be performed and the type of work dictates the selection of personal and physical facilities.

3. **Responsibility and Authority :** Responsibility means accountability. It may be considered as the obligation of a subordinate to his boss to do a work given to him. *Authority* means right and power to act.
   The responsibilities and authority should go hand in hand. One without other leads to demotivation and chaos.

4. **Span of Control :** *Span of control* or span of management refers to the number of subordinates that report to an executive or the number of subordinates that an executive can supervise directly.

5. **Dividing and Grouping Work**
   Dividing : Divisionalisation provides a broader perspective, a greater sense of responsibility on the part of the personnel and more clear-cut control over profits.
   Grouping : The process of grouping is essential for specialization and co-ordination.

6. **Effective Delegation :** Effective delegation is said to be existing when an executive instead of doing all the thinking for the unit himself, passes down to his subordinates any task on which they can take decisions themselves and perform it efficiently and effectively.

7. **Communication :** Communication means transmitting instructions and information within the organisation and to all those are affected Communication serves as a linking process by which parts of an organisation are tied together. Good Communication is essential if all employees are to know what to do in order to achieve the goals of the organisation.

8. **Line and Staff function :** All the activities of an organisation are divided in to two groups (i) Line function (ii) Staff function.
   - Line functions are those which contribute directly and vitally to the objectives of an organisation.
   - Staff functions are those that aid the line or are auxiliary to line functions.

9. **Balance, Stability and Flexibility :** All the units of organisation should be balanced. Also organisational stability refers to the capacity to withstand the losses of key personnel without serious loss to the effectiveness of the organisation in performing its work.

1.8.4 Authority

Authority

Different people interpret authority in different ways. In the legal sense, authority means the right of the person to take an action.

The following are the types of Authority

1. **Technical Authority :** It means recognition of person's opinion in certain specialized field.
2. **Ultimate Authority :** It deals with the original source from which the person derives the right to take certain action.
3. **Administrative Authority :** It means the right to act the company in the specified areas. Administrator should be clear as to what rights are associated with the task that is to be delegated.
4. **Operational Authority :** It is the permission given to the subordinates to do certain jobs.
    - Authority means right and power to act.
    - Authority is the right to make decisions direct the work of others and gives orders. It is a right to direct, act and control.
    - The authority is the rightful legal power to request subordinates to do a certain thing or to refrain from doing that, and if he does not follow these instructions the manager is in a position, if needed, to take disciplinary action, even to discharge the subordinate. Without authority, only anarchy and chaos would result.
5. **Rational – Legal Authority :** The authority which is defined legally.
6. **Traditional Authority :** It is the authority which comes through traditions. People are emotionally attached to this authority.
7. **Charismatic Authority :** This is the authority due to influence of some leaders on the public.
    - Authority is given by the Institution and is therefore, legal or legitimate.
    - Authority is not endless or unlimited.
    - Authority should invariably be in writing, through in small organisations, it may be verbal.
    - Authority must be commensurate with responsibility.
    - Authority may be centralized or de-centralized.
    - Authority is given to the position and not to the position holder.

1.8.5 Delegation of Authority

- Delegation may be defined as 'the entrustment of responsibility and authority to another and the creation of accountability for performance'.
- Delegation may be defined as 'dividing his load and sharing his responsibilities with others'.
- Delegation of Authority merely means 'the granting of authority to subordinates to accomplish a particular assignment while operating within prescribed limits and standards established'.

Delegation is important because it is both the gauge and the means of a manager's accomplishment. Once a man's job grows beyond his personal capacity, his success lies in his ability to multiply himself through other people.

The Essential Element of Delegation

- Assignment of work to another for performance.
- Grant of authority to be exercised.
- Creation of an obligation or accountability on the part of the person accepting the delegation to perform in terms of the standards established.

Principles of Delegation of Authority

- Parity between authority and responsibility.
- Responsibility in terms of results.
- Principle of Unity of Command.
- Delegation of responsibility.
- Overlapping of responsibilities.
- Free flow of information.
- Delegated authority.

Problems of Delegation of Authority

Problem in Delegation of Authority is classified under the following heads.

1. **On the part of management / executive**
   - (a) Felling of perfection.
   - (b) Lack of ability to direction.
   - (c) Lack of confidence in subordinate.
   - (d) Fear of being exposed.
   - (e) Absence of controls.
   - (f) Conservative attitude.
   - (g) Desire of dominance.

2. **On the part of the subordinate**
   - (a) Dependence on boss.
   - (b) Fear of criticism.
   - (c) Lack of self-confidence.

(d) Overburdened with work.
(e) Lack of proper facilities.
(f) Lack of incentives.

3. **On the part of the organisation**
   The process of delegation of authority may suffer due to some internal organisational problems such as
   (a) Defective organisation structure and non-clarity of authority-responsibility relationships.
   (b) Defective and inadequate planning and policy formulation.
   (c) Lack of unity of command.
   (d) Lack of effective control mechanism in the organisation.

1.9 TYPES OF ORGANISATION

The structure of one industrial organisation differs from that of another organisation and it depends upon following.
- Size of the organisation,
- Nature of the product being manufactured,
- Complexity of the problems being faced

Common Types of Organisation
- Line, Military or Scalar Organisation
- Functional Organisation
- Line and Staff Organisation

(a) **Line, Military or Scalar Organisation :** It was called military organisation because it resembled to old military organisation. It is the simplest form of organisation structure. Line organisation is based upon authority and responsibility rather than on the nature and kind of operation or activities. Line organisation is direct and people at different levels know to whom they are accountable.

This type of organisational structure is followed in most government departments and autonomous engineering organisations. (Structure is given above).

Advantages of Line, Military or Scalar Organisation
- It is simplest and easy to understand.
- It makes clear division of authority.
- It encourage speedy action.
- It is flexible, easy to expand and contract.
- It fixes responsibility on an individual therefore it is strong in discipline.
- It is capable of developing the all round executive at the higher levels of authority.

Disadvantages of Line, Military or Scalar Organisation
- Speculation is not considered in this type of organisation.
- It overloads a few key executives.
- It is limited to very small concerns.

- It encourages dictatorial way of working.
- For controlling work high supervision is required.

Application of Line, Military or Scalar Organisation
- All types of small firm.
- Automatic and continuous process industries such as construction company, sugar factory, paper mill etc.

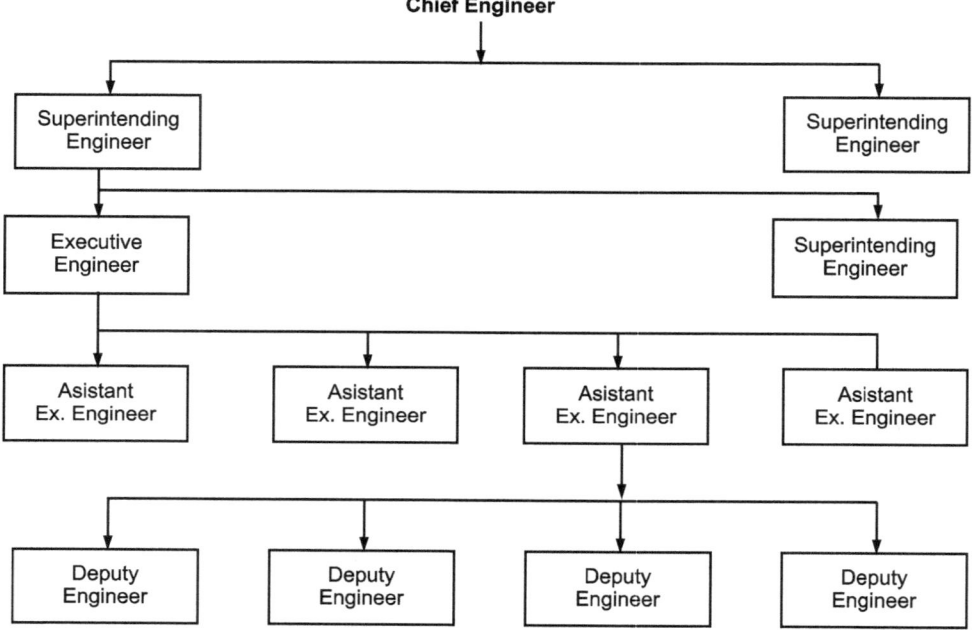

Fig. 1.5 : Line, Military or Scalar Organisation

(b) Functional Organisation : F.W. Taylor suggested functional organisation because it was difficult to find all round person qualified to work at middle management levels in the line organisation. The basic functional organisation is specialization. In such an organisation, work is carried out on a functional basis and each functional is carried out by a specialist. According to Taylor the ideal situation in such an organisation would be when each person performs a specified function only. This removes the staff personnel from his assisting capacity and gives him authority and responsibility for supervision and administration. The idea behind this type of organisation is to divide the work in such a manner that each person has to perform a minimum number of functions and is fully responsible for those aspects of work.

All similar and related work is grouped under one person. In order to perform his function effectively, a person has to report to several superiors for different phases or aspects of the work. Thus, a subordinate anywhere in the organisation will be commanded directly by a number of superiors, each with authority in his own field.

Advantages of Functional Organisation
- In Functional Organisation one person or department is responsible for one function therefore he / they can perform his their duties in a better manner.
- Functional Organisation makes use of specialists to give expert advice to worke₹
- Functional Organisation relives line executives of routine, specialized decisions.
- It reduces wastages, time and increase profit.
- By using Functional Organisation quality of work is improved.

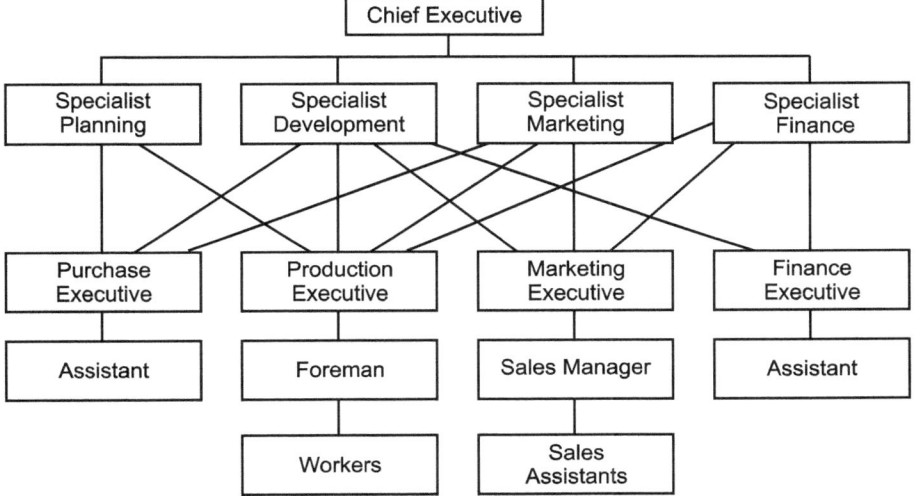

Fig. 1.6 : Structure of Functional Organisation

Disadvantages of Functional Organisation
- Co-ordination of the efforts of various functions is difficult.
- Discipline is difficult to maintain by using this type of organisation.
- Fixing of responsibility is very difficult in case something goes wrong.
- Workers are not given opportunity to make use of their ingenuity, initiative and drive.
- All round executives cannot be developed.
- In functional organisation maintain an industrial relationship is more complex.

Application of Functional Organisation

Due to large disadvantages it is not used in construction industry but modified form is used in same most modern and advanced concerns.

(c) **Line and Function Organisation :** Line organisation is unsuitable for large and complex projects, where the key men need to be assisted by specialists in different fields. The individuals who constitute the staff in an organisation are experts, who have no line authority but whose function is largely advisory. This type of organisation comes into existence because line authority cannot assume direct responsibilities for all functions such as research, design, planning, scheduling and recording of performance etc. All these activities are performed by functional staff, while the line authority maintains discipline and stability in an organisation. The authority by which the staff performs its advisory functions is delegated by the 'line' and their advice is generally accepted keeping in view their experience and expertise.

Advantages of Line and Functional Organisation

- Staff executive take advices of experts.
- Less wastages of material, money and man power.
- There is no confusion as exist in functional organisation.
- Quality of work is improved.
- More attention is given on work.

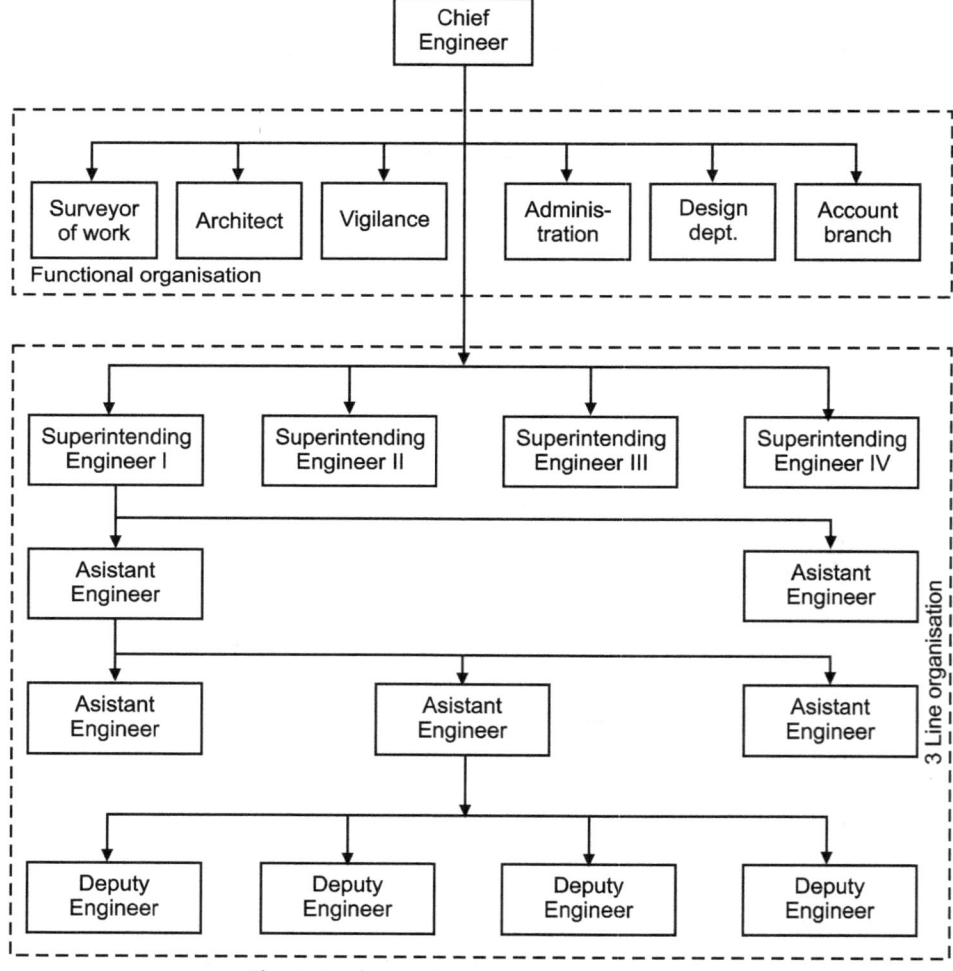

Fig. 1.7 : Line and Functional Organisation

Disadvantages of Line and Staff Organisation

- Product/consultancy cost will increase because of high salaries of functional staff executives.
- Line and functional organisation may get confusion in case functions are not clear.
- In this type of organisation staff may lose their initiative, drive and ingenuity.

Application of Line and Staff Organisation

Line and functional organisation is very common among the medium and large company/ consultancy/ project.

QUESTIONS

1. State the importance of construction industry.
2. Describe the construction team and importance of each member in it.
3. What are the different types of construction ?
4. Explain various stages in a project life cycle.
5. State the importance of management in construction.
6. What are the different functions of management ?
7. Explain different functions of management any one in brief.
7. Explain the process of value engineering.
8. Explain the process of value engineering.
9. What is leadership ?
10. What are the qualities to be possessed by leader ?
10. What are the different types of leadership ?
11. What is the importance of organisation.
12. State the principles and characteristics of organisation.
13. What is meant by 'Authority' and 'Delegation of Authority' ?
14. What are the types of organisation ?

15. Write short notes on following :

   (a) Project Life Cycle.

   (b) Importance of Management in Construction.

   (c) Value Engineering.

   (d) Indian Construction Industry.

   (e) Principles of Organisation.

   (f) Qualities of Leader.

   (g) Line Organisation.

   (h) Functional Organisation.

Unit - II
NETWORK TECHNIQUE

2.1 INTRODUCTION

Planning is the most important part of management processes. Without proper planning, successful completion of any project or running of any organisation will not be possible. The objective of planning is to complete the project in a better manner in proper time and to make logical decisions which will help to understand the complexity of situation in execution in a better way. In construction management, the work must be completed in a fixed predecided duration at previously estimated cost. The analytical methods of planning include system analysis, operation research, system engineering and the like. However, in very simple language, the planning of any project includes

1. What to do ?
2. When to do ?
3. How to do ?
4. Who will do ?
5. Where to do ?

The planning, therefore, deals with execution of any project after it has been decided to undertake the same. Any project consists of different activities which will have inter-dependence. A system is a sequence of arrangement of different activities of work considering their interdependence. Planning is proper sequencing of these activities. Proper scheduling of the different activities before commencement of the work and controlling the operations in a systematic manner is the heart of planning. Early era of scientific management and planning may be pointed to introduction of Gantt charts. This may be said to be beginning of scientific project management technique. This method of scheduling was developed by Henry Gantt sometime in 1899. Modern techniques of management include Critical Path Method (CPM) and Project Evaluation and Review Technique (PERT). These techniques aid the managers in planning, scheduling and control of large and complex projects wherein there may be different constraints on various resources.

2.2 HISTORICAL REVIEW OF MANAGEMENT TECHNIQUES

Historical construction projects were undertaken in ancient Egyptian and Roman Empires. The projects were architectural brilliance. Very little is known about the planning of these monumental projects, the scheduling and controlling during construction. It took nearly nineteenth century for the planners to think of work and time relationship through graphical representation. Credit goes to W. Taylor sometime in 19th century for establishing graphically work-time relationship in construction management.

However, the popularisation of this graphical representation on scientific basis was made by Henry L. Gantt and Fedric. This may be said to be commencement of work scheduling on scientific basis. The present day bar chart is modification of the Gantt chart which is an excellent and very easy representation of different activities in any project. With different limitations of this bar chart regarding interdependence of activities and resource limitations, different other methods of scheduling like 'line on balance', 'mile stone' and 'curves' were some developments over the Gantt chart. But their use was limited and were not of much help in controlling and hence served only as a preliminary method of scheduling. To suit with the complex problems in construction or any other project and different rapidly changing methods in construction, it was very necessary that the scheduling methods should have built-in provisions for showing clearcut inter-relationship of different activities, scope for decision making with due consideration for the shortening of the time to do so. This evolved the new techniques like CPM and PERT. Many other forms of this techique such as Graphic Evaluation and Review Technique (GERT), Resource Allocation and Manpower Planning System (RAMP'S) etc. have been evolved and have also become popular.

Since ancient period when gigantic construction projects have been completed and today also they are in existence, there must have been some management techniques used. Management must be an age-old science which must have been applied to simple and complex problems and everyday problems to long duration projects. Without being put into words and in books, this science must have been in use for many thousands of years. It may be that the ancient day-to-day problems were simpler and very big projects were a few. Also the persons involved were also handful in number as such they used to follow their own techniques based upon previous experience, their innovative ideas and process of contemplation. However, after the industrial revolution, there was tremendous growth in the complex problems related to development of industries, small as well as large and especially development of factory system. It also led to big construction project needed for big industries, steel, cement etc. and even small industries for consumer goods. With the advent of industrial revolution, the population in the urban areas went on increase in geometrical proportion and this also lead to construction of big complexes and construction projects for Government and other public establishments. This also needed projects for public amenities and completion of such complex projects and even simple projects in comparatively small duration economically was a challenge. Proper management was the only tool to face this situation and with the completion of such complex project, the methodology used and the experience was shared and was studied. This systematic study, probably, became science of management. The importance of this science was evident when it was being studied and used. Later on scientific analysis and studies were conducted and this science was based on firm principles and different aspects were further studied in details and scientific technology was evolved on different aspects. This led to modern science of Project Planning and Management and its different aspects such as :

- Project Planning
- Project Management Techniques
- Organisation
- Material Management
- Work Study
- Financial Management
- Safety Engineering
- Personnel Management
- Management Information System (MIS)
- Communication in Management
- Maintenance and Replacement Studies
- Industrial Budgeting and Cost Analysis
- Marketing Management
- Forms of Industrial Enterprises
- Plant Layout
- Production Planning and Control
- Production System Analysis Techniques.

2.3 PROJECT AND ITS OBJECTIVES

A project is composed of different jobs, tasks, functions or activities which are related to each other. The job has some objectives so that completion of all these related jobs or tasks successfully will lead to completion of the project and the objective of the project is fulfilled. Any project has to commence at a specific moment and will be finished when all the related jobs are completed. For working and completion of any project, basic things required are
1. Material resources including raw material and machinery, and
2. Manpower resources.

Availability of both of the above is absolutely necessary for successful completion of the project. However, availability, quality and proper use of human resources is most important determinant factor in completion of the project and thereby accomplishing the project objectives. In project planning, technology and management both are very important. The technology considers the recent innovations in using the material and working of processes while the management deals with the manpower resources and its critical use in handling materials and processes. It is, therefore, necessary that the rapid accumulation of scientific techniques and innovations should match the corresponding improvement in the sphere of human group relation and this can be achieved through proper management. Management is necessary to increase the productivity using technological innovations and critical use of the manpower resources available.

Any project will have following objectives
- The project should be completed at a minimum capital investment i.e. the project should be economical.

- The project should be completed within as minimum time period as possible.
- It should be completed with the critical use of the available manpower.

Project Management is the process of achieving the above three objectives in completion of the project. This involves planning before the project commences and also planning during the execution of the project. The phases of planning before commencement of the project are

1. Project Planning and
2. Project Scheduling.

The phase of planning during the execution involves

1. Project Controlling.

This phase involves recognising the different difficulties encountered during the execution and to overcome these difficulties by applying suitable measures so that the execution confirms to the pre-execution schedule and the pre-execution phases.

2.4 PROJECT PLANNING

The first of the precommencement phases of the project is planning. Planning consists of the following steps

1. Defining clearly the objective of the project.
2. Dividing the project into different independent tasks or unit jobs for completion of the project.
3. Determination of total requirement of different types of material for completion of the unit jobs.
4. Determination of machinery needed.
5. Determination of needed manpower.
6. Preparing estimates of cost of different tasks.
7. Determination of duration of completion of different unit jobs or tasks.
8. Decide on a plan.

The above steps are absolutely necessary for successful completion of the project. This planning is important as it will decide the direction of the implementation, help in preparing framework of jobs and will be able to reveal the possible breaks. It will also be useful in setting some performance standard. The starting point of planning in many projects is available resources. Sometimes this becomes a problem which has to be solved in planning phase before proceeding to the next phase which is scheduling for the project.

2.5 SCHEDULING

Scheduling is the sequencing of different independent tasks with their time relationship with reference to each other. With the available manpower and other resources, the time duration for each individual task will have to be determined. Alternatively, the required resources will have to be planned if the duration of the individual task is to be fixed if there is any constrain for the same. However, normally the available resources will decide the duration of the task. With this step completed, the sequencing of the different operations or activities will have to be decided and according to the duration of activities the allocation of available resources will have to be decided. Scheduling forms a very important phase of the project and especially in this phase attention will be needed to those resources whose availability is limited as they will be imposing a constrain in the project. Skilled technical manpower and the capital investments are the two important limitations of the resources. Scheduling is very important part of the project planning as it deals with inter-relationship between the individual tasks and realistic estimates of the duration of the same in commensurating with the available resources. Allocation of the available resources to the different concurrent activities will also decide the duration of the different activities and it will have to be given due consideration that concurrent activities are simultaneously taken up with allocation of resources and the project is not delayed because of undue delay of any of the activities.

2.6 CONTROLLING

The planning and scheduling form the two important steps before the actual project commences. The controlling phase starts after the project starts and is undertaken during the conduct of the different project operations, activities or tasks. As far as possible, it is necessary to see that the project performs as per the predecided schedule. But because of the different difficulties faced during the operation due to different unavoidable reasons, it may not be possible to adhere to the schedule. It is, therefore, necessary at different stages of the operation of the project to review the difference between predetermined schedule and the actual performance. This will be effective to determine the precise effect of the deviation of the actual performance from the schedule. It will also be necessary to review, to replan and to reschedule so that the deviations are compensated and the project is completed, as far as possible in the predecided duration. Project control can, therefore, be defined as 'a formal mechanism in determining the deviations in actual performance compared to the basic plan and predetermined schedule and to determine the precise effect of the deviation with respect to the duration of completion of the project so that, if necessary the project can be replanned and rescheduled to compensate for the deviation for completion of the project in the predetermined duration.

The different steps in accomplishing controlling can be summarized as below
1. Establishing standards and targets in terms of the time for completion of different phases of the project.
2. Actual measure of performance compared to the set down target and standard at the end of different stages.
3. To identify the deviations from the standards in terms of time and other measures.

4. To suggest and select the correcting measures. This will consist of problem of identifying the bottle necks and the different drawbacks and shortcomings in terms of resources, decision making, organising the needed correction especially in terms of resources. This will include the skills necessary for the decision maker. In fact, the controlling of any project consists of
   1. Time control
   2. Cost control and
   3. Quality control.

2.6.1 Decision Making – A Key in Project Management.

In all the phases of project planning, decision making is most important. It will be necessary to make right decisions at all the stages of management which include planning, organising, staffing, scheduling and controlling. The decisions to be taken will depend upon the available resources at any stage and should lead to the goal to be achieved. The success or failure of the project will depend upon the decisions taken by the management at different stages. Even though the decision mainly depends upon the available resources, it is very necessary at each stage to identify the central problem and find out the different alternatives to solve the same. It is also necessary to analyse the different alternatives and considering the short falls and strength of different alternatives, final decision will have to be made.

2.7 METHODS OF PLANNING

It is not very easy to manage complex projects and also research and development projects which may have certain uncertainties. It is, therefore, very necessary to plan the project properly, prepare work schedules and control the project-accordingly while in execution. It will be necessary to see that the project is completed as far as possible in the estimated duration and at the estimated cost and achieve its technical performance objectives. For this, it is necessary that improved modern techniques of management be employed from the conception of the project and also at any intermediate stage. These modern improved techniques in any form consist of the following
1. Defining clearly the work to be performed, with the help of work breakdown structure.
2. Developing more realistic schedule and cost estimates based on available resources to perform the work.
3. Determining the optimum use of available resources to achieve the best in terms of time, cost and technical performance objectives.
4. Identifying areas which may develop potential delays and cost overruns in time so that corrective measures and action can be taken in time.

The modern techniques to achieve above objectives of project management are as below
1. Bar chart and its modifications.
2. Network diagram and its modifications.

2.8 WORK BREAKDOWN STRUCTURE

The most important function of management is "Planning" which involves listing of activities, finding logic and interdependence and assigning the durations to each activity. As the project grows larger, number of tasks increases and it becomes necessary to break them into smaller manageable units called as "activities" which can be easily supervised and estimated. Hence this method is called as work breakdown structure. This method is used by project managers to simplify the project execution.

The general steps which are followed in the process of work breakdown structure are as follows

- A team of project managers and Subject Matter Experts (SME) who are involved in the project, is formed.
- Breaking down the tasks is started from the end product in its entirely and work downwards to increasing levels of detail. This is usually can be the title of the project e.g. Construction of Bungalow at Lonavala. (Bungalow at Lonavala)
- Define the main deliverables i.e. the main components of the projects end product e.g. substructure, superstructure, landscaping etc.
- This step defines the 'main branches' of the project.

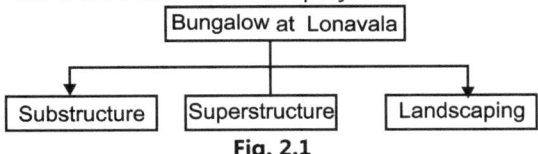

Fig. 2.1

- These 'main branches' are again broken down into their subcomponents using as many sub-branches as needed until manageable 'activities' are defined. These need not be sub-divided further.

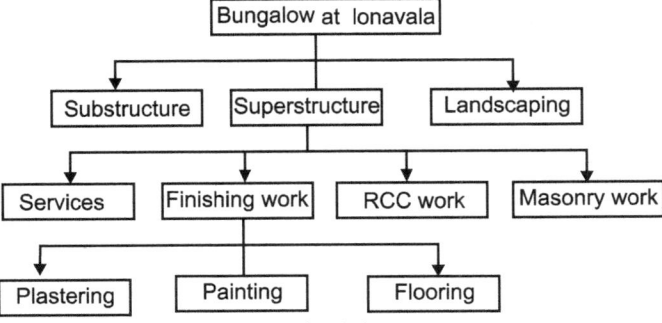

Fig. 2.2

- There are no hard and fast rules that are to be followed while break-down the tasks. One has to rely on his experience, type of project and the management style followed for the project. Generally, 8/80 rule is used, which says, no task should be smaller than 8 hours of work (i.e. 1 day approx.) and should not be larger than 80 hours of work (i.e. 10 days approximately)

- A detailed "WBS" is as shown in the following Fig.

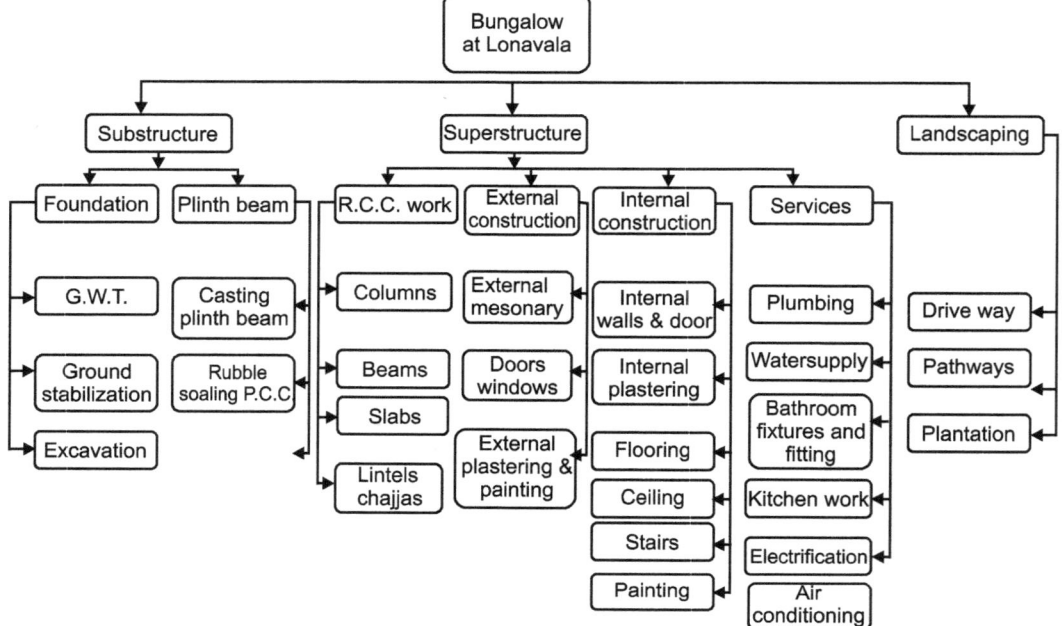

Fig. 2.3

2.8.1 Advantages of Work Breakdown Structure

- It assigns accurate responsibilities to the project team.
- WBS indicates project mile stones and control points.
- It also helps to estimate cost, time and risk.
- WBS defines the project scope so that the stakeholders can have a better understanding of the same.
- It provides the foundation for planning, resource allocation and scheduling.
- It gives us the information of necessary work that is distribute between elements of the project, distribution of cost and budget between different elements of the project, division of larger elements into smaller ones.

WBS can also be represented on a list as shown below

Project : Construction of Bunglow at Lonavala

- 1.0 Structure
- 1.1 Foundation
  - 1.1.1 Excavation
  - 1.1.2 Ground Stabilisation
  - 1.1.3 Construction of Footing
- 1.2 Plinth beam
  - 1.2.1 Casting of plinth beam

    1.2.2 Rubble soling
    1.2.3 PCC
2.0 Superstructure
2.1 RCC work
    2.1.2 ....
    2.1.3 ....

2.9 BAR CHART

A project, whatsoever, complex can be easily divided into number of well-defined manageable jobs or units called activities. These activities have to be performed in a definite sequence for successful completion of the project.

These different activities consume resources and take time for their completion. Bar chart developed by A. Gantt was the first introduction of scientific management technique for project controlling.

It was an improved method of planning and controlling than the available method of production of ordinance factories introduced and developed by Henry L. Gantt for U.S. Army sometime around 1900.

This simple method consisted of preparation of a chart which displayed different activities by horizontal bars representing the schedule of different activities. The duration of the different activities were represented by the horizontal length of the bars. This pictorial representation of scheduling was probably one of the earliest methods of scheduling on some rational basis and therefore, was named after the innovator as Gantt's chart or more popularly as Bar chart as the different activities were represented by horizontal rectangular bars.

The different activities of any project or the horizontal bars were represented on Y-axis against the duration of respective activities on X-axis. Horizontal lines of duration on X-axis are plotted to scales whereas on the Y-axis the activities are represented as to suit the representation of pictorial view and are arbitrary.

Each bar represents one specific unit job or activity to be performed and the beginning and the end of each bar represent the time of commencement and completion of the activity on the horizontal time scale. Hence, the length of the bar represents the time of completion of that activity as indicated earlier.

These bar charts can be explained with the help of following examples

Bar Chart 1

A Gantt chart is shown in Fig. 2.4. A project consisting of 8 different activities A, B, C, D, E, F, G, H is represented in the figure. The duration of the activities are 10, 12, 6, 6, 16, 8, 16, 12 days respectively.

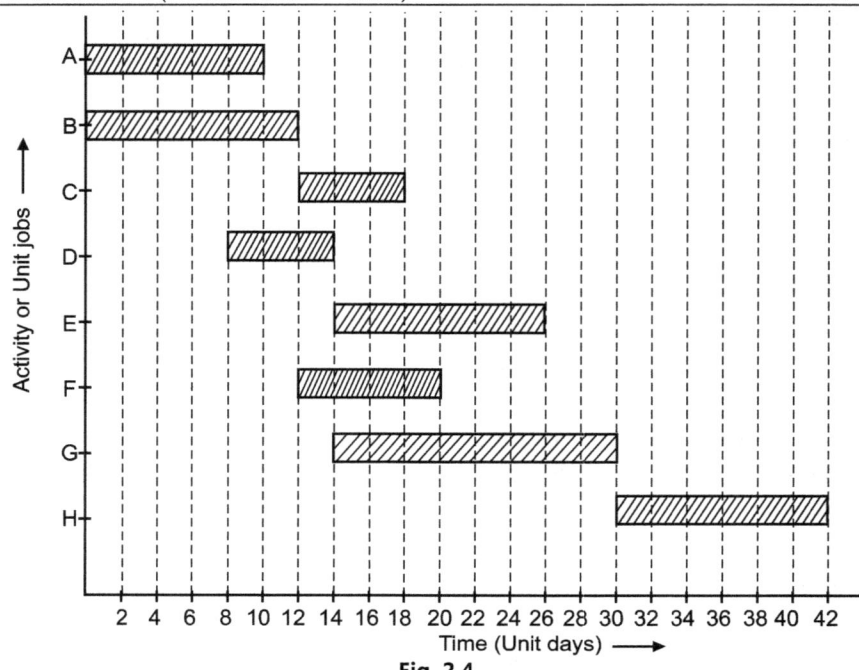

Fig. 2.4

These activities are analysed and sequence of the activities are decided using work break down structure. The analysis is given below
1. Activities A o activities D and G are completed.
8. End of activity H is completion of the project.

The above analysis of the different activities can be tabulated as shown below

Sr. No.	Name of Activity	Duration in Days	Preceding Activity	Succeeding Activity	Remark
1	A	10	NIL		
2	B	12	NIL		
3	C	6	B		
4	D	6	NIL	E	8 days after A and B have commenced
5	E	12	D		
6	F	8	A		
7	G	16	A, D		
8	H	12	D, G		

After this tabulation the bar chart is prepared as shown below. For any activity if there is any preceding activity, the succeeding activity should start at the same instant, the preceding activity is completed so that the project is completed in minimum period. However, if there is no preceding activity, such activities can start simultaneously but the resources should be taken into consideration.

2.9.1 Salient Features of Bar Chart

Advantages of Bar Chart
- It is very simple and easy method of scheduling.
- Each activity is shown separately. Actual progress of work can be easily compared with the proposed schedule. Hence, modifications can be carried out easily if required.
- Interdependence of the different activities can be represented to a limited extent.
- Achievements on a particular date in progress can be easily represented.
- Cumulative progress can be represented on bar chart.
- It can represent possible delays.

Limitations of Bar Chart
- Interdependence of the various activities cannot be shown absolute clearly and sequence of activities is not clear.
- By itself it does not indicate the progress of the project and hence cannot be used for effective controlling.
- It cannot represent and reflect tolerance and uncertainties in time estimation for various activities.
- It does not give optimum duration of the project.
- Different alternatives cannot be evaluated from bar chart.
- It is not possible to locate critical activities.
- In some the projects there are activities wherein estimation of time required for completion of these activities cannot be precisely determined. This is so in case of projects involving research or development projects or projects like space vehicle launching and the like. In case of such projects the bar chart may not be useful as there may be frequent rescheduling in case of many activities because of change in time of completion of such activities. It is not possible to incorporate such rescheduling flexibility in the bar chart and hence bar charts are not useful in research and development or innovative projects.
- Bar chart diagrams, though very simple to construct and understand, are useful only in case of small-size conventional projects in which number of activities are limited and time duration of completion of them are definite. These bar charts are, therefore, used in construction and manufacturing projects wherein the time estimation can be made with fair degree of accuracy.
9. Along with research and development projects, bar charts are not normally used in case of complicated projects involving multifarious activities large in number which are interdependent even though their time estimation may be finite.

2.9.2 Remedial Measures for Removal of Shortcomings of Bar Chart

Lack of Degree of Details

Too many activities cannot be separately shown on the bar chart as it may become clumsy. Hence, different small activities are coupled into major activities and such major tasks are only represented in the bar chart. Hence, in big projects where there are too many activities, representation on bar chart is difficult and hence bar chart cannot be used for big projects. A particular activity is shown by a single bar, the subactivities cannot be separated out and hence effective control over the activities is not possible and cannot be achieved.

One example of such major activity involving different subactivities may be cited. In the project of renovation of a workshop, a major activity may be replacement of old machine by a new one. This activity in a bar chart may be represented by a single bar. But this activity involves the following different subactivities

1. Ordering a new machine.
2. Getting delivery of new machine.
3. Incorporating power and other changes for fixing new machine.
4. Removing old machine.
5. Installation of new machine.
6. Testing new machine.
7. Disposal of old machine.

A separate bar chart as given below may be prepared for this single activity.

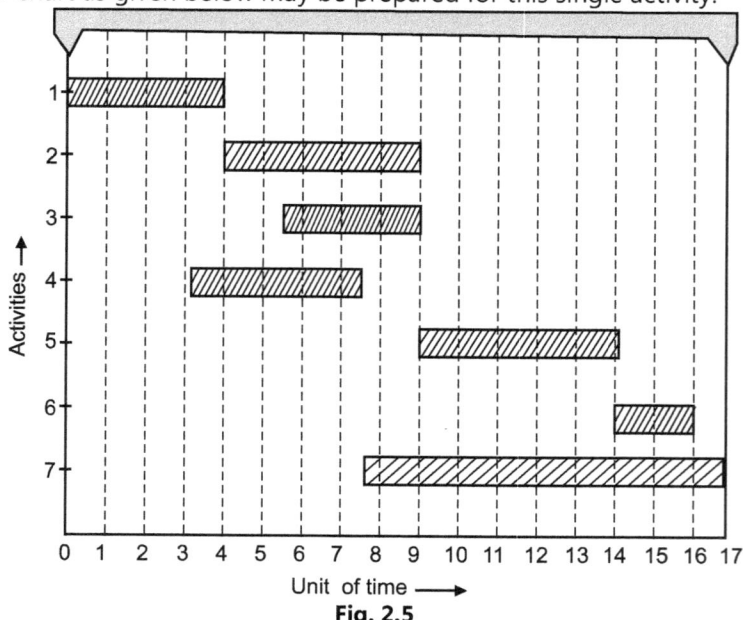

Fig. 2.5

2.9.3 Comparison of Project Progress with the Schedule and Review

As the bar chart itself duly represents the schedule, it cannot show the progress of work and hence it is not a useful device in control of the project. It is absolutely necessary that the actual progress of the work has to be compared with the schedule at specific instances of time so that if necessary some rescheduling can be thought of. The remaining activities may be rescheduled suitably if the actual progress differs much from the designed progress. The actual progress of work at a particular instant of time can be depicted on the existing bar chart prepared prior to the start of the project representing the proposed schedule. The progress of different activities can be shown on this bar chart by hatched lines on the top half of the bar rectangle representing the same activity or in short the bar chart of actual progress is superimposed on the bar chart of the proposed schedule and can be shown by different colours. Fig. 2.6 represents a bar chart with 4 activities. The proposed progress and actual progress is compared after completion of 11th week of the project. The actual progress of each activity at the end of 11th week is represented on half the width of the same activity by hatching.

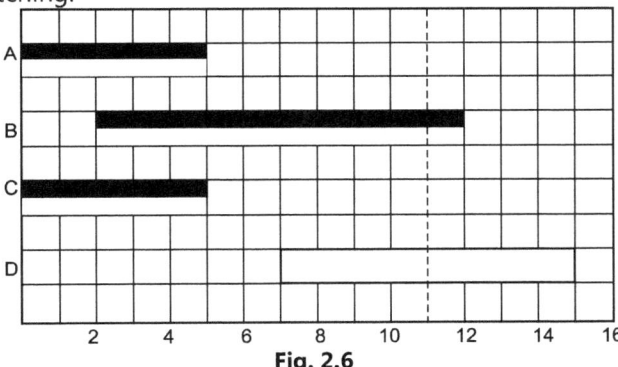

Fig. 2.6

The following table gives the complete information regarding the comparison of proposed progress with actual progress.

Sr. No.	Activity	Proposed Duration in Weeks	Proposed Progress after 11th Week	Actual Progress after 11th Week	Comparison
1	A	7	7 weeks work completed	5 weeks work completed	2 weeks lagging
2	B	11	9 weeks work completed	10 weeks work completed	1 week ahead of schedule
3	C	5	5 weeks work completed	5 weeks work completed	As per schedule
4	D	8	4 weeks work completed	Nil, not started	4 weeks lagging

Activity A is 2 weeks behind the schedule. Activity D is succeeding activity of A. Hence its start is 4 weeks lagging and the actual work is also lagging by 4 weeks, hence the project is likely to be completed behind the schedule by 4 + 4 = 8 weeks even though the progress of activity B is 1 week ahead of the schedule and activity C is as per schedule.

2.9.4 Inter-relationship of Activities

In any project some activities are inter-dependent i.e. a particular activity can commence only after some other activity is completed. Such activities whose start and end depend upon each other, have to be represented serially in bar chart as their interdependence is clearly established. However, many other activities can run simultaneously or are cocurrent activities and as such they are shown by bars over same time scale. This concurrency cannot be clearly depicted as it is not very clear whether these activities, though concurrent, start simultaneously or there is only some overlap of time. As such the overlap cannot represent the degree of concurrency and the inter-relationship cannot be clearly represented in bar chart. These activities which are shown by the overlapping bars on time scale may be completely independent or may have some interdependency. However, this cannot be represented on bar chart or the parallel bars cannot give any information about independency or interdependency of these concurrent activities.

This will be clear from the example of project of canal construction which includes layout, excavation and lining.

The different activities are

A   Layout of the canal on proposed central line according to the section – 6 weeks

B   Excavation for canal – 12 weeks

C   Lining of canal – 12 weeks

Activity C is succeeding activity of B which is further a succeeding activity of A. Independently, the different events would take durations as given above. If all the activities would be undertaken serially, the project would take 31 weeks for completion. However, since work in the project is in linear extension, it could be divided in sections and for each section all the above three activities can be undertaken serially and the bar chart would be as shown below after staggering the activities.

Activity B is started 2 weeks after commencement of activity A. After completion of activity A, 9 weeks work of activity B is left. Similarly activity C has 4 weeks work left after completion of activity B. Now, if due to some difficulties, the time of completion of activity A is delayed by 2 or 3 weeks, what effect it will make on the succeeding activities B and C?

How will these activities be affected ? This cannot be clearly depicted in the bar chart and inter-dependence of the different activities cannot be clearly indicated in the bar chart or can be revealed from the bar chart.

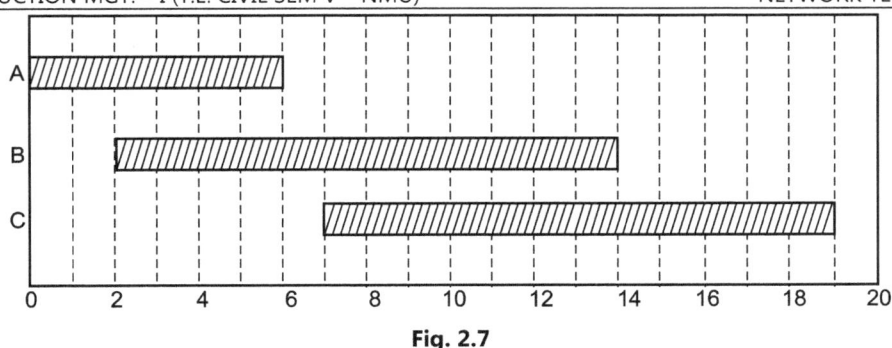

Fig. 2.7

However, by modifying the bar chart, this difficulty can be overcome. Each activity in the bar chart can be suitably divided into different equal sections so that all the three activities can be taken up sequentially for these sections. This is represented in Fig. 2.8.

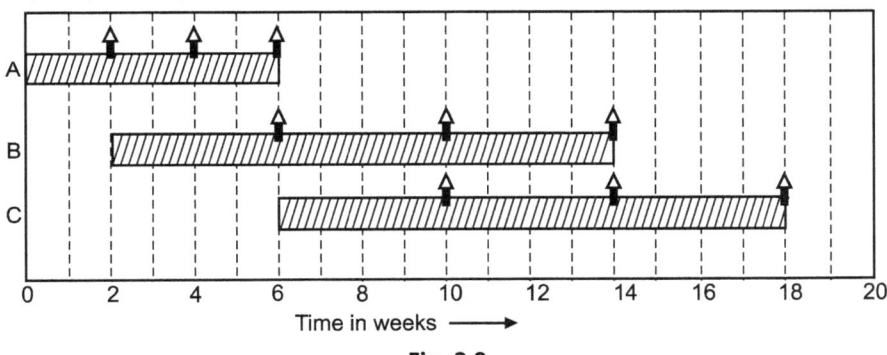

Fig. 2.8

Each activity is divided in three sections. For activity A each section will require 2 weeks for completion, for activity B each section will require 4 weeks for completion and for activity C each section will require 4 weeks for completion. With this modification, effect of delay in work of activity A can be very easily contemplated on next activity B or that of delay in activity B can be easily found out on activity C. With this, control measures necessary can be easily worked out so that the project may not be unnecessarily delayed.

2.10 MILE STONE CHARTS

The mile stone chart came up as a modification and an improvement over the Gantt or Bar chart. It came up sometime in 1940. A project is divided into different activities and each of the activity can be further divided suitably into key events of that activity. These key events in a particular activity are specific achievements in that activity and are marked in the bar – representing that activity which are specific points in time.

These points can be easily identified in the main bar as they represent certain specific achievement or completion of a particular portion of that activity. It is not necessary that these mile stones are spaced equidistant with respect to time. In short, a particular activity represented in bar chart may consist of combination of many small activities. The bar representing such compound activities is divided such that each specific point on time scale represents completion of a subactivity. Such subactivities can be easily recognised during the progress of the project and then controlling of the project is easier. The specific points representing the beginning or end of such subactivities are termed as *mile stones*. In mile stone chart, bars are divided and the events are arranged in monological sequence. Different mile stones may be connected by means of arrows according to then logical sequence which may even look like a network. A mile stone chart consisting of 4 activities A, B, C and D is represented in Fig. 2.9 and Fig. 2.10 in two different ways.

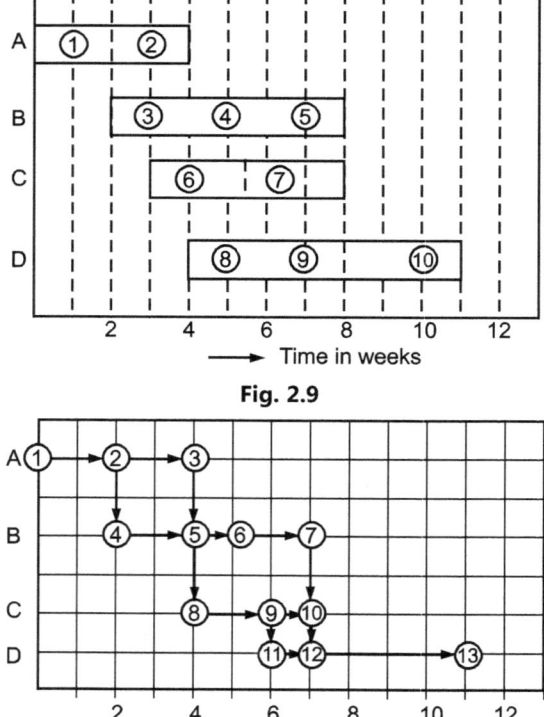

Fig. 2.9

Fig. 2.10

The two figures are two different ways of representing the mile stone chart. Fig. 2.9 is just a modification of bar chart wherein activity A is divided into 2 subactivities. Activity B is divided into 3 different subjobs, activity C is divided into 2 different tasks and activity D is broken into 2 different subactivities. Each subactivity is a specific task and can be easily recognised in preparation of the diagram and also during the progress of the project. It is not necessary that a particular activity be divided into only such subactivities for which duration is equal. The time duration for the different mile stones of any activity may be different but the achievement during such time duration should be specific so that the subactivity could be easily recognised. In Fig. 2.10, it is possible that sequential completion of subactivities may be

(1) → (3) → (6) → (8) → (9) → (10)

(2) → (4) → (5) → (7) → (9) → (10)

Subactivities (2) and (3) may be undertaken simultaneously, subactivities (4) and (5) are sequential which may be concurrent with subactivities (6) and (8). This type of mile stone chart was a definite improvement over the conventional bar chart.

Another way of representing a mile stone chart is as shown in Fig. 2.13. In this chart, the commencement and end of an activity or subactivity is represented by sequential number. Thus, activity A is divided into two subactivities (1) – (2) and (2) – (3). Similarly activities B, C and D have been divided into 3, 2 and 2 subactivities. The diagram is self explanatory. It indicates once (1) – (2) subactivity is completed, the subactivity (4) – (5) can commence and so on. The project will be completed after subactivity (12) – (13) is concluded in a period of 11 weeks. The circles representing commencement or conclusion of any subactivity are termed as nodes and this chart may be called as Nodal Mile Stone Chart.

Though there is definite improvement in mile stone chart over bar chart, it still possesses the same drawbacks as that of bar chart. Interdependencies between the events is not represented very clearly in modified bar chart.

The different subactivities in a particular activity are sequential and mark a particular achievement in that activity and is definitely a point in monitoring the progress of the project but inter-relationship between the different subactivities of different activities cannot be adequately represented. Attempt is made to overcome this difficulty by using a nodal mile stone chart where some attempt is made to represent this interdependency and event oriented network is prepared, which is termed as PERT Network.

2.11 INTRODUCTION TO NETWORK

The necessity of better planning and scheduling has increased due to increasing complexity of the extent of project. The method of planning and rescheduling in case of complex large projects should enable the management to view the whole project and if necessary the management should be able to review and reschedule the project during the process of execution. The network technique is one of the most modern tools of project management which enables the planners to View at a glance, Review and Reschedule.

This network planning and scheduling technique developed sometime in 1940 in western countries is used extensively now in planning of complex projects and controlling the execution of various activities and operation in the projects. The main advantages of this network technique are simplicity, flexibility and necessary overall control on the work. This technique is a useful tool for management of a project.

To determine the date of completion of any Civil Engineering project, or a Mechanical Engineering Project an Electrical Engineering Project, it is not only enough to prepare an estimate of cost of the project but most important is the planning of various operations or activities involved, time required for the completion of all these activities and the knowledge of inter-relationship and interdependency of each activity is also essential. The total time required for the completion of the project depends upon the time required for the different activities and on their interdependence. Network planning and scheduling technique is the study of all such activities, their inter-relationship and interdependency.

2.11.1 Objectives of Network Planning and Scheduling

It is necessary for successful completion of any project that schedules and objectives of the different operations involved should be defined in a project with reference to the targets to be achieved taking into account all the problems which may creep in at the time of planning stage or during the execution of the project. Network planning and scheduling requires efficient integrated management. The main objectives can be summarized as below

- There should be a detailed integrated planning of the different unit jobs or activities involved.
- Realistic schedules should be developed.
- Exercising effective control : There should be periodical checking and evaluation of the progress of work in comparison with the planned schedule.
- The effect of current progress of work on the time of completion of project. This review may need some remedial action and if necessary reschedule with the necessary changes in the allocation of resources.
- There should be optimum utilisation of scarce resources, time and money.

The above objectives can be achieved by proper planning, analysing and scheduling and controlling. Network Technique is the tool towards the objective.

2.11.2 Development of Network from Bar Chart

To overcome the limitation of bar chart for not showing the interdependence of activities clearly, a modification is done in which arrows are used. Consider an example in which activity (1) is the starting activity, (2) and (3) Starts only after completion of activity (1), Activity (4) can not start before completion of activities (2) and (3). This can be shown with the help of arrows as below

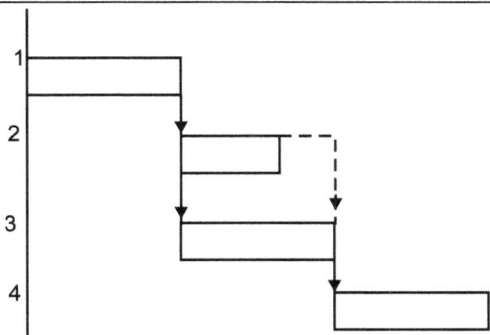

Fig. 2.11

If the bars are represented as a node, the same bar chart can be shown as a network using arrows and circles as below

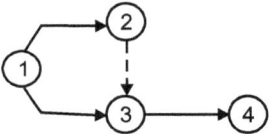

Fig. 2.12

2.11.3 Basics of Network

Network technique is one of the modern methods of project management. Any complex project can always be broken down into a number of distinct, well-defined jobs or tasks. These different tasks when completed successfully end into completion of the project. These unit tasks are called "Activities." The beginning and end of any, such unit job or activity is an important point in the network and is called an "event." Thus, activity is a unit job or task which flows between two successive events. A project, therefore, can be said to consist of different events which mark the beginning or end of different activities and the network is a flow diagram which connects the different events logically and sequentially through different activities. The network diagram is graphical representation of the different events or activities which should be completed in a sequential manner for the successful completion of the project. The event being either beginning or end of a unit job, is only a point and hence is represented by a circle. It does not consume any time or any resource and only indicates either beginning or end of an activity. The activity on the other hand is a unit job or task end of which is an event.

2.11.4 Types of Network

Networks are of two types.

(1) Critical Path Method (CPM)

(2) Programme Evaluation and Review Technique (PERT)

The CPM network is activity oriented whereas the PERT network is event oriented depending upon the importance of the activities and events in those methods. Fundamentally, the CPM and PERT networks are the two techniques of project management which are used in planning, scheduling and controlling the different operations involved in the project. The basic theory and the method of graphical representation of the network in both the above methods are same.

2.11.5 Characteristics of Projects Amenable to Network Planning

A project which has to be analysed by network planning either by CPM or PERT should have following characteristics.

- It should be possible that the project can be broken down into clearly recognisable distinct unit tasks or operations so that the sequential completion of all such unit jobs will end in completion of the project. Such unit jobs or tasks are named as activities. They consume time and resources.

- These different recognisable unit jobs or activities should have definite point of commencement and a definite point of conclusion. All the activities into which a project is divided should have a definite start and should have a definite end which can be distinctly recognised. This commencement or conclusion of any activity which can be defined precisely is called as *event*. which is a definite accomplishment in the project.

- For completion of the project, the different events must occur in some definite sequence which is decided by logic. This logic is decided by technological sequence in which the different events should occur so as to complete the project, which are derived by "work breakdown structure."

Thus, the basic elements of the project network are

- Activities or definite unit jobs or tasks.
- Events : Definite accomplishment in the project.

It is very clear that the activities and events are securely connected with each other. Start and end of any activity is a definite accomplishment in the project and therefore, marks an event. Any two sequential events can occur only if the unit job or activity between them is completed. So that the connection between two successive events is an activity. An event is represented by a circle or a square and an activity by a arrow joining two successive events.

Critical Path Method i.e. CPM

Any project consists of clearly recognisable unit jobs or operations which are called activities which consume time and resources. Commencement or completion of any activity is a definite point which is termed as event : One or More activities may commence simultaneously and may emerge from a single event whereas in the similar manner one, two or many activities may end simultaneously i.e. merge to a single event. After the project is broken down in different activities, their sequence is decided. An activity is represented by an arrow and all the activities are represented sequentially by arrows which form a CPM network. In this network, the junction between the different activities represent different events.

CPM network is generally used for such project in which it is possible to make fairly accurate estimate for the time duration required for the different activities constituting the project. Knowing the resources necessary for completion of different activities, cost estimates for the different activities can also be made to a fair degree of accuracy and hence with this knowledge, it is possible to make a very accurate estimate for the duration of completion of the project and also the estimated cost of the project. It is obvious that such information can be accurately collected from similar type of projects already executed and hence CPM networks are generally used for repetitive type of projects and have been effectively used for construction projects whatsoever complex. However, in case of research and innovative development projects, the duration of the different activities, as well as resources needed cannot be precisely decided and hence for such projects the CPM network cannot be used. Where duration of the different activities cannot be precisely decided, an optimistic, normal and pessimistic duration may be decided and most probable time for completion of the activities is decided. As such in repetitive type of projects, stress is on completion of activities and hence CPM networks are activity oriented. In research or innovative development projects, the stress is on events and in such projects which are event oriented 'Project Evaluation and Review Technique' (PERT) is used.

2.12 TYPES OF CPM NETWORK

2.12.1 CPM Method of Project Planning

CPM Method of Project Planning involves identification of specific activities, their time of completion i.e. duration and their interrelationship. In general, there are two types of networks used. They are

- Activity On Arrow (AOA) type of arrow diagramming.
- Activity On Node (AON) type of precedence diagramming.

1. Activity On Arrow Type Network

As said earlier the events are shown by numbers in geometrical figure like circle or square and the activity shown and by an arrow. The head and the tail of an arrow represent event. The event is a point and it does not consume any time. The event is also called as *Node* or *connector*. The activity is represented by letters like A or B or C or D ... etc. They are also represented by pair of numbers as 1 – 2, 2 – 3, 3 – 4 etc. In activity 1 – 2, the points 1 and 2 are the two nodes of the activity. Out of the two nodes, 1 is a 'From' node and 2 is a 'To' node and the From node must be a lower number than To node. In this way, the direction of activity arrow is clearly established. The project is divided into different activities, inter-relationship between the activities and the sequence is decided and the CPM diagram is prepared.

Fig. 2.13 shows construction of network by Activity On Arrow method (AOA).

Activity Symbol	Activity Description	Inter Dependancy	Duration in Days
A	Study of plan layout	Start Activity	1
B	Clearance of site	Follows A	1
C	Earthwork in Excavation	Follows B	6
D	Laying of foundation concrete	Follows C	5
E		Constant after B	3
F	Procurement of Bricks Brick work	Follows D and E	10

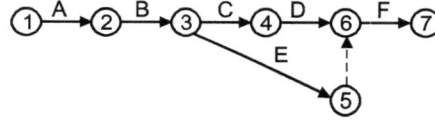

Fig. 2.13

2. Activity On Node Type Network

The problem in Activity On Arrow type or AOA network is necessity of Dummy activities for maintaining the logic and the right sequence in the network. This increases the length of the tables, enlarges the network graph and takes time for calculation work and increase the complexity of the network for large and complex projects. Another type of network is the Activity On Node diagram or precidence diagram which overcomes the problem of AOA network.

In AON network diagram, the activities are represented by boxes and arrows, and are used for designating the inter-relationship between the activities. The AON diagram is simpler to prepare and is easier to explain. It presents a clearer picture of the project as compared to AOA diagram. The AON diagram for the same problem (used for AOA) is represented in Fig. 2.14.

Both methods have their own advocates. The principal under both the methods should be understood. But the A – O – A method was first developed and is very widely used. Further, the use of numbers for events in A – O – A method has made it amenable to programming on computer and the Dummy activities used make the logic more clear. Hence A – O – A or Activity on Arrow method is more popularly used in CPM.

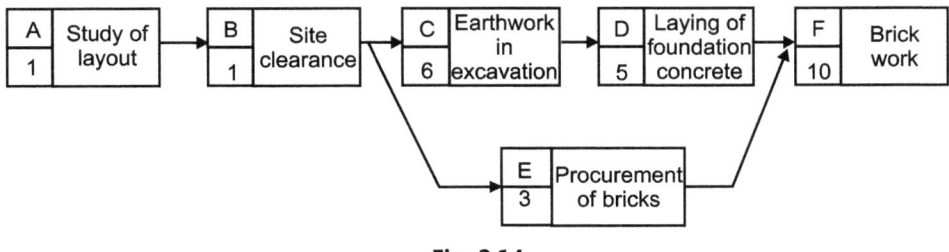

Fig. 2.14

2.13 TERMINOLOGY IN NETWORK

1. Event and Activity

Event is well-defined point or stage or accomplishment of the project. An event is that particular instant of time at which some specific part of a plan has been or is to be achieved. It is, therefore, the commencement or completion of an activity. Specifically, it is a definable specific accomplishment in a project plan which is recognisable at a particular instant of time. It should be definitely distinguishable as a specific point in time and should be readily understood by all those who are concerned with the project. It does not consume time or resources.

Activity is a specific job or unit task in any project and event is start or end of the activity. In construction project, excavation for foundation is an activity whereas starting of excavation for foundation is an event.

Activity	Event	
1. Location of site.	(a)	Site located.
2. Excavation for foundation.	(b)	Commencement of excavation for foundation.
	(c)	Completion of excavation for foundation.
3. Installation of new machinery.	(d)	New machinery installed.
4. Laying of sewer pipeline.	(e)	Sewer pipeline laid.

2. Representation of Event

An event is a well-defined point in a project and hence is represented by a node. The shape used to represent the node may be (i) circular, (ii) square, (iii) rectangle, (iv) oval shape or (v) any other regular geometrical figure such as triangles. However, generally a circle has been chosen to represent the nodes. Events are numbered for their identification and these numbers are written inside the geometrical figure representing the node.

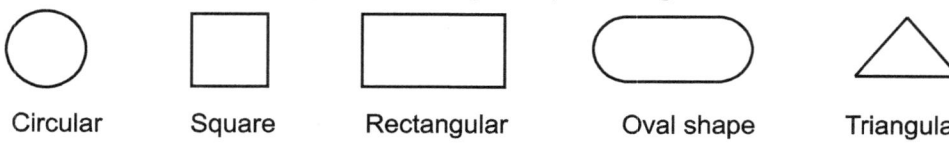

| Circular | Square | Rectangular | Oval shape | Triangular |

Fig. 2.15

3. Activity

It is the actual performance of a task or a unit job. It is a recognisable part or item or operation of the project. It, therefore, consumes time and resources in the form of manpower, material, use of machinery or any other facility. It is a positive specific tangible and meaningful effort having a proper description understandable by all concerned with the project.

4. Representation of Activity

Activities are represented by simple arrows in network diagram. The arrow runs from left to right generally so that the tail is towards left and the arrow head is towards right. The tail of the arrow represents the start of the activity and arrow head represents the end of the activity. However, the length of the arrow neither represents the magnitude of the work completed in the activity nor time required for completion of that activity. The length of the arrow is chosen to suit the convenience of drafting and proper representation of the complete network in the available space for drawing.

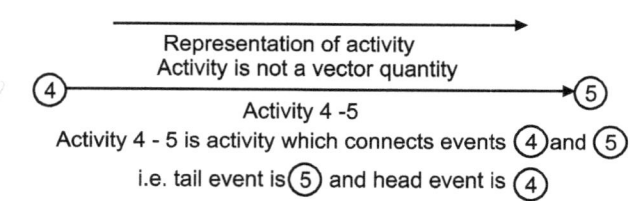

Representation of activity
Activity is not a vector quantity
Activity 4 -5
Activity 4 - 5 is activity which connects events ④ and ⑤
i.e. tail event is ⑤ and head event is ④

Activities can be identified with the use of English alphabets such as above activity is A.

- Activity A — Excavation of earth work
- Activity B — Foundation concrete
- Activity C — Construction of brick work in foundation and plinth
- Activity D — Laying of D P C
- Activity E — Brickwork in superstructure

2.13.1 Different Types of Activities and Their Inter-Relationship

A project is broken into different types of unit tasks or activities. Depending upon their interdependency, some activities are to be taken serially whereas some of the activities can be undertaken simultaneously which are subsequently called as predecessor Activities and Successor Activities.

Depending upon their way of occurrence, the different activities can be termed as below

Parallel Activities

Activities which can be undertaken and completed simultaneously and independently to each other are called parallel activities.

Serial Activities

Those activities which are performed immediately one after the another are called serial activities. They are dependent on each other and cannot be performed independently.

Predecessor Activities

Activity or number of activities which are necessary to be performed before a particular activity is undertaken, they are called predecessor activities. Unless these predecessor activities are completed, the next activity cannot commence.

Successor Activities

Any activity or activities which immediately begin after the performance of predecessor activities are termed as successor activities to those predecessor activities.

In Fig. 2.13,

C and E are parallel activities, D and E are also parallel activities.

A and B are serial activities.

A is predecessor activity of activity B.

B is predecessor activity of activities C and E.

B is successor activity of activity A.

C and E are successor activities of activity B.

F is successor activity of activities D and E.

Dummy Activity or Dummy

Dummy is a device to identify a dependence amongst the activities. It is not performance of any actual job or task and hence does not consume any time or resources. It is necessary to maintain the logic and uniqueness of the different activities in the project and serves as a connecting link for the control purposes. Dummy is, therefore, an activity without any actual job to be performed.

To differentiate the same from other performing activities, the Dummy Activity is represented by a dashed arrow. It is identified in the same way as other activities but the dashed arrow clearly represents that it is a dummy activity. With the help of dummy activity, logical sequence is maintained and confusion is avoided. Dummy serves the grammatical purpose as well as logical purpose.

Grammatical Purpose of Dummy

It will be illustrated with following example. Two persons are to leave place A and to go to place B. The first person uses a scooter and second uses a car. Event (1) is leave A whereas event (2) is reach B. This cannot be properly represented for the two persons as the diagram would be as shown below

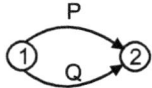

Fig. 2.16

Activity P – Person with scooter going from A to B. (Activity 1 – 2)

Activity Q – Person with car going from A to B. (Activity 1 – 2)

With this type of representation, uniqueness of the identification is lost as Activity P and Activity Q though different, are represented and treated like one single activity. (1-2) This inconvenience leads to mistake and has to be solved suitably for which dummy activity is used. To avoid the said confusion, Dummy activity is introduced as shown below

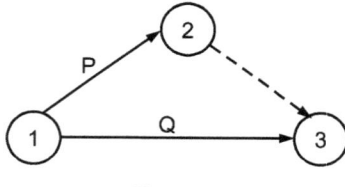

Fig. 2.17

Event (1) – Leave A

Events (2) and (3) – Reach B

The two activities P and Q are represented as below

Activity P – represented as 1 – 2

Activity Q – represented as 1 – 3

Since Activity 2 – 3 is a dummy activity practically event (2) and event (3) are same i.e. reach B. But to represent that activities A and B are different, a dummy activity 2 – 3 is introduced so that activity P or 1 – 2 represents activity that person with scooter is moving from A to B and activity Q or 1 – 3 represents activity that person with car is moving from A to B. Activity 2 – 3 is dummy activity for first person with scooter. The same can also be represented meaningfully as below

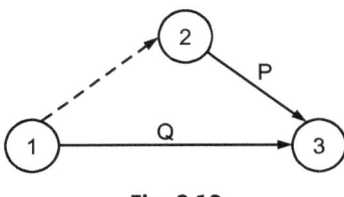

Fig. 2.18

Events (1) and (2) – Leave A

Event (3) – Reach B

Activity 1 – 2 is Dummy activity.

Activity P is 2 – 3 activity for person with scooter.

Activity Q is 1 – 3 activity for person with car.

Activity 1 – 2 is Dummy activity for first person.

However, it should be noted that dummy activities should be provided only if it is necessary. Provision of redundent dummy in the network may lead to confusion. Hence in initial stages, dummy activities may be introduced liberally which can further be removed by careful inspection of the network wherever such dummy activities are unnecessary.

Examples of dummy provided in initial stage and then dummy removed in the final network are as below

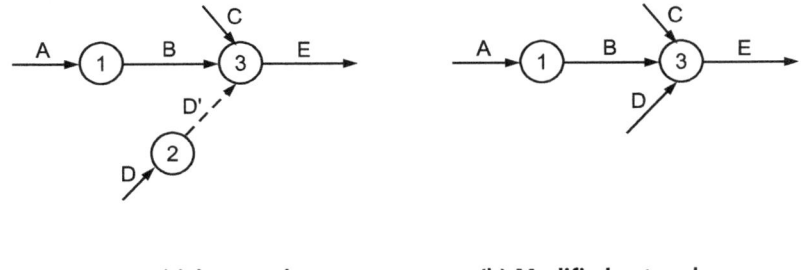

(a) Initial network　　　　　　(b) Modified network

Fig. 2.19

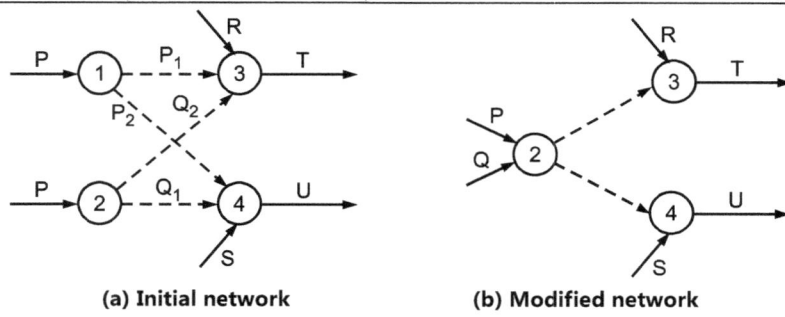

(a) Initial network (b) Modified network

Fig. 2.20

Example 2.1 : Convert the following Activity On Node (AON) Network into Activity On Arrow (AOA) Network.

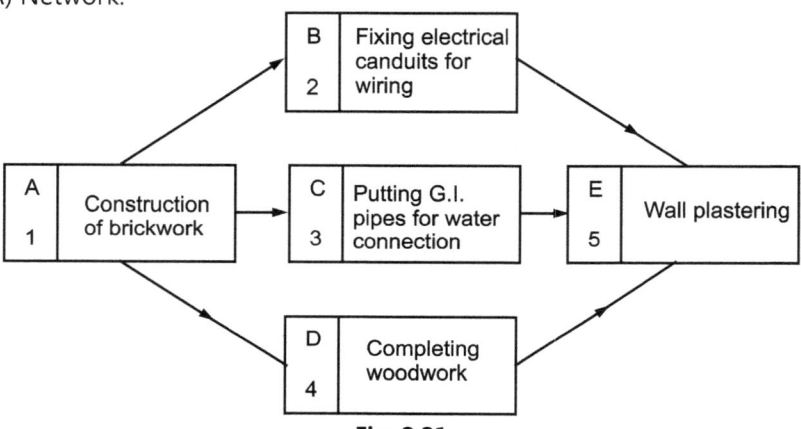

Fig. 2.21

Solution :

Activity 1 – 2 : Construction of Brickwork.
Activity 2 – 3 : Fixing Electrical Conduits.
Activity 2 – 4 : Fixing GI pipes for water connections.
Activity 2 – 5 : Completing woodwork in doors and windows.
Activity 5 – 6 : Plastering the brickwork.

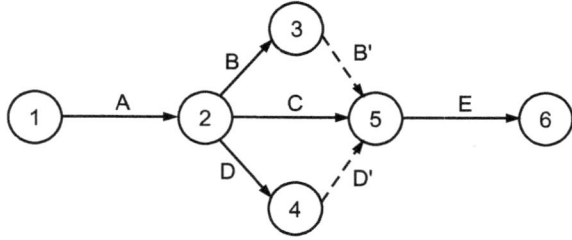

Fig. 2.22

2.14 FRAMING NETWORK FOR A PROJECT

The different steps in framing the network for any project can be summarized as below

1. **Objective :** The project objective is the specific achievement which must be very clear, specific and well-defined. It is a complete task to be accomplished which is to be achieved by completing the different unit jobs sequentially.

    Example :   1. Erection of a statue in a public place.

    2. Replacement of an old machinery by a new one.

    3. Construction of a residential building.

2. **Breakdown of the Project into Different Unit Tasks or Activities :** The complete project is the sequential accomplishment of different unit jobs. Therefore, by careful thinking the whole project should be broken down into simple unit jobs or activities with the help of work Breakdown Structure, where specific and the sequential accomplishment will make the project complete and the objective is achieved. The commencement and completion of these specific activities will be the different events in the completion of the project and they are the specific stepwise achievements of the project.

3. **Sequencing :** After breaking down the project into different activities, an analysis is to be made about the sequencing of the events and activities. This will lead to interrelationship between the different events and also activities. A clearcut picture should be worked regarding the predecessor events and the successor events and also predecessor activities, succeeding activities, parallel activities. A table may be prepared showing the inter-relation between the events. Such a table may also be prepared showing relation between the activities.

4. **Drawing of Network :** With above information ready and knowing the rules of framing the network, one can start locating the events sequentially starting with the first event on the left hand end and the proceeding towards right and locating the different events sequentially. Thus, starting from the first event, which is commencement of the project, one will be able to reach the last event which is completion of the project. The different unit jobs or activities will be arrows joining the successive events. Thus, the network for the project can be completed.

5. **Checking the Network :** After the network is completed, it has to be checked for the contents, sequence and sense. In content it is to be checked that all the necessary unit jobs are incorporated and no job or activity is missing. It should also be seen that logic and grammer of the network is maintained and network correctly represents the sequence. If necessary, for maintaining the sequence, dummy activities are used but there should not be redundant dummy activities and any error such as looping, or cycles and dangling. After checking the network if any such

mistakes or errors are found they are removed suitably and network is corrected and redrawn. After the final network is drawn, the events are numbered using Fulkerson's Rule. It should be noted that number of activities may be equal to or more than the number of events. In good network, $\frac{\text{No. of Activities}}{\text{No. of events}}$ should be between 1 to 1.6.

2.14.1 Rules for Framing Network

While framing network, following rules should be borne in mind

1. Initial event is starting of the project. Hence, the different activities will emerge from this initial node. Hence, there is always a single initial node in network. (Fig. 2.23)

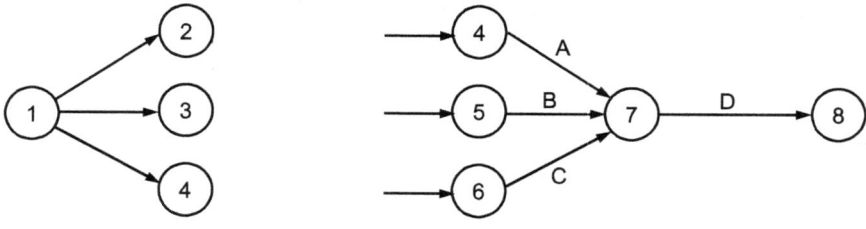

Fig. 2.23   Fig. 2.24

2. An event cannot be said to have occurred unless all the activities merging in that event are completed. Event (7) can be said to have occurred when all the activities A, B, C are completed. (Fig. 2.24)

3. No event depends for its occurrence on the occurrence of any succeeding event. This means that there cannot be any path in the network looping back from a succeeding event to a preceding event. Such a situation is known as **"Looping"** which should not occur anywhere in the network.

In Fig. 2.25 there is looping from event (5) to event (2) through event (4).

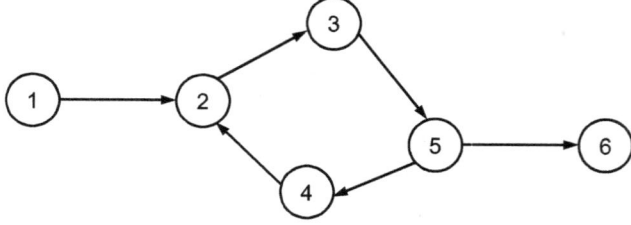

Fig. 2.25

If such a situation occurs, the logic underlying the diagram must be re-examined and the inter-relationship between the activities may be properly decided.

4. No activity can start unless the tail event has occurred. In Fig. 2.24, activity D cannot commence unless event (7) has occurred.

5. There should not be dead end loop for any activity except the final event node which is completion of the project. If there is any other dead end in the network that is called **"Dangling."** There should not be any dangling in the network. This dangling situation can be corrected with the use of dummy.

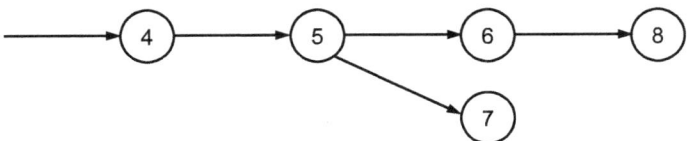

Fig. 2.26 : Dangling

Activity 5 – 7 is a dangling activity. It cannot remain separate from other activities before project concludes. This can therefore be connected to some other activity in the project by a dummy activity. (Fig. 2.27).

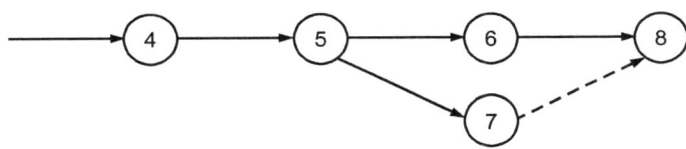

Fig. 2.27

6. Any activity in the project should be represented by a single arrow and each arrow should represent a singular activity and hence the number of arrows must be equal to number of activities.

7. Dummy activities should properly represent the interdependency and constraints between the different events.

8. Logic of the network be maintained. Initial event is start of the project which is shown at the left hand end and final event is project concluding which is shown at the right hand side. Hence, the activity arrow heads will point towards progress of the project i.e. from left to right.

9. This leads to usual practice that the line flows from left to right.

10. Arrow representing activities are not vectors and hence their length does not indicate the duration of any activity to any scale. Length is chosen to suit the drafting requirements.

11. As far as possible straight lines are used for arrows representing the activities, curved arrows are avoided.

12. Orientation of angles between the arrows representing the different activities does not lead to any specific information and is chosen to suit the drafting convenience and proper use of the available space.

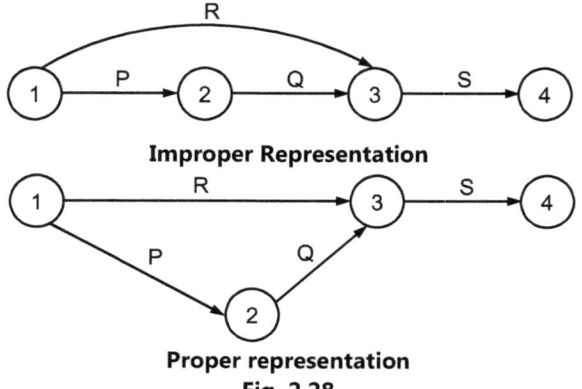

Improper Representation

Proper representation
Fig. 2.28

13. Activity arrows, as far as possible, should not cross. But if the interdepen-dency of the activity demands the same and crossing is unavoidable, the activity arrow should be broken to bridge over the other.

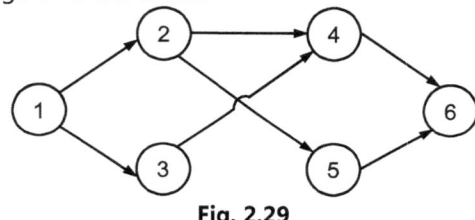

Fig. 2.29

14. Head events have always higher numbers than the tail events.

2.14.2 Shapes of Network Diagram

Normally, with the above cited guidelines, the network shape is angular where activity arrows are horizontal and making some acute angle with horizontal. However, network diagram can also be drawn in rectangular shape where activity arrows are either horizontal and vertical.

However, to maintain the logic and the requisite flow of the progress of activities, these horizontal and vertical arrows are required to be given a right angle turn. Such a type of rectangular network is quite compact but may sometimes become little clumsy. The angular type of network shows natural flow from left to right and is easy to understand.

Fig. 2.30 represents the above two networks.

Network technique is a flow diagram consisting of events and activities which must be accomplished in a planned sequence representing the interdependency and inter-relationship between the different activities and events in the project. In the network diagram activities, dummy activities and events that constitute the project are represented with the help of three symbols which have been already discussed.

Activity is represented by arrow ⎯⎯⎯⎯>
Dummy activity represented by broken arrow ---▶

Event is represented by circle : ○

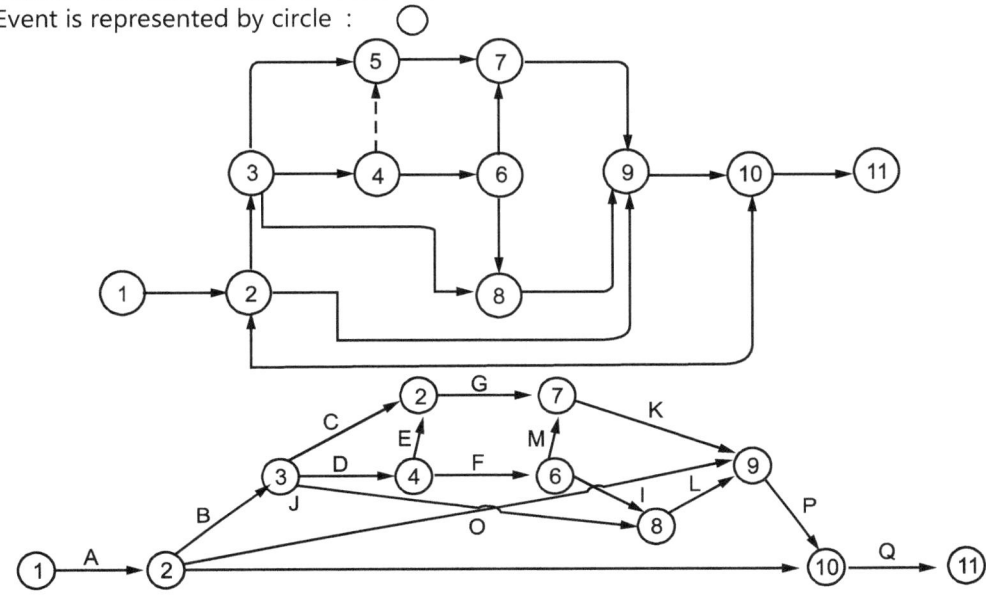

Fig. 2.30

2.14.3 Numbering of Events

In network diagram, events are numbered so that they can be identified. Different activities joining the events or nodes are identified with alphabets or with the event numbers at the tail and head of the activity. In numbering events, **'Fulkerson's Rule'** is followed.

1. The single initial event which is starting point of the project is numbered 1.
2. Initial event is head event for different activities. The head of arrows will lead to different other events which can be numbered serially 2, 3, 4 ……
3. These new events will be head events for further activities in the project. The head events of these activities will be numbered serially.
4. The process will continue till the last event which is completion of the project.
5. In this process all the events will be numbered serially. It is to be remembered that the head event will have a lower number than the head event.
6. In bigger network extensive modifications may be necessary and some additional activities or events may be required to be introduced in this modification. This will, therefore, need renumbering of events. This will be avoided by numbering events serially with numbers 10, 20, 30 …… etc. in place of serial numbers 1, 2, 3, …… so that in case some events are required to be added they can be suitably numbered in between the predecessor and successor events. This method of numbering events is called Fulkerson's method.

Example 2.2 : Using Fulkerson's method, number the events in the network shown below

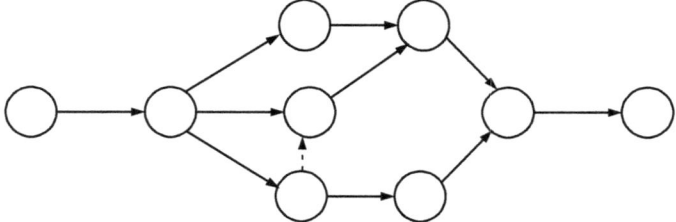

Solution :

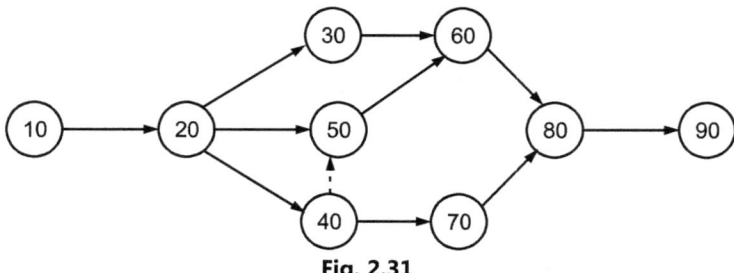

Fig. 2.31

Example 2.3 : Draw a network diagram for project laying a drainage pipeline.

Solution : The project can be broken into different activities and events as shown below

Activities :
    A - Layout (10 – 20)
    B - Excavation for trenches (20 – 40)
    C - Procurement of pipes (10 – 30)
    D - Pipe laying in excavated trenches (40 – 50)
    E - Pipe testing (50 – 60)
    F - Refilling of trenches (60 – 70)

Events :
    A - Start of the project
    1 - Starting layout
    2 - Layout completed, excavation started
    3 - Procurement of pipe started
    4 - Pipes procured
    5 - Excavation completed, Pipe laying started
    6 - Pipe laying ended testing of pipes started
    7 - Pipe testing started earth filling started
    8 - Earth filling completed

Event	Predecessor Event	Successor Event
Start of layout	–	Layout completed
Start of Excavation	Layout completed	Excavation completed
Procurement of pipe started	–	Procurement of pipe completed
Pipe laying started	Excavation completed, pipe procured	Pipe laying completed.
Pipe testing started	Pipe laying completed	Pipe testing completed.
Refilling started	Pipe testing completed	Refilling of trench ends.

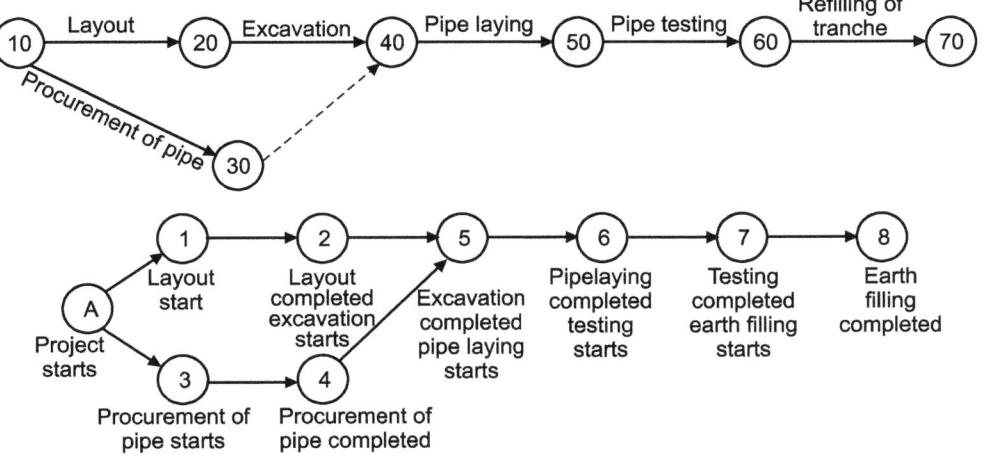

Fig. 2.32

Example 2.4 : Draw the network for the activities and events shown in the table given below

Activity	Events / Nodes		Duration in Days	Activity Inter-relationship		
	I Node	J Node		Preceeding	Succeeding	Parallel
A	10	20	3	–	B, C	–
B	20	30	3	A	D, E	C
C	20	40	4	A	F	B
D	30	40	0	B	F	E
E	30	50	6	B	G	D
F	40	50	2	D, C	G	–
G	50	60	4	E, F	–	–

Solution :

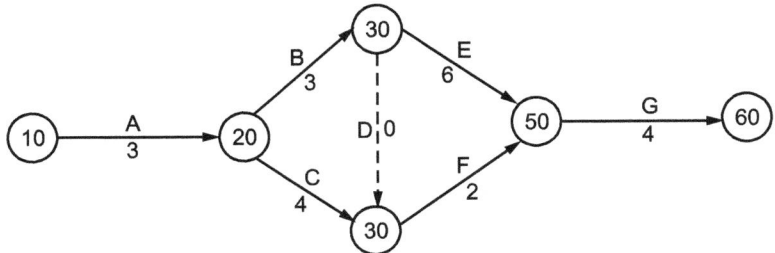

Fig. 2.33

Activities are denoted by Letters A, B, C ... and also by the tail node and head node. The tail nodes and head nodes are in general denoted by I nodes and J nodes. The duration of the activity is shown below the activity arrow and identification of the activity above the arrow. Duration of an activity is the estimated time required to complete the activity.

2.15 TIME ESTIMATES

The time duration used for different activities is any convenient unit consistent throughout the network. The unit is usually either days or weeks. For estimating time duration, a normal work crue depending upon the type of the work and experience is assumed. Generally in CPM the duration of the different activities in the project are deterministic and can be estimated fairly precisely. Depending upon the duration of different activities, the project duration will be decided.

2.15.1 Event Times

For each event two type of times are expressed depending upon occurrence of that event. Earliest Occurrence Time (EOT) of any event is the time wherein all the activities emerging to the event are completed in the least period possible. This is computed by adding the duration of all the activities along an activity path leading to that event. If more than one activity path is leading to that event, then the maximum of earliest occurrence time of the different activity paths is taken as Earliest Event Occurrence time and is denoted by T_E.

$$\text{EOT for an event} = \text{EOT of preceding event} + \text{Duration of activity}$$

$$EOT_j = EOT_i + t_{ij}$$

or

$$T_E^j = T_E^i + t_{ij}$$

Similarly, Latest Occurrence Time (LOT) for any event is the maximum time for completion of any event without causing any delay in completion of the project. This time is computed by subtracting the duration of all activities along the activity path from the concluding event to the event in question. If more than one event is emerging out, then the latest occurrence time is least of the time calculated from different activity paths.

$$LOT_i = LOT_j - t_{ij} \quad \text{i.e.} \quad T_L^i - T_L^j = t_{ij}$$

EOT for an event = EOT of preceding event + Duration of leading activity.

LOT for an event = LOT of following event − Duration of leaving activity.

In case more than one activities are leading to an event, EOT is taken maximum of all leading paths. Whilst LOT is taken minimum of all activity paths leaving the node. EOT is calculated by forward pass method and LOT is calculated by backward pass method.

2.15.2 Forward Pass

The minimum or expected duration of any project is the earliest occurrence time of the last event. Hence, to find out the duration of the project, one has to find out EOT of last event in the network of the project. This is done by calculating the EOT for each event of the network by forward pass method till the last event is reached. In case of merge events, EOT is calculated by all the possible paths and the maximum of values of EOT calculated from different paths is considered EOT for that event. This will give the duration of the project.

$$EOT_{(j)} = EOT_{(i)} + t_{ij}$$

Where, $EOT_{(j)}$ = Earliest occurrence time of jth event i.e. succeeding event

$EOT_{(i)}$ = Earliest occurrence time of ith event i.e. preceeding event.

$t_{(ij)}$ = duration of activity $i-j$ i.e. intervening activity

The first event in the network occurs at zero time and with this basis the EOT of all the subsequent events and project duration can be calculated. This is the minimum period in which the project can be completed.

2.15.3 Backward Pass

Normally, the earliest event occurrence time of last event is the project duration and the same is taken as the latest event occurrence time of the last event. However, if there is any imposed duration for the project that is taken as the latest event occurrence time for the last event. Assuming this latest event occurrence time of the last event, sequentially the latest event occurrence time for successive predecessor events can be calculated. The latest event occurrence time for any event in the network is the latest allowable event occurrence time for the succeeding event minus the duration of intervening activity.

$$LOT_{(i)} = LOT_{(j)} - t_{ij} \quad \text{i.e.} \quad T_L^i = T_L^j - t_{ij}$$

where, $LOT_{(i)}$ = Latest event occurrence time of ith event i.e. preceding event

$LOT_{(j)}$ = Latest event occurrence time of jth event i.e. succeeding event

$t_{(ij)}$ = duration of activity $(i-j)$ i.e. intervening activity.

In case there are more than one bursting activities originating from event i, the $LOT_{(i)}$ is calculated by all possible paths and whichever is minimum is taken as the LOT for that event. Thus, starting from the last event, LOT of all the events can be calculated and this will lead to finding LOT of first event as zero. This will help in finding the allowable delay in occurrence of different events without affecting the overall duration of the project. The allowable delay in occurrence of any event is the difference between the LOT and EOT for the event. This allowable delay is the slack period of the event.

2.15.4 Activity Times

For the different activities there is a time of start and time of finish.

For forward pass,

$$\text{Activity finish time} = \text{Activity start time} + \text{Duration}$$

and for backward pass,

$$\text{Activity start time} = \text{Activity finish time} - \text{Duration}$$

For the different activities, following times are calculated:

- EST – Earliest Start Time
- EFT – Earliest Finish Time
- LST – Latest Start Time
- LFT – Latest Finish Time

EST and EFT are the time of earliest start and earliest finish respectively of any activity without changing the sequence of the activities in the network.

Similarly, LST and LFT are the time of latest start and latest finish respectively without delaying the project duration without changing the sequence of the activities in the network.

An activity can start only after the tail event has occurred.

Hence, Earliest Start Time of any activity is the Earliest Occurrence Time of Tail Event of the activity.

∴   EST of an activity = EOT of tail event

     EFT of any activity = EST of that activity + Duration

Similarly, an activity must conclude before the time of occurrence of head event.

Hence the Latest finish time of any activity is the Latest Event Occurrence time of head event of the activity.

     LFT of an activity = LOT of head event

     LST of an activity = LFT of the activity – Duration

The above terminologies can be very well explained with the help of following network.

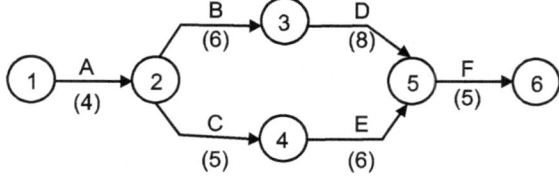

Fig. 2.34

Explanation of this network is
- Activity A is the starting activity.
- Activities D and E ends the project.
- Activities B and C emerges from A.
- Activity D will start only after completion at activity B.
- Activity E is the succeeding activity of C.
- Activity F starts only after completion of activity D and E.

The duration of each activity is shown below the arrow and the activity name.

Now, let us calculate EST, EFT, LST and LFT using forward and backward pass. The nomenclature which we will be using is as follows

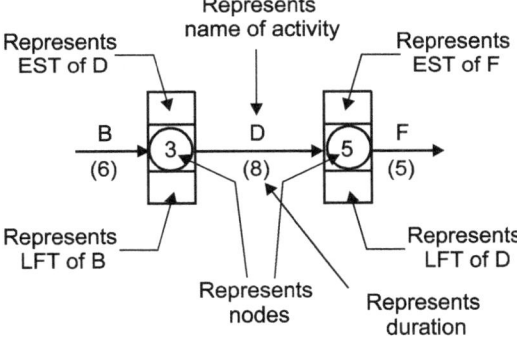

Fig. 2.35

Forward Pass

In this, we will move from left to right.

(1) The project starts at 0th time i.e. starting time on first day.

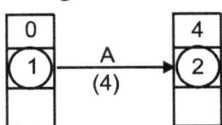

Fig. 2.36

∴ Activity will start earliest at 0th day.

∴   EST of A = 0

As activity A has EST = 0, it will finish earliest at 0 + 4 = 4 days.

i.e. EST of A+ duration of A. This is called as Earliest Finish Time (EFT) of A.

(2)

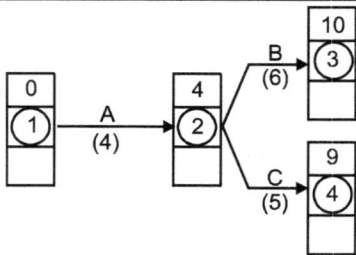

Fig. 2.37

As 'A' finishes at 4th day, activities B and C will start on 4th day. Hence EST for B and C both is '4'.

∴ $(EFT)_B$ = $(EST)_B$ + duration of B
= 4 + 6 = 10

Similarly, $(EFT)_C$ = $(EST)_C$ + duration of C
= 4 + 5 = 9

(3)

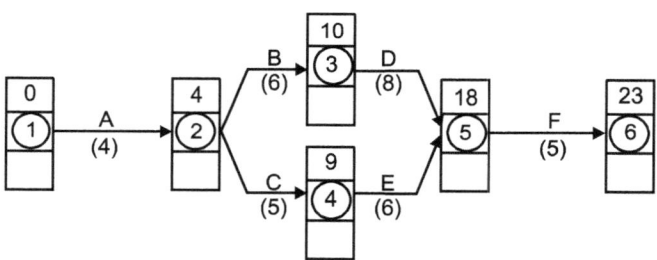

Fig. 2.38

Activity D will start after completion of activity B which is EFT of B. Similarly, activity E will start after completion of activity C which is EFT of C.

∴ EST of D = 10
EST of E = 9

∴ EFT of D = (10 + 8) = 18
And EFT of E = (9 + 6) = 15

Now, as per the logic of the network, activity F will start only after completion of both the preceeding activities D and E i.e. 18 days which is the "highest" of both the EFTs.

∴ EST of F is 18 which gives EFT of F as (18 + 5) = 23 days. This is the total project duration.

Backward Pass

In backward pass, we will calculate the time estimates from right to left. Duration of project is 23 days which means the activity F should be finished latest by 23 days.

∴ LFT of F is 23 days, hence it has to start latest by (23 − 5) = 18 days, which is LST of F.

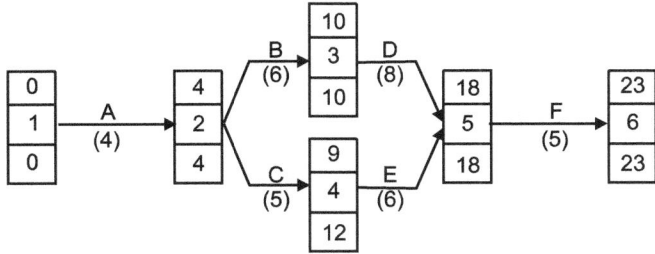

Fig. 2.39

LST of F as 18 indicates that, activities D and E should be finished latest by 18.

∴ LST of D = IFT of E = 18 as these are parallel activities

∴ LST of D = (18 − 8) = 10 and LST of E = (18 − 6) = 12.

Similarly, LST's and LFT's of all remaining activities are calculated as under

LFT of B = 10 ∴ LST of B = (10 − 6) = 4
LFT of C = 12 ∴ LST of C = (12 − 5) = 7

In the backward pass, we have to consider the minimum time of all for calculating LFT of A.

i.e. 4. ∴ LFT of A = 4, LST of A = (4 − 4) = 0

2.15.5 Floats

As there can be allowable delay or slack in case of events without affecting the duration of the project, similarly there can be some allowable delay in completion of any activity and measure of such delay is called *Float*. It is a measure of time by which an activity may be delayed without affecting the logic of the project or the total duration of the project. There are four types of floats with different identification. They are Total Float (TF), Free Float (FF), Interfering Float (IF) and Independent Float (F_{ind}).

Total Float

'It is the time by which a particular activity can be delayed without causing any effect on the duration of the project'. It is, therefore, the difference between the maximum time available for any activity and its duration. The maximum time available for any activity without causing delay to the project is difference of its Latest Finish Time and the Earliest Start Time.

Hence, Total Float = (LFT − EST) − Duration
∴ TF = (LFT − Duration) − EST

$$= \text{LST} - \text{EST}$$
$$= (\text{LST} + \text{Duration}) - (\text{EST} + \text{Duration})$$
$$= \text{LFT} - \text{EFT}$$
$$\therefore \quad \text{TF} = \text{LST} - \text{EST}$$
$$= \text{LFT} - \text{EFT}$$

It can also be pointed out,

Total Float = (LOT of head event – EOT of tail event) – Duration of activity.

Free Float

'It is the amount of time by which the commencement of any activity may be delayed without any effect or interference on the start of the next activity'. If there has to be no effect on the subsequent activity, the time of earliest occurrence of the head event of the activity must be maintained. Hence, free float is the difference between EOT of the head event and EFT of the activity so that if the start of the activity is delayed by this duration, it will get just completed before EOT of the head event.

$$\text{FF} = \text{EOT of head event} - \text{EFT of the activity}$$
$$= \text{EST of the following activity} - \text{EFT of the activity}$$

Hence, free float of any activity i – j is the difference between its earliest finish time and the earliest start time of the succeeding activity.

$$\text{FF} = \text{EOT of Head Event} - \text{EOT of Tail Event} - \text{Duration of Activity}$$
$$= \text{EOT of Head Event} - (\text{EOT of Tail} + \text{Duration of Activity})$$

Hence $\quad \text{FF} = \text{EOT of Head Event} - \text{EFT of Activity}$

Free float is that portion of positive total float that can be used by an activity without affecting the earliest start time of succeeding activity.

The concept of free float is based on the possibility that all activities start at their EST and all the events occur at their earliest time.

Interfering Float

It is the slack of head event. It is equal to difference of LOT and EOT of the head event and is also difference of Total Float and Free Float.

$$\text{IF} = \text{TF} - \text{FF}$$

Interfering float is the potential downstream interference of any activity. If the full interfering float is made, subsequent activities become critical and if it is exceeded the total duration of the project will increase and the project will be delayed.

Independent Float

It is the excess time that is available if the preceeding activity ends as late as possible and the succeeding activity starts as early as possible. The independent float is defined as the excess of minimum available time over the required activity duration.

Minimum available time for any activity

$$= \text{EOT of Head Event} - \text{LOT of Tail Event}$$

∴ F_{ind} = EOT of Head Event − LOT of Tail Event −

Duration of the Activity

= EOT of Head Event − EST of Activity + EST of Activity − LOT of tail event − Duration of Activity

= EOT of Head Event − (EST of Activity + Duration of Activity) − (LOT of tail event − EST of Activity)

= (EOT of Head Event − EFT of Activity) − (LOT of Tail Event − EOT of Tail Event)

= Free float − Slack of Tail Event

∴ Independent Float = Free Float − Slack of Tail Event

If tail event is i^{th} event and head event is j^{th} event and the activity is denoted by i − j,

T_L^j = LOT of jth event

T_E^j = EOT of jth event

T_L^i = LOT of ith event

T_E^i = EOT of ith event

t_{ij} = Duration of Activity

Total Float of an activity is the excess of maximum available time for activity over activity duration

∴ $TF = \left(T_L^j - T_E^j\right) - t_{ij}$

= LFT − EFT of the activity = LST − EST of the activity

Free Float of an activity is the excess of available time over the activity duration when all the activities start at their earliest start line.

∴ $FF = \left(T_E^j - T_E^i\right) - t_{ij}$

= EST of following activity − EFT of the activity

= EOT of head event − EFT of the activity

Independent Float of an activity is the excess of minimum available time over the activity duration.

$$\therefore \quad F_{ind} = \left(T_E^j - T_L^i\right) - t_{ij}$$

$$= \left(T_E^j - T_E^i + T_E^i - T_L^i\right) - t_{ij}$$

$$= \left(T_E^j - T_E^i\right) - t_{ij} - \left(T_L^i - T_E^i\right)$$

= Free Float − Slack of tail event

Interfering Float of an activity is the difference between the Total Float and Free Float. It is equal to slack of head event.

$$IF = TF - FF$$

$$= T_L^j - T_E^j = \text{Head event slack}$$

The above floats are represented diagrammatically in Fig. 2.40.

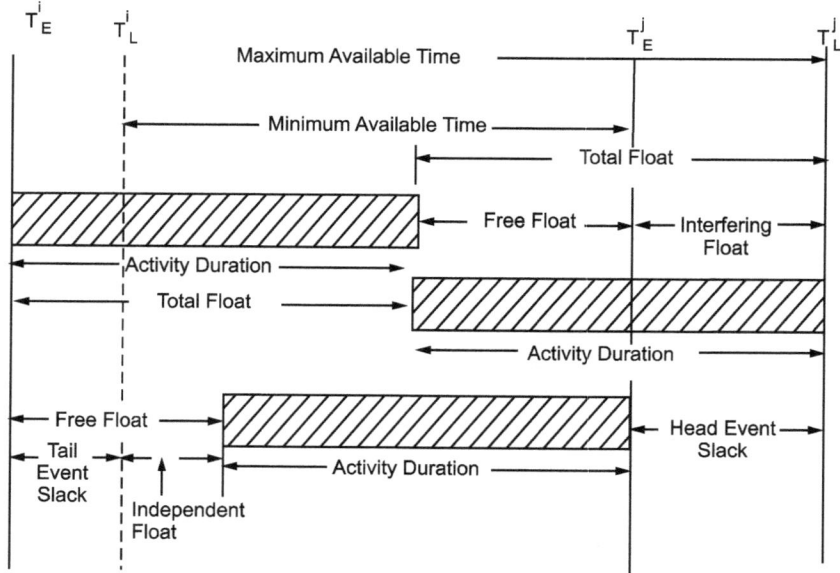

Fig. 2.40

Floats are used in scheduling to show where flexibility exists. This flexibility is meaningful and can be made use for large one time projects such as construction of a highway or dam or developing a new missile or launching a satellite. Out of the four floats, only two of them namely, total float and free float are of practical use. Total float is most useful since it is difference of maximum available time for any activity and its duration. There may be three possibilities regarding total float.

- It may have a negative value if the maximum available time is less than activity duration.
- It may have zero value if the maximum available time is equal to activity duration.
- It may have positive value if the maximum available time is greater than activity duration.

When the float is negative, such activities are most important and they demand special attention and special action. Such activities are termed as "Super Critical Activities." The activities where float is zero, they are called "Critical Activities." They demand good attention and no freedom of action can be taken with such activities as it may result in delay of the project. The activities with positive float are "Subcritical Activities" and hence some freedom in terms of delay may be possible with such activities. They demand normal action.

Negative float indicates that the activity duration is more than maximum available time in the project which is little abnormal situation and attempt may be made for compressing the duration by rearranging the resources or arranging additional resources to bring the negative float to positive or at least to zero. Critical path is one which joins the critical activities for which float is zero. These critical activities control the project duration. Any delay in the execution of critical activity than the scheduled duration will extent the project duration by the same time slab. Critical path starts from the initial event and passes through all such events where there is no slack and ends in the last event. In order to identify the critical path, float concept provides the necessary and sufficient conditions for activities to be critical. It may be possible that some activities joining event with zero slack may not be found critical with float concept. It should also be noted that there can be more than one critical path in the network.

The activity times and floats for the previous example are tabulated as under

Activity	Duration	EST	EFT	LST	LFT	TF	FF	Int F	Ind F
A	4	0	4	0	4	0	0	0	0
B	6	4	10	4	10	0	0	0	0
C	5	4	9	7	12	3	0	3	0
D	8	10	18	10	18	0	0	0	0
E	6	9	15	12	18	3	3	0	0
F	5	18	23	18	23	0	0	0	0

The activities which are having Total Float (TF) = 0 are termed as critical activities. Hence, as per the above table, activities A, B, D and F are critical activities. If we join these activities, we get a continuous path which is termed as critical path and total duration of the project is 23 days. The network with critical path will be shown as below

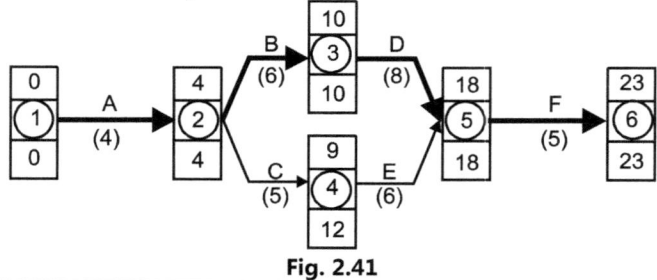

Fig. 2.41

Example 2.5 : Draw an AOA network diagram and find critical path, total duration of project and all floats.

Activity	Duration in Days	Preceeding Activities	Succeeding Activities
A	3	–	C, D, F
B	10	–	E, H
C	4	A	E, H
D	6	A	G
E	4	B, C	G
F	6	A	J
G	8	D, E	I
H	2	B, C	I
I	6	G, H	K
J	8	F	K
K	8	J, I	–

Solution : The network is drawn as given below

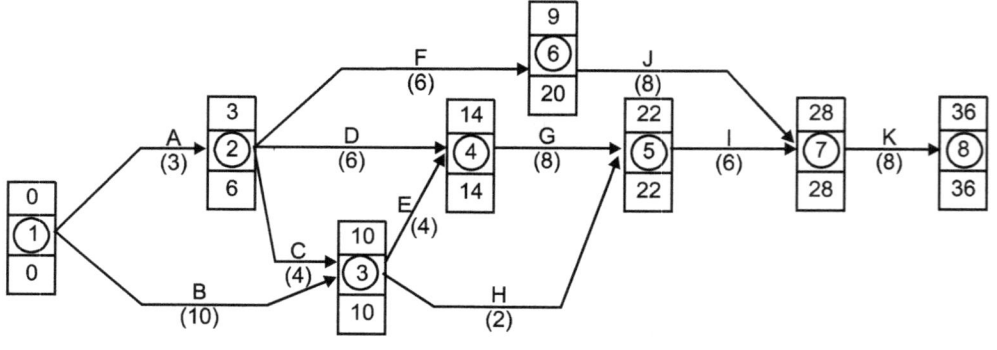

Fig. 2.42

Activity	Duration	EST	EFT	LST	LFT	TF	FF	Int F	Ind F
A	3	0	3	3	6	3	0	3	0
B	10	0	10	0	10	0	0	0	0
C	4	3	7	6	10	3	3	0	0
D	6	3	9	8	14	5	5	0	2
E	4	10	14	10	14	0	0	0	0
F	6	3	19	14	20	11	0	11	−3
G	8	14	22	14	22	0	0	0	0
H	2	10	12	20	22	10	10	0	10
I	6	22	28	22	28	0	0	0	0
J	8	9	17	20	28	11	11	0	0
K	8	28	36	28	36	0	0	0	0

Example 2.6 : Analyse the work of construction of a Steel Rolling Mill and construct a CPM Network for the same. Calculate the project duration after marking the critical path. Also calculate the Total Float and Free Float.

Solution : The work of erection of a steel mill on analysis can be divided into different independent jobs as shown below. The estimated duration of completion of these activities is also indicated in table below. The duration of each activity has been estimated by proper analysis and with experience of duration of similar activities undertaken in earlier projects. The correlation and sequence of different activities is properly studied and if necessary dummy activities are introduced to maintain proper flow and sequence of work.

The details of preparing the network and calculation of floats will comprise of the following steps

- Step No. 1 : Table of inter-relation between different activities.
- Step No. 2 : Preparation of network with the help of above table.
- Step No. 3 : Calculation of EST and EFT of different activities by Forward Pass Method.
- Step No. 4 : Calculation of LFT and LST of different activities by Backward Pass Method.
- Step No. 5 : Marking the Critical Path.
- Step No. 6 : Calculation of Project Duration.
- Step No. 7 : Calculation of Total Float and Free Float.

All the above are worked out in tabular form

Sr. No.	Description of Job or the Activity	Activity Symbol	Estimated Duration in Weeks
1	Preliminary Investigation	A	5
2	Design of Building	B	10
3	Preparation of specifications of machinery and equipment	C	4
4	Procuring Machinery and Equipment	D	32
5	Construction of Building Foundation	E	12
6	Construction of Machinery Foundation	F	7
7	Construction of Building Superstructure	G	14
8	Laying underground pipes, conduits and other anciliary utility	H	4
9	Installation of Machinery and Equipment	I	18
10	Installation of Electrical Driving Unit	J	12
11	Installation of Wiring and Control Equipment Final Checking and Testing	K	10
12	Clearing site	L	9
13		M	2

Step No. 1 :

Sr. No.	Activity	Duration	Preceding Activity	Succeeding Activity	Remarks
1	A	5	–	B, C	Starting Activity
2	B	10	A	E, F, H	
3	C	4	A	D	
4	D	32	C	J, I	
5	E	12	B	G	
6	F	7	B	J, I	
7	G	14	E	L	
8	H	4	B	R	
9	I	18	D, F	K	
10	J	12	D, F	P	
11	K	10	I, P	L	
12	L	9	K, G, R	M	
13	M	2	L	–	End Activity
14	P (Dummy)	00	J	K	Dummy
15	R (Dummy)	00	H	L	Dummy

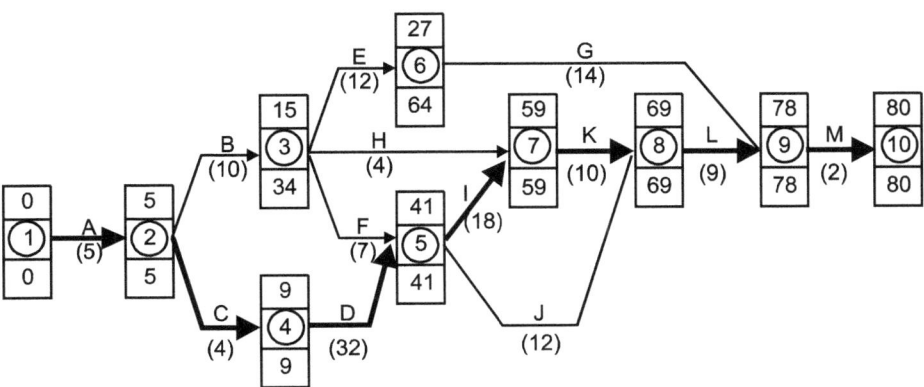

Fig. 2.43

Total duration of project : 80 days.

Activity	Duration	EST	EFT	LST	LFT	TF	FF	Remarks
A	5	0	5	0	5	0	0	Critical
B	10	5	15	24	34	19	0	
C	4	5	9	5	9	0	0	Critical
D	32	9	41	9	41	0	0	Critical
E	12	15	27	52	64	37	0	
F	7	15	22	34	41	19	19	
G	14	27	41	64	78	37	37	
H	4	15	19	55	59	40	40	
I	18	41	59	41	59	0	0	Critical
J	12	41	53	57	69	16	16	
K	10	59	69	59	69	0	0	Critical
L	9	69	78	69	78	0	0	Critical
M	2	78	80	80	80	0	0	Critical

Critical path : A-C-D-I-K-L-M

Example 2.7 : Work out the project duration and indicate the critical path. Also calculate the interfering float.

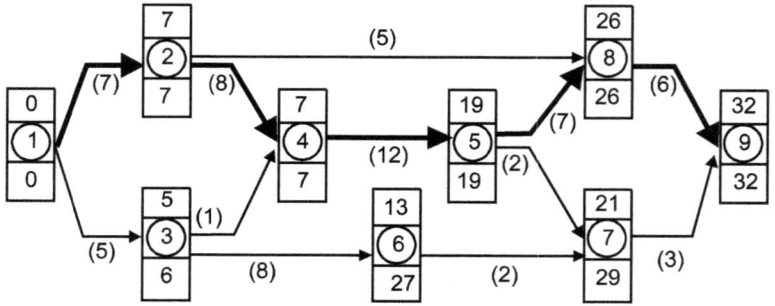

Fig. 2.44

Project Duration = 32 days

Activity	Duration	EST	EFT	LST	LFT	TF	FF
1-2	07	0	7	0	7	0	0
1-3	05	0	5	1	6	1	0
2-4	00	7	7	7	7	0	0
3-4	01	5	6	6	7	1	1
2-8	05	7	12	21	26	14	14
3-6	08	5	13	19	27	14	0
4-5	12	7	19	7	19	0	0
5-8	07	19	26	19	26	0	0
5-7	02	19	21	27	29	8	0
6-7	02	13	15	27	29	14	6
8-9	06	26	32	26	32	0	0
7-9	03	21	24	29	32	7	8

Example 2.8 : For construction of a small residential block, prepare the network and calculate the duration of the project by CPM.

Solution : The project is broken into different unit jobs or activities and depending upon the resources available, the activity duration is decided.

Table is prepared for the different activities with the predecessor and successor activity as shown below

Sr. No.	Activity	Description	Duration in Weeks	Preceding Activity	Succeeding Activity
1	A	Excavation, Foundation, Plinth, Masonry and DPC	3	–	C
2	B	BB work in superstructure including fixing door and window frames, casting lintels, shelves	4	C, D	K, J, G
3	C	R.C.C. work in beams and slab	4	A	B
4	D	Preparation of door, window frames and panels	2	–	B
5	E	Inside Plaster in CM 1 : 5	3	J	F
6	F	Marble Mosaic tile flooring	2	E	I
7	G	Outside Plaster in CM 1 : 5	3	B	I
8	H	Distempering inside and outside & oil painting to doors & windows	2	I	–
9	I	Fixing doors and window panels	2	F, G	H
10	J	Providing water supply and sanitary fittings	3	B	E
11	K	Providing electrical wiring and fittings (concealed)	4	B	–

L, M, N and P are dummy activities.

The network diagram is as shown below in Fig. 2.45.

The critical path and duration of the project is determined as shown in Table below.

Solution :

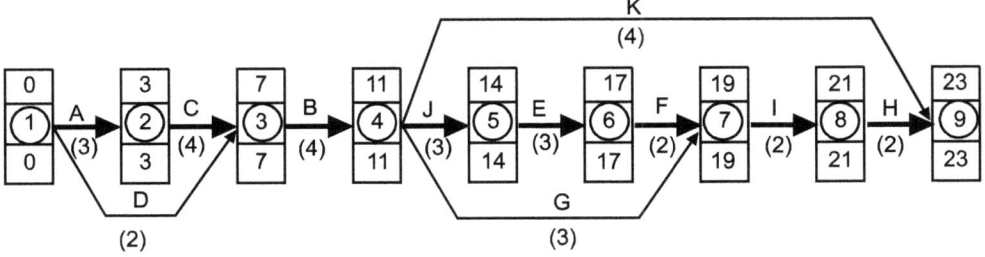

Fig. 2.45

Activity	Duration (Weeks)	EST	EFT	LST	LFT	TF
A	3	0	3	0	3	0
B	4	7	11	7	11	0
C	4	3	7	3	7	0
D	2	0	2	5	7	5
E	3	14	17	14	17	0
F	2	17	19	17	19	0
G	3	11	14	16	19	5
H	2	21	23	21	23	0
I	2	19	21	19	21	0
J	3	11	14	11	14	0
K	4	11	15	19	23	8

Total duration of project = 23 weeks.

Critical path A – C- B – J – E – F – I – H

2.16 PERT

2.16.1 Programme Evaluation and Review Technique (PERT)

This method was developed for U.S. Navey Special Project Office for Polaris Missile Programme. The Lockhead Missile System Division along with management consultant firm Booz, Allen and Hamilton developed this programme for evaluating the feasibility of existing schedule for reporting the progress.

As discussed above, the PERT emphasises events which is start or completion of an activity and commencement of further activities. The method of development network for CPM and PERT are to some extent identical but the basic difference is, for CPM, since the time duration of activities are fairly accurately known, the emphasis is on activities whereas in PERT since probabilistic time duration for the different activities are evolved the network has to be event oriented as the point where a specific part of programme is achieved or activity completed is important.

Basically there is not much difference between CPM and PERT. In place of activities in CPM, the PERT consists of number of events arranged in sequential order joined by arrows. The most important part of PERT is selection of specifically identifiable events which are planned to accrue in the completion of the project.

The sequential arrangement of these events will, of course, depend upon inter-dependency in the similar manner as interdependence of activities is decided in CPM. The most important job is estimation of duration of moving from one event to next event throughout the project wherein uncertainties are involved. Hence, the probabilistic duration of completion of events is considered in PERT. Rest of the procedure of forming network and analysis, highlighting the critical activities in CPM and critical events in PERT, is same. Since PERT depends on probabilistic duration of occurrence of events, it is used for such project where the management cannot be guided by past experience. PERT network is, therefore, suitable for non-repetitive or once-through projects which are research or innovative form.

Three Time Estimates in PERT

Due to uncertainty of the project, three times estimates are made as follows :

1. **Optimistic Time (t_o) :** 'It is the shortest possible time in which activity can be completed when everything goes smoothly'. No provisions are made for delays or setbacks.

2. **Pessimistic Time (t_p) :** 'This is the longest time the activity takes if everything goes wrong'. Major hurdles like labour strikes or natural calamities are excluded from this time.

3. **The Most Likely Time Estimate (t_m) :** 'This is the time required by the activity under normal circumstances'. It assumes that things are going in normal ways, a few setbacks, no excitements and no dramatic breakthroughs.

The beta distribution of PERT time estimates is as given below

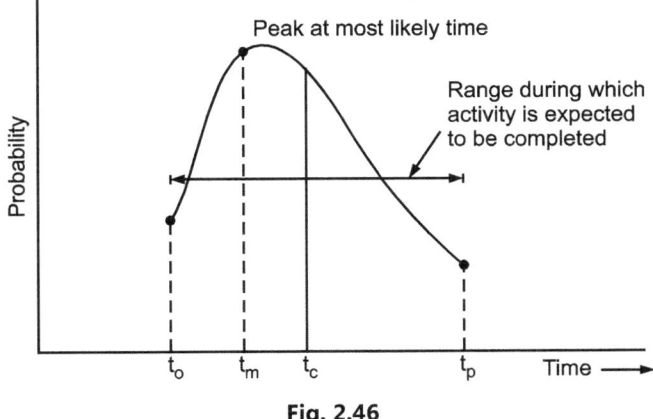

Fig. 2.46

The expected time $\quad t_e = \dfrac{(t_o + 4t_m + t_p)}{6}$

Standard Deviation

'It is the statistical measure of the uncertainty being the spread of distribution curve about the mean value'.

$$\therefore \quad S.D. = \sigma = \frac{(t_p - t_o)}{6}$$

Variance (V)

'It is a function of difference between t_p and t_o'. If $(t_p - t_o)$ is small, there is certainty of meeting the schedule. But if it is large, there are less chances of meeting the time schedule.

$$\therefore \quad V = \sigma^2 = \frac{(t_p - t_o)^2}{6^2}$$

Using the standard deviation, the probability of meeting scheduled event time is calculated as follows

$$Z = \frac{\text{Scheduled date} - \text{Expected data}}{\sqrt{\text{Variance of evetns involved}}}$$

For corresponding values of Z, the probability can be read from standard normal distribution as follows

Z	Probability	Z	Probability
2.8	0.997	− 0.2	0.421
2.6	0.995	− 0.4	0.345
2.4	0.992	− 0.6	0.274
2.2	0.986	− 0.8	0.212
2.0	0.977	− 1.0	0.159
1.8	0.964	− 1.2	0.115
1.6	0.945	− 1.4	0.085
1.4	0.919	− 1.6	0.055
1.2	0.885	− 1.8	0.036
1.0	0.841	− 2.0	0.023
0.8	0.788	− 2.2	0.014
0.6	0.726	− 2.4	0.008
0.4	0.655	− 2.6	0.005
0.2	0.579	− 2.8	0.003
0.0	0.500		

PERT consist of the following steps
- Project is broken down in events.
- Events are arranged in logical sequence.
- Network is drawn and events are numbered.
- Using three time estimates, expected time is calculated.
- Standard deviation and variance is calculated.
- Network is marked with expected time of each event, and forward and backward pass is made as in CPM.
- Critical path is marked on network and project duration is found out.
- The probability of completing the project on due date is calculated.

2.16.2 Extension of PERT

There are three major developments in the use of PERT. They are as follows
1. Introduction of possibility of realisation of an activity in PERT.
2. Use of PERT in mass production.
3. Auto PERT.

   When the PERT network for a complex project is found to be complicated, the analysis of network becomes very difficult and time consuming. In order to eliminate such situation a possible method has been devised for automatically producing a type of standard network in the computer. This innovation is named 'AUTO PERT'. This was first time used by Shell Chemical Co. of U.S.A. under the guidance of G. Mechenzie who is the father of this technique.
4. GERT means Graphical Evolution and Review Technique. It is the latest tool in the hands of the management. This not only deals with the uncertainties in the completion time of the activities but also deals with the probability of realisation of the activity itself. This approach combines the concept of PERT type of network with flow graph concept. Application of GERT has been made in the following fields.
   - Space vehicle count down analysis.
   - Manufacture of semiconductor material analysis.

However, this latest technique is yet to become popular in the industry.

2.16.3 Successful Application of PERT

For successful use of PERT technique the following conditions are necessary
1. **Support of Top Management :** It is absolutely necessary that there must be whole hearted support to the use of this technique. The top management should understand the potentials and also the limitations of PERT that it can provide encouragement in use of PERT in planning stage of innovative projects. With unwillingness on the part of top management it is worthless to spend time and effort in use of PERT.
2. **Publicity :** Proper publicity is made throughout the organisation and all the persons involved in the programme should be informed well in advance about the use of

PERT for the project. All the managerial and supervisory personnel should know about the launching of PERT which will help in creating the necessary involvement of all concerned in the use of this tool and will create necessary climate in the organisation.

3. **Team Effort and Co-ordination :** The nature of PERT calls for a co-ordinated effort by all the departments involved in the plan. It is very necessary that the project manager should provide leadership and take all the concerned heads of the department into confidence so that best co-ordination is available from them.

4. **Training :** A thorough training is must for all concerned who are actively associated with the planning and execution of the project. There should be proper training which may take sometime for developing the necessary skills to work on the network at the time of planning and execution.

5. **Abuses :** PERT is a planning technique as well as an information system, as such there should not be mistakes in preparing the extensive reports on progress. This may defeat the basic purpose of planning mechanism. Time estimates are likely to give longer duration to be on safer side which may also defeat the purpose of PERT. There is no trouble with this if new activities take more time than the average time estimations. This may be counterbalanced for catching up subsequent events as there is bound to be some flexibility.

6. **Use of Computers :** In complex projects of very long duration the activities may increase to a large extent. If the number exceeds even 200, it will not be possible to handle the project without the use of computer However, small projects can be handled even without any use of computer. But the use of computers may make the work handy and easier.

Example 2.9 : Following is the data for a small project having 10 activities. Draw PERT diagram. Find t_e, σ, variance.
What will be the probability of completing the project in (i) 35 days, (ii) 40 days.

Activity	t_o	t_m	t_p
1 – 2	3	8	13
1 – 3	2	5	8
2 – 4	3	8	7
2 – 5	4	7	10
3 – 5	2	3	10
4 – 6	7	9	11
5 – 7	4	6	8
6 – 8	6	9	12
6 – 7	5	7	9
7 – 8	2	5	14

Solution : 1. Draw the network

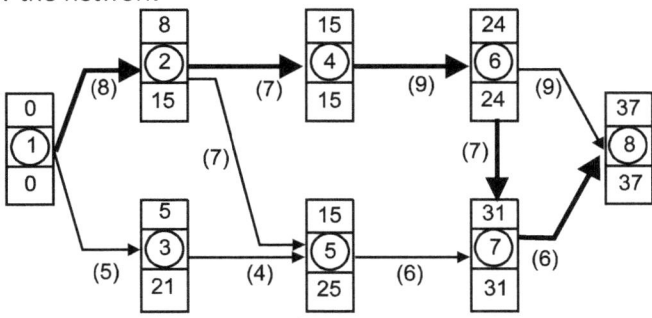

Fig. 2.47

Calculation of various parameters are as follows

Activity	t_o	t_m	t_p	t_e	σ	V
1 – 2	3	8	13	8	1.67	2.78
1 – 3	2	5	8	5	1.00	1.00
2 – 4	3	8	7	7	0.67	0.44
2 – 5	4	7	10	7	1.00	1.00
3 – 5	2	3	10	4	1.33	1.47
4 – 6	7	9	11	9	0.67	0.44
5 – 7	4	6	8	6	0.67	0.44
6 – 8	6	9	12	9	1.00	1.00
6 – 7	5	7	9	7	0.67	0.44
7 – 8	2	5	14	6	2.00	4.00

Critical path : 1 – 2 – 4 – 6 – 7 – 8
Duration : 37 days

Sum of variance along critical path
1 – 2 – 4 – 6 – 7 – 8 = 2.78 + 0.44 + 0.44 + 0.44 + 4 = 8.1

Standard deviation = σ = $\sqrt{\text{Variance of the project}}$ = $\sqrt{8.1}$ = 2.846

Probability of completing the project

(i) $$Z = \frac{\text{Scheduled date} - \text{Expected date}}{\sqrt{\text{Variance of events involved}}}$$

$$Z = \frac{(35 - 37)}{2.846} = -0.7027$$

Probability corresponding to Z from the table of standard normal distribution
= 0.243 i.e. 24.3%

(ii) $$Z = \frac{(40 - 37)}{2.846} = 1.05$$

Probability corresponding to Z from the table of standard normal distribution
= 0.852 i.e. 85.2%

2.16.4 Comparison of CPM and PERT

Though the method of framing the network and location of critical operations or unit jobs and events are similar, the CPM is an activity oriented network system and the PERT is an event oriented network system. In both the systems, unit jobs i.e. activities and points of start or completion of unit jobs i.e. events are used in framing of the network diagram. The method of representation of the activities by arrows and events by circles is also similar. However, in CPM emphasis is given on activities as their duration period can be precisely decided while in PERT the emphasis is on events as point where a particular unit job is completed is important. The methodology of preparation and analysis of network is mostly similar and utilises the same logic. Though many things are common, the points of difference in the above two systems of network can be summarized as below

- CPM is activity oriented and PERT is event oriented.
- In CPM, the time estimates i.e. duration of completion of different activities can be decided with fair degree of accuracy whereas the time of completion of different events cannot be precisely decided in PERT.
- CPM is used for repetitive type of projects wheras PERT is used for research or innovative type of project.
- In CPM, cost estimates for the different activities can be precisely arrived at. By varying the resources the duration of completion of the project can be changed. As such the cost optimisation is possible in CPM. In CPM, cost may not be proportional to the time and hence cost optimisation is given prime importance in CPM. In PERT, on the other hand since duration cannot be specified precisely, the cost goes on increasing as the duration of the project increases and to some extent the cost is directly proportional to the duration. To minimise the cost, therefore, it is necessary to pay attention to minimise the duration of the project.
- In projects where cost is controlling factor, CPM is used and in projects where time is controlling factor, PERT is used.
- CPM is used for deterministic projects whereas PERT is used for probabilistic projects. Where long developed well-seasoned components and stable technology is used, CPM is always preferred. In such projects any changes made during the execution can be easily incorporated in CPM network. In case of projects where extreme degree of uncertainty rules in deciding the event durations, PERT has to be used. In such projects, control over time overweighs the control over the cost.
- PERT is therefore, frequently used for Research and innovative development projects wherein uncertainties reign time required for different events and eventually in completion of the project.

QUESTIONS

1. Explain importance of management in project planning and execution.
2. Bring out the development of management science.
3. Explain the different phases of project management.
4. Explain the two important methods of project planning in brief and bring out the difference between the two.
5. Explain salient features of CPM and PERT and the circumstances in which each is used.
6. What do you understand by Bar chart ? With suitable example, describe the process of construction of Gantt's chart.
7. What are different strong points and shortcomings of a Gantt's chart ?
8. How the different shortcomings of bar chart can be removed ?
9. How milestone chart differ from a bar chart ? How it overcomes some of the shortcomings of bar chart ?
10. Give out the advantages and limitations of milestone chart.
11. Differentiate between CPM, PERT, Bar chart and Mile stone chart.
12. Draw the bar chart for a project with 8 different activities as shown below and calculate the total time of completion.

Sr. No.	Name of Activity	Duration in Days	Preceding Activity	Succeeding Activity	Remark
1	A	3	–	C, D	
2	B	5	–	–	
3	C	3	A	E* G	
4	D	5	A	F	
5	E	8	C*	H	*Cannot start unless 60% work of C is completed.
6	F	5	D		
7	G	6	C		
8	H	5	E		Last Activity

If there is increase of 3 days in the time of completion of activity A, calculate the corresponding delay in completion of the project.

13. What do you understand by Event and Activity ?
14. What is AOA network and AON network ? Explain with suitable examples.
15. Differentiate between CPM and PERT network. Explain where each is used.

16. What are different types of events? Explain with examples.
17. Describe the different types of activities in a network and explain the use of dummy activity.
18. What are difficulties in logic in the network? Explain looping and dangling.
19. What are the different rules to be observed in framing of network?
20. A project consists of 6 events and inter-relationship between them is as shown below. Draw the network.

Event	Predecessor Event
(1)	–
(2)	(1)
(3)	(2)
(4)	(2)
(5)	(3) (4)
(6)	(5)

21. Write about characteristics of CPM and PERT networks.
22. Inter-relationship between the different activities in a project is as shown below. Draw the network and find the critical path.

Activity	Predecessor Activity	Successor Activity	Duration
A	–	B, C	6
B	A	E, H	8
C	A	D	9
D	C	I, J	4
F	B	I, J	3
G	E	L	6
H	B	R	10
I	D, F	I, J	8
J	D, F	P	1
K	I, P	L	2
M	L	–	4
R	H	L	6
P	J	K	5

23. What do you understand by CPM and PERT? Give the points common to both and also the points of differentiation.
24. Compare CPM and PERT.
25. Explain the procedure of construction of CPM network with example of erection of statue of a national leader in a square of a city.
26. Define the following
    (i) Optimistic time (ii) Most likely time (iii) Pessimistic time (iv) Expected mean time
27. Differentiate between the following terms
    (i) Activity and Event   (ii) Dummy activity and Critical activity
    (iii) Total float and Free float
    (iv) Looping and Dangling.

28. Define the following
    (i) Earliest Event Occurrence Time and Latest Event Occurrence Time.
    (ii) Latest Start Time and Latest Finish Time of an Activity.
    (iii) Slack of an Event and Independent Float for an Activity.
29. Define Free Float and bring out its importance. How is it determined?
30. How is probability of completion of a project in given definite period is determined?
31. Different activities and their duration for construction of a residential building is given below. Frame the network and work out the period of completion of project. Mark Critical Path.

Name of Activity	Description	Duration in Weeks
A	Select plot for construction	2
B	Selection of Architect	2
C	Purchase of Plot	3
D	Preparation of Plan and Estimate	2
E	Approval of plan from local authority	2
F	Preparation of material requirement	4
G	Place order for different materials	1
H	Obtain timber for shutters	3
I	Obtain glass	1
J	Obtain door window frames	3
K	Obtain building materials (bricks, cement, aggregate)	2
L	Obtain marble mozaic tiles	2
M	Clear site	1
N	Give layout	1
O	Construction of foundation concrete	1
P	Construction of plinth and DPC	2
Q	Construction of superstructure till lintels	2
R	Casting of lintels	2
S	Construction of superstructure above lintel till slab	2
T	Construction of RCC roof including beams and slab	2
U	Preparation of timber shutters	1
V	Fitting of shutters	1
W	Construction of tile flooring	2
X	Inside and Outside plaster	1
Y	Obtaining pipe and sanitary fittings	1
Z	Obtaining Electrical fittings	1
A'	Fixing water supply and sanitary fittings	1
B'	Fixing electrical fittings	1
C'	Interior decoration	3
D'	Clean up	1

32. Different activities in construction of a small culvert with 2 spans are listed below with their period duration. Prepare a CPM network and construction schedule starting from 1st day of next month. Find out the period of completion of the project.

Activity Identi-fication	Name of Activity	Duration Days
A	Excavation for abutments	4
B	Procurement of sand, cement and aggregate	3
C	Excavation for piers	2
D	Foundation concrete of abutments	2
E	Curing of PCC of abutments	2
F	Foundation concrete for pier	1
G	Curing of PCC for pier	2
H	Excavation for wing walls	2
I	Foundation concrete for wing walls	2
J	Curing of PCC for wing walls	2
K	Procurement of Rubble	4
L	UCR masonry of first abutment	3
M	UCR masonry for second abutment	3
N	UCR masonry for pier	3
O	UCR masonry for wing wall for first abutment	2
P	UCR masonry for second abutment	2
Q	Earth filling for first wing wall	4
R	Earth filling for second wing wall	4
S	Rolling of Earth filling	4
T	Formwork of Deck slab	6
U	Procuring steel	4
V	Placing reinforcement	4
W	Concreting Deck slab	2
X	Curing Deck slab	21
Y	Procuring and fixing hand rails	6
Z	W.B.M. and Surfacing	7

33. Fig. 2.48 shows the network for a construction project. The three different time estimates for each activity are marked. Determine the critical path and probability of completion of the project in 80 days.

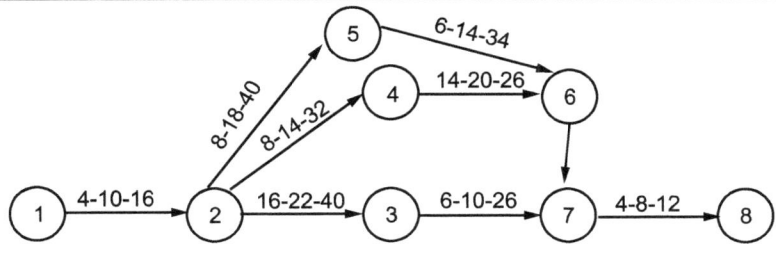

Fig. 2.48

34. Justify the importance of planning and network technique in Civil Engineering works.

35. What do you understand by CPM and PERT ? Give the points common to both and also the points of differentiation.

36. Compare CPM and PERT.

37. Define the following
    (i) Optimistic time
    (ii) Most likely time
    (iii) Pessimistic time
    (iv) Expected mean time

38. How is probability of completion of a project in given definite period is determined ?

1. (a) Draw the network for the following data. Show the critical path. Also find the expected project duration of the project.

Activity	Estimated Duration in Days		
	Optimistic Time (t_o)	Most likely Time (t_m)	Pessimistic Time (t_p)
1 – 2	2	5	8
1 – 3	3	87	7
1 – 4	3	8	13
2 – 4	2	3	10
2 – 5	4	7	10
3 – 6	4	6	8
4 – 6	7	9	11
5 – 7	6	9	12
6 – 7	2	5	14
6 – 8	5	7	9
7 – 8	4	6	8
8 – 9	8	10	12

(b) Explain Three times estimates in PERT.

39. (a) For small construction project, the time estimates of different activities are given below

Activity	Estimated Duration in Days		
	Optimistic	Most Likely	Pessimistic
1 – 2	4	10	22
2 – 3	2	5	8
2 – 4	4	7	16
2 – 5	4	7	10
3 – 5	4	7	22
4 – 5	5	8	17
5 – 6	6	9	18

Draw the network and determine the critical path and expected minimum duration.

(b) What are the different points on which site documentation depends.

(c) What is PERT ? Explain its applications.

40. Explain 'super critical' and 'sub-critical' activities.

41. What are predecessor activities, successor activities, concurrent activities and zero-time activities ? Explain giving a suitable example.

42. The table below gives activities and their durations.

Activity	Duration (Days)
1 – 2	5
2 – 3	5
2 – 4	9
2 – 5	11
3 – 5	7
4 – 5	0
5 – 6	8
6 – 7	6
6 – 8	15
7 – 8	12

(i) Draw a network and calculate project duration and highlight the critical path by heavy ruling line.

(ii) Calculate EST, EFT, LST, LFT for the activities.

(iii) Calculate Total float, Free float, Independent float and Interference float for the activities.

43. What do you mean by Project life cycle phases ?
44. Write a note on 'Gantt Chart and its limitations'.
45. Write short notes on
    1. Tools and Techniques of Project Management.
    2. Gantt chart and its limitations.
    3. Total float, Free float, Interference float and Independent float.
    4. Network Analysis.
    5. Critical, Subcritical and Super Critical activities.
    6. Categories of Project.
    7. Importance of Project Management in Construction Industry.
    8. EST, EFT, LST, LFT and TF.
    9. Project life cycle phases.
    10. Merits and Demerits of Matrix Structures. =
46. Listed below are the activities of a project along with dependence.
    (i) Draw a network and calculate total project duration and highlight the critical path.
    (ii) Calculate EST, EFT, LST, LFT and Total Float for the activities.

Activity	Duration (Days)
1 – 2	8
2 – 3	12
2 – 4	12
3 – 5	0
4 – 5	0
3 – 6	16
5 – 7	20
4 – 8	12
6 – 9	16
7 – 9	10
8 – 9	16

47. Differentiate CPM and PERT.
48. What do you mean by Dummy activity ? What is the use of providing dummy activity in a network ?
49. What are the basic tools and techniques of project management ? Explain in brief.
50. Explain Critical, Sub-critical and Super Critical activities.
51. Describe the procedure for preparing CPM network for any construction project in Civil Engineering.

52. What are predecessor activities, Successor activities, Concurrent activities and Zero-time activities ?
53. (a) What do you mean by dummy activity ? What is the use of providing a dummy activity in a network ?
    (b) What possible errors of logic do you predict while drawing a network ? Describe these with neat sketches.
54. Discuss the merits and demerits of matrix structure.
55. Compare Bar chart and CPM on the following points
    (i) Activity dependence
    (ii) Resource allocation
    (iii) Interpretation and ease in reading
    (iv) Time control
56. Enlist six different factors affecting duration of an activity.
57. Explain the following principles of Management
    (i) Division of work.
    (ii) Decentralisation of authority.
    (iii) Unity of direction.
58. What is project ? Explain the concept of project.
59. What is meant by 'Project Life Cycle' ? Explain the 'Planning and Organising phase' of project life cycle.
60. The following constraints are given for the activities of a project.
    (i) 'G' follows 'F' but precedes 'H'.
    (ii) 'G' follows 'D' but precedes 'J'.
    (iii) 'M' follows 'H' but precedes 'L'.
    (iv) 'K' follows 'A' but precedes 'L'.
    (v) 'F' follows 'A'.
    'A' and 'D' are starting activities. J and L are terminal activities. The duration of the activities are in weeks.
    A = 3, H = 3, F = 2, L = 2, G = 1, M = 4, D = 6, K = 5, J = 7.
    (a) Draw a network, compute project duration and show critical path.
    (b) Tabulate the statement showing therein EST, EFT, LST, LFT and TF of each activity.
    (c) Also calculate Free Float, Independent Float and Interference Float of each activity.
61. (a) Define 'Updating' and explain in detail with the help of one example.
    (b) What are logical errors in case of CPM ? Draw sketches to illustrate your answer.
62. Listed below are the activities of a project along with their respective duration and dependence. Sketch the network diagram showing critical path by heavy rule line and find the project duration.

Also prepare a mathematical table showing EST, EFT, LST, LFT, Total float for activity in a project alongwith critical and non-critical activities of a network you have drawn.

Preceding activities	Activity	Duration (Days)	Following Activity
–	A	9	K, G, H, J
–	B	6	E, F
–	C	11	K
–	D	5	–
B	E	3	K, G, H, J
B	F	5	K
A, E	G	3	L
A, E	H	6	M
A, E	J	3	–
A, C, E, F	K	4	–
G	L	10	M
L, H	M	3	–

63. (a) What are logical errors in case of CPM ? Draw sketches to illustrate your answer.
    (b) Define
       (i) Interfering floats
       (ii) Independent float
64. What is the importance of Management in case of Construction Industry ?
65. Explain various states of the life cycle or product.
66. What are the principles of Scientific Management ?
67. Explain the term : Delegation of Authority.
68. Define Authority. What are the different principle of Delegation of Authority ?
69. Explain the importance of management to an enterprise.
70. State different types of organisation. Explain scalar organisation.
71. Discuss F.W. Taylor's principles of scientific management.
72. Explain any three functions of management.
73. What is a product life cycle ? Discuss its usefulness in determining the production strategy.
74. State the qualities of a successful manager.
75. Explain in brief, "Life Cycle of Product".
76. Write a note on functions of Management.
77. Enlist different types of organisation and suggest a suitable type of organisation for a construction industry.
78. Explain "Functional organisation with respect to its merits and demerits".
79. What is Management. Give its importance.
80. Write a note on contribution of F.W. Taylor to management.
81. Listed below are the activities of a project along with their durations.

Activity (i – j)	Duration (Weeks)
1 – 2	6
1 – 3	5
2 – 4	10
3 – 4	3
3 – 5	4
4 – 5	6
4 – 6	2
5 – 6	9

    (i)   Draw AOA network and calculate the total project duration. Highlight the critical path.
    (ii)   Calculate EST, EFT, LST, LFT, Total Float, Free float and Independent Float.

82. (a) The activities of a small project can be described by the following relationships.
    (i)   A, B and C can start simultaneously.
    (ii)   A and B precede D.
    (iii)   B precedes E, F and H.
    (iv)   F and C precede G.
    (v)   E and H precede I and J.
    (vi)   C, D, F and J precede K.
    (vii)   K precedes L.
    (viii)   I, G and L are terminal activities of the project.
    Draw a network diagram for the project.
  (b) Explain the types of organisation.
  (c) Explain the project life cycle.

83. How does PERT differ from CPM, State the areas where PERT can be applied and its limitations.
84. Differentiate between public sector and private sector.
85. Explain characteristics and principles of organisation.
86. Draw the network with the help of following information

Activity	A	B	C	D	E	F	G	H	J	X	Y
Duration	10	12	16	18	9	15	12	16	19	5	8
Preceding Activity	–	–	–	A	A, B	C	A	DEF	G	J, H	J, H

  (a) Draw the neat network.
  (b) Show critical activities and critical path with the help of table.
  (c) Find the total duration of project.

87. State the differences between AOA and AON.
88. Explain the project life cycle with example of any construction site.
89. Show with example, total float and free float. Also give definition of the same.

CONSTRUCTION MGT. – I (T.E. CIVIL SEM V – NMU)　　　　　NETWORK TECHNIQUE

90. What are the qualities required for a Project Manager ?
91. What is PERT ? Give any 3 applications of PERT.
92. Suggest a suitable organisation chart for Construction Industry.
93. Explain in brief types of organisation.
94. Explain evolution of Scientific Management.
95. The following table gives the time estimates of the various activities of a project

Activity	Duration in Weeks		
i – j	t_o	t_m	t_p
1 – 2	1	2	3
2 – 3	3	6	9
2 – 4	2	4	6
3 – 5	4	6	9
4 – 6	4	6	8
5 – 6	0	0	0
5 – 7	3	4	5
6 – 7	2	5	9

(i) Draw the project network and find the total project duration.
(ii) Calculate the variance along with critical path.
(iii) What is the probability that the project will be completed in the estimated time ?

96. (a) Compare Gantt chart with CPM network.
    (b) Explain, what is a Matrix Structure ?
    (c) Explain with sketches, the various relationships in a Precedence Network.

97. A project has the following time schedule

Activity (i – j)	Duration (Weeks)
1 – 2	3
1 – 3	4
1 – 4	14
2 – 4	2
2 – 6	5
3 – 5	4
3 – 6	6
4 – 6	1
5 – 6	1

(i) Draw AOA network and calculate the total project duration. Highlight the critical path.
(ii) Calculate EST, EFT, LST, LFT, total float and free float.

98. Explain the Evolution of Scientific Management.

99. Explain Line and Staff Organisation w.r.t. its merits and demerits.
100. Give definitions of following with suitable example of each
    (i) Dummy activity,
    (ii) Critical activity,
    (iii) Critical path,
    (iv) Concurrent activity,
    (v) Preceding activity,
    (vi) Succeeding activity.
101. Show following logic with the help of AOA network.
    (i)   Activity C depends on A and B.
    (ii) Activity P depends on C and D but activity Q depends on C only.
    (iii) Activity C cannot be started before completion of activities Y and X whereas D depends on X and Z.
    (iv) Activity S must not start before Q gets completed. Activity X depends on S but will start only after 3 days after completion of S.
    (v)   Activities M and N depends on Q, P and O.

UNIT III

CRASHING, UPDATING, RESOURCE LEVELLING AND LINE OF BALANCE

3.1 INTRODUCTION

The duration of a project or for that matter duration of a activity is related to cost. In general, time is related to cost in performance of any job. In using CPM, one of the objectives is to develop optimum time-cost relationship so that the project can be scheduled in a way so as to complete the same at the minimum cost without any undue delay in completion of the project. Network technique is used to bring improvement in planning, scheduling, controlling, at the same time directing all above objectives. Hence, planning techniques should be used to arrive at a feasible and desirable time-cost relationship so as to complete the project at the total minimum cost. All clients always have monetary limitations and the investments are of primary concern for all the programmes. For any project the earliest possible and practicable date of completion is of great importance. The financial resources should be made available during the various time periods throughout the development of any programme. Without availability of the funds in time, there will not be orderly progress and the completion of the project may be delayed. In this context, the modern methods of planning like CPM system are useful. Upon completion of the network each activity must be studied with respect to its duration and the cost. In most of the projects, approximately 30% of the activities are found to be critical and remaining 70% of the activities have some float. The policy of every organisation and every owner is to reduce the duration of the project so that the utilisation of the project may be started before the schedule and time saved may be utilised gainfully. The overall project duration can be reduced by reducing the time period for the critical activities which control project duration. It would be useless to pay attention to non-critical activities and spend extra resources to expedite them. There are two ways of reducing the duration of critical activities. They are : (1) By increasing and employing more resources so that the activity duration is reduced. (2) By relaxing technical specifications of the activity.

However, it is not the aim and objective that the project duration be reduced at the cost of the quality and therefore, the only way of reducing the project duration is by utilising and developing more resources of all the critical activities. Of course, there is a limit for reduction of completion time of any activity irrespective of availability of all possible resources and hence there is a range of time duration for completion of any activity and for completion of the project depending upon the available resources. Larger the duration of the project, lesser is the cost and reduction in the period of completion will increase the cost. It is, therefore, necessary to strike golden mean between the cost and the duration and optimum duration is the one which will give most economical total cost of the project.

3.2 PROJECT COST

3.2.1 Introduction

For any project two types of costs are involved. They are

1. Direct cost
2. Indirect cost

Direct cost is the cost spent or accomplished for that particular activity or project whereas the indirect cost is related to control or direction of that work, financial overheads, losses if any and the like. The total cost can, therefore, be divided as below

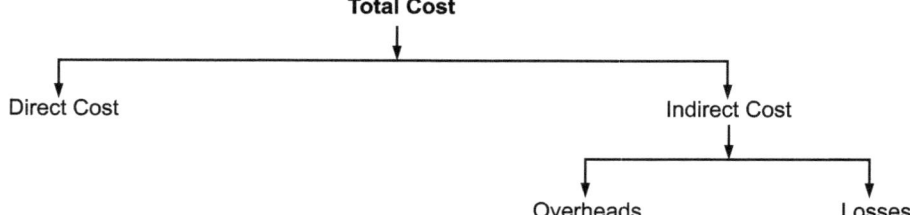

3.2.2 Direct Cost

It is the expenditure which is charged to the specific activity and can be identified to be so. It consists of direct investment made for the completion of that activity or the project in terms of material, labour and the equipment. Material required for any activity will not change, hence the direct cost on materials will remain unaltered. However, if more equipment and labour are employed, it reduces the duration of activity upto a certain minimum. Hence, less the duration, more is the direct cost and the graph of variation of direct cost against duration is as shown in Fig. 2.1.

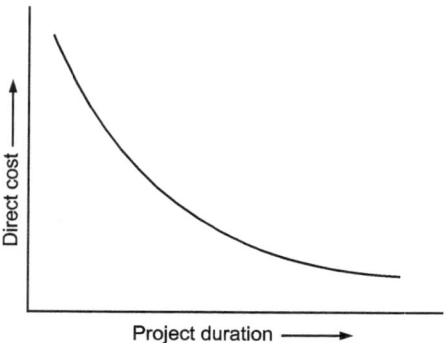

Fig. 3.1 : Project Duration

3.2.3 Indirect Cost

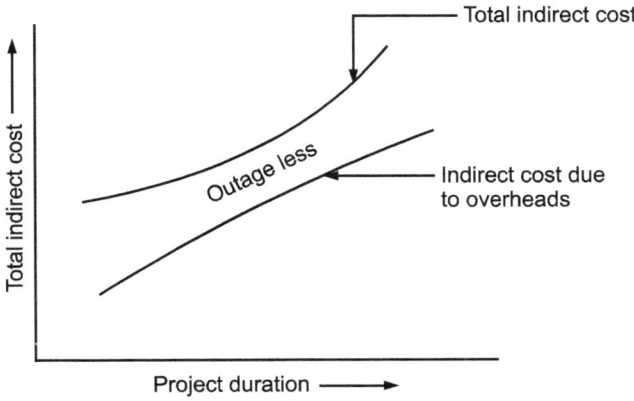

Fig. 3.2

Indirect costs on a project are those expenditures which are related to control and direct the project. It consists of overheads such as supervision charges, office establishments, electricity charges indirect labour and material, loss of revenue, lost profit, penalty etc. Indirect costs are those expenditure which cannot be appropriated or clearly allocated to any individual activity of the project but are assessed as a whole. This indirect cost is directly proportional to the time and, therefore, rises with duration. Considering only overhead and supervision, the indirect cost is represented by a straight line with a slope equal to daily overheads. But if the loss in profits and the other charges such as penalty etc. are added which are termed as an outage loss, the indirect cost graph may become curved as shown in Fig. 3.3.

Generally for any project, presuming there are no outage losses, the indirect cost variation is taken to be straight line only. With the available resources, the duration of the different activities represented in the network are the normal durations. However, if the resources are increased, activities can be completed in minimum possible period. This is known as 'crashing of the activity' and the cost associated is known as 'crash cost'. Thus, by crashing different critical activities, the project can be completed in minimum possible duration and the associated total cost which is sum of direct and indirect cost is the crash cost. Crash duration is, therefore, the minimum duration and the crash cost is the maximum cost of the project.

The total cost at the normal duration is the normal cost but this normal cost is not the minimum cost of the project. The optimum cost of the project is the minimum cost as represented on the total cost curve and the duration corresponding to this optimum cost is called *the* optimum duration of the project. It can be seen from the total cost curve that the total cost of the project goes on increasing on either side i.e. whether the duration is increased or decreased the total cost of the project increases. This will be clear from Fig. 3.3.

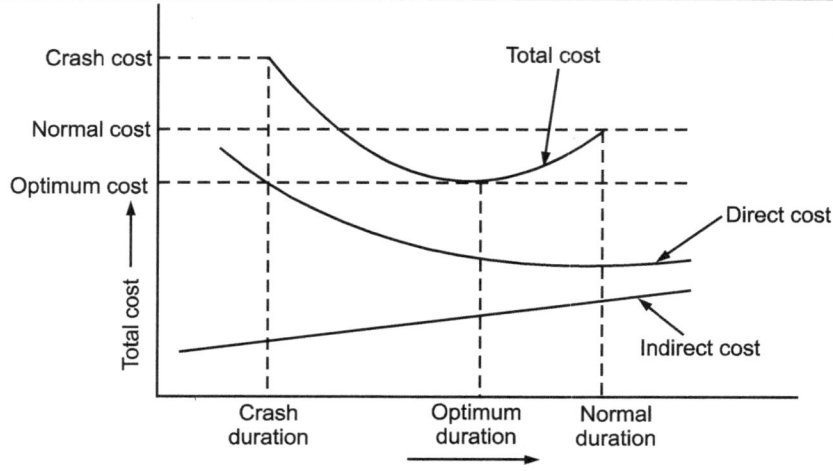

Fig. 3.3

If the network analysis indicates that the project duration and the project completion date do not match and duration has to be reduced, following alternatives are considered

1. Examine the estimated duration of different activities and study the possibility whether the estimated duration may be reduced without any extra cost.
2. The logic of the network and interdependency of the different activities to be examined to check where some of the interdependent and sequential activities may be converted into independent and concurrent activities.
3. Examine whether some of the critical activities may be crashed by utilising extra resources involving extra costs.

3.3 COST SLOPE FOR DIRECT COST

The direct cost curve can be approximated by a straight line. Depending upon the flatness of the curve, a single straight line or number of broken straight lines can be used for this approximation. The cost slope is the slope of the cost curve approximated as a straight line.

$$\text{Cost slope} = \text{Slope of straight line AB} = \frac{C_s - C_n}{t_n - t_c}$$

where,
- C_s = Crash cost
- t_c = Crash duration of activity
- C_n = Normal Cost
- t_n = Normal duration of activity

That critical activity with minimum cost slope is crashed first until other parallel activities are non-critical.

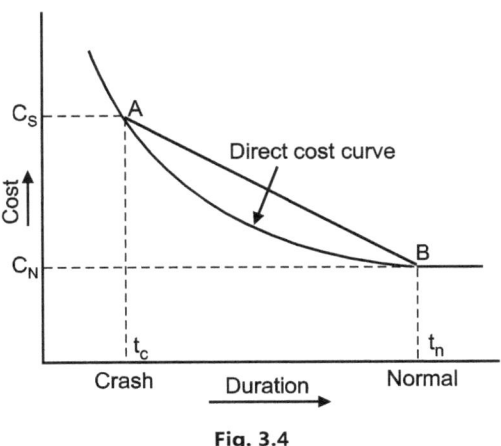

Fig. 3.4

3.4 CRASHING OF NETWORK FOR COST OPTIMISATION

As seen in the previous section, to decrease the schedule duration of the project, the duration of critical activities or crashing the critical activities is done. This may cause increase in the cost beyond the optimum limit. Crashing any activity is completing the activity in the minimum possible time limit.

However crashing of the project can be carried for the following objectives
- For finding the minimum duration of the project and the corresponding cost of the project.
- For optimisation of the project i.e. for finding optimum duration and optimum cost of the project.
- For finding the extra cost of reducing the project duration by a particular duration.

It may be possible that while crashing the activities, some activities which are non-critical may become critical. However, for reducing the project duration, the focus is directed on the critical activities as critical path decides the project duration. Let us, understand the procedure of crashing of network by solving following example.

Example 3.1 : Frame the CPM network for the data given in the table below

Also find

1. Critical path and Normal duration of the project.
2. Calculate the normal cost and optimum cost. Assume the total cost of the project ₹ 11,000 and indirect cost ₹ 300/- per day. Calculate the optimum duration.

Activity	Events		Duration (Days)		Slope of Cost Curve in ₹/Day
	Preceding	Succeeding	Normal	Crash	
A	10	30	7	3	100
B	10	20	9	7	60
C	30	50	4	1	150
D	20	50	5	3	250
E	20	40	3	1	20
F	50	60	6	4	332
G	40	60	2	1	1,000

Solution : Step I : The network as shown below

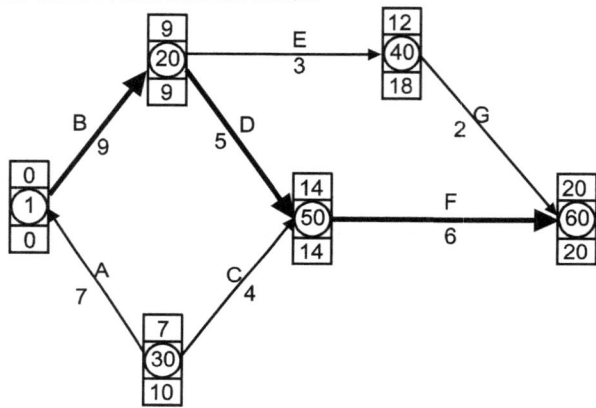

Fig. 3.5

Step 2 : The EST and LFT for the different events are calculated by the forward pass and the backward pass methods and are indicated near the events. The critical path is 10 – 20 – 50 – 60 and the critical activities are B, D and F. (Refer Table No. 3.1)

Table 3.1

Sr. No.	Activity	Duration	EST	EFT	LST	LFT	TF	Crash Slope	Remarks
1	A	7	0	7	3	10	3	100	
2	B	9	0	9	0	9	0	60	Critical
3	C	4	7	11	10	14	3	150	
4	D	5	9	14	9	14	0	250	Critical
5	E	3	9	12	15	18	6	20	
5	F	6	14	20	14	20	0	332	Critical
6	G	2	12	14	18	20	6	1000	

Hence, the normal duration – 20 days; Normal cost = Rs. 11,000/-

Step 3 : Transfer the network as a squared network to understand the concurrency of activities and the float available with non critical activities.

Remember following points while drawing squared network.

(a) The critical path is drawn as a straight line starting from 0 to normal duration (critical path B-D-F).

(b) All the nodes on critical path are shown on it (nodes (10), (20), (50) and (60)).

(c) Non critical paths are shown above or below the critical path.

(d) All the activities are starting at its EST. Activities A and C spans between nodes (10) and (50). Total duration of activities A and C is 11 days while the duration between nodes (10) to (50) is 14 days.

Therefore, Total float = 3 days.

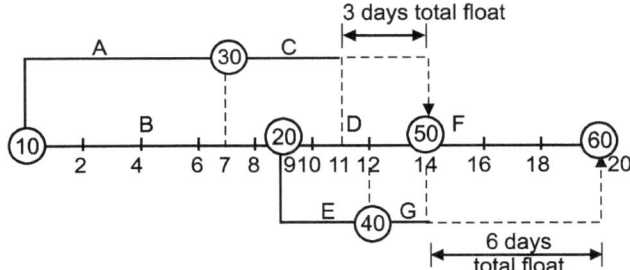

Fig. 3.6

Similarly, total duration of activities between nodes (20) and (60) is 11 days while that of activities E and G is 5 days.

Therefore, total float = 6 days.

It is very important to note that total float is a 'shared float' i.e. this float is shared between the serial activities between two nodes. i.e. Activities A and C have total float as 3 days, if Activity A uses float on 1 day, C will have remaining float as 2 days and so on. Similarly, total float of 6 days is shared between E and G.

Step 4 : Crashing of activities will start by compressing the critical activity with minimum crash slope. i.e. by increasing the total cost at minimal for each day's crashing.

∴ Out of B, D and F activities, activity B will be crashed since it has minimum cost slope i.e. Rs. 60/- days. Now, once we have decided that activity B is to be crashed, the next question is "by How many days? " To answer this questions, study the squared diagram carefully. If we crash activity B by 2 days (from 9 days normal duration to 7 days crash duration), the float available for A and C will be come 1 day (3 days – 2 days). This ensures that activities A and C do not become critical activities.

∴ Crash activity B by 2 days (its duration becomes 7 days).

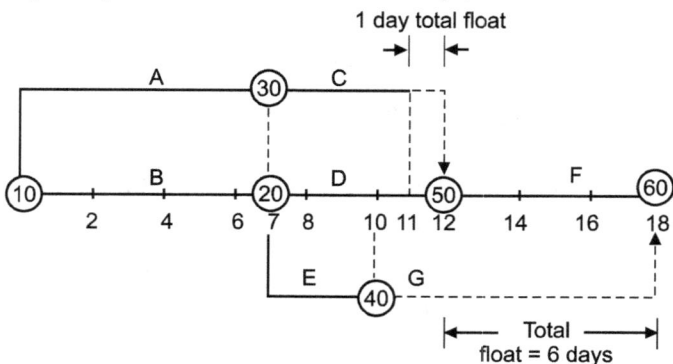

Fig. 3.7

Note that total float for activities E and G are 6 days as before.

∴ (Duration) = 18 days

(Cost)$_1$ = 11000 + 2 (crash slope of activity B) = Rs. 11,120/-

Step 5 : As activity B can not be compressed further, the critical activity with next higher cost slope is D, which can be crashed by 2 days. Activity D is a Concurrent activity with A, C (1 day TF) and E, G (6 days TF). As TF for A, C is only 1 day, we can crash activity D by only 1 day though activity D can be crashed by 1 more day. Activities A and C will also become crticial then this can be shown as follows

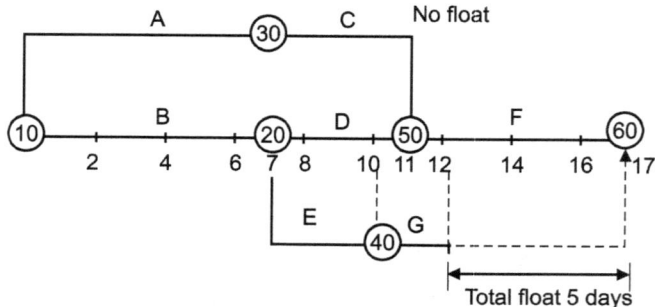

Fig. 3.8

Total Float = 5 days

∴ (Duration)$_2$ = 17 days

(cost)$_2$ = Rs. 11,120 + 250

= Rs. 11,370/-

Step 6 : Now if we want to compress activity D, it is to be crashed along with A and C as they are parallel to D and critical. Hence, the options available are

(a) Crash activities D and A (by 1 day) ⇒ Crash slope = 250 + 100 = 350

(b) Crash activities D and C (by 1 day) ⇒ Crash slope = 250 + 150 = 400

(c) Crash activity F by 2 day ⇒ Crash slope = 332.

Minimum cost slope out of the above options is considered.

∴ Crash activity F by 2 days.

∴ $(Duration)_3$ = 15 days

$(Cost)_3$ = Rs 11370 + Rs 332 × 2

= Rs. 12,034/-

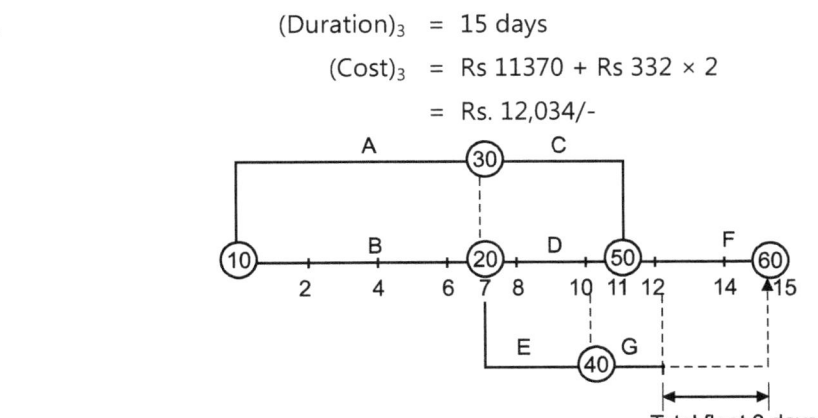

Fig. 3.9

Step 7 : Now, at present the scenario is

(a) Critical activity B is completely crashed.

(b) Activity F is completely crashed.

(c) Activity D can be crashed by 1 more day. But as it is parallel with A and C any one activity which gives minimum cost slope is to be crashed along with D.

(d) Activities E and G are non-critical activities and hence they will not play any role in crashing. Considering the minimum crash slope (Rs. 350 per day) A from the previous step, the squared network after crashing D and A by 1 day will become.

∴ $(duration)_4$ = 14 days

$(cos)_4$ = Rs. 12,034 + Rs. 350

= Rs. 12,384/-

This ends the crashing steps as critical activities B, D and F are completely crashed and can not be crashed further. This is called as "All crash solution."

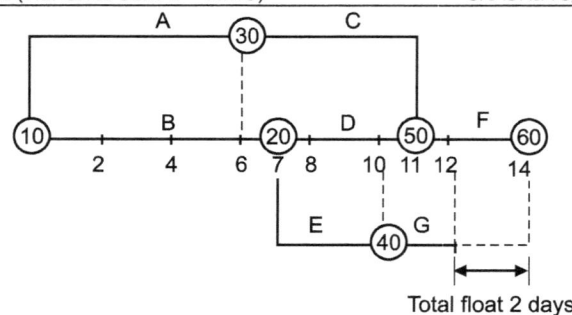

Total float 2 days

Fig. 3.10

Summary of all the steps along with indirect cost and total cost is as follows

Duration	20	18	17	15	14
Direct Cost	11,000	11,120	11,370	12,034	12,384
Indirect Cost	6,000	5,400	5,100	4,500	4,200
Total Cost	17,000	16,520	16,470	16,534	16,584

    Minimum Cost = Rs. 16,470/-

And   Optimum Duration = 17 days

Hence, the solution of this crashing problem is,

(a) Crash activity B by 2 days.

(b) Crash activity D by 1 day.

Example 3.2 : For the network shown in Fig. 3.11 the data about the cost is given in the table. The indirect cost of the project is ₹ 3,000 per week. Determine the optimum cost and optimum duration.

Activity	Normal Duration in week (t_n)	Crash Duration in week (t_s)	Normal Cost C_n	Crash Cost C_s
10 – 20	12	6	14,000	29,000
10 – 30	16	10	8,000	17,000
20 – 30	8	2	12,000	18,000
20 – 40	10	6	16,000	30,000
30 – 40	10	6	10,000	22,000

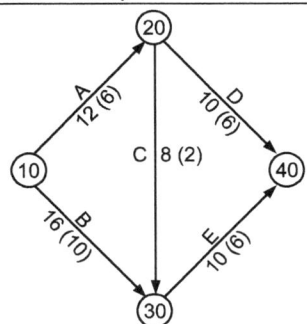

Fig. 3.11

Solution : The EST and LFT of different activities are calculated and critical activities are noted. Cost slopes of different activities are also calculated.

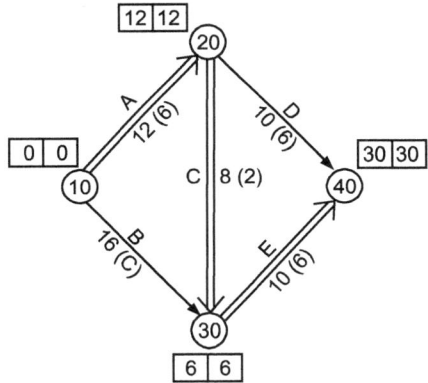

Critical events are 10, 20, 30, 40 and
Critical path 10 – 20 – 30 – 40
Critical Activities are A, C and E

Fig. 3.12

Activity	Normal Duration (week)	Crash Duration (week)	Normal Cost (C_N)	Crash Cost (C_S)	Cost Slope $\dfrac{C_S - C_N}{t_N - t_S}$ ₹/week	Remark
A	12	6	14,000	29,000	2,500	Critical
B	16	10	8,000	17,000	1,500	–
C	8	2	12,000	18,000	1,500	Critical
D	10	6	16,000	30,000	3,500	–
E	10	6	10,000	22,000	2,000	Critical

Indirect cost is ₹ 3,000/- per week. All the activities have cost slope less than the indirect cost. Hence, crashing of any activity may reduce the total cost. However, the reduction in duration will be achieved only in crashing the critical activities. Skipping the detailed description as done in the previous example, the step by step crashing of network is given on below

Step 1 : The squared of Network for the different durations are as below. The total cost for the different durations are as per table given below. The optimum duration, as found from the table and the graphs, is 22 weeks.

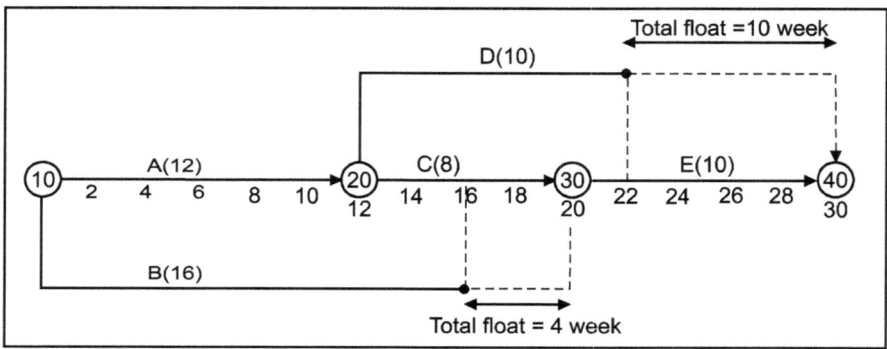

Schedule No. 1

Fig. 3.13

$$(\text{Duration})_1 = 30 \text{ weeks}$$
$$(\text{Cost})_1 = \text{Sum of costs of all activities}$$
$$= \text{Rs. } 60,000/-$$

Step 2 : Crash activity C by 4 weeks so that activity B will critical.

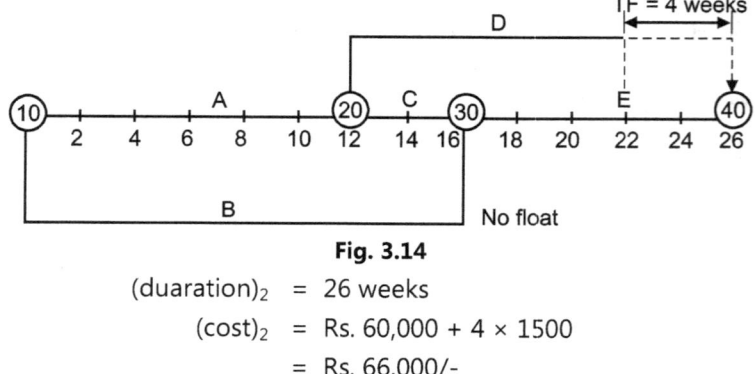

Fig. 3.14

$$(\text{duaration})_2 = 26 \text{ weeks}$$
$$(\text{cost})_2 = \text{Rs. } 60,000 + 4 \times 1500$$
$$= \text{Rs. } 66,000/-$$

Step 3 : As activity B is also become critical activity, alternatives available are as follows
(a) Crash activities A and B by 6 weeks ⇒ crash slope = 4,000/-
(b) Crash activities C and B by 2 weeks ⇒ crash slope = 3,000/-
(c) Crash activity E by 4 weeks ⇒ crash slope = 2,000/-

The alternative with minimum rash slope is considered i.e. crash activity E by 4 weeks.
Therefore, the squared network will become,

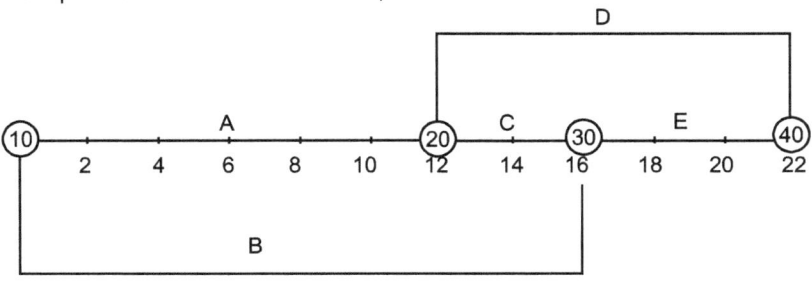

Fig. 3.15

$$(Duration)_3 = 22 \text{ weeks}$$
$$(Cost)_3 = Rs.\ 66,000 + 2000 \times 4$$
$$= Rs.\ 74,000/-$$

Step 4 : Now the whole network is critical in which following scenario is existing
(a) Activity E is completely crashed.
(b) Activity C can be crashed by 2 weeks further along with activity B and D ⇒ crash slope = 6500/-
(c) Activity A and B can be crashed simultaneously for 6 weeks ⇒ crash slope 4,000/-.

The maximum crash slope is Rs. 4,000/- per day. Hence, activities A and B can be crashed by 6 weeks and the network will be,

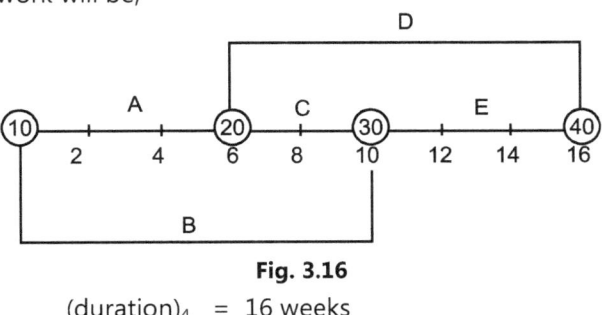

Fig. 3.16

$$(duration)_4 = 16 \text{ weeks}$$
$$(cost)_4 = Rs.\ 74,000 + 6 \times 4,000$$
$$= Rs.\ 98,000/-$$

Step 5 : As activities E and B are completely crashed, further compressing the network is not possible. Hence, it is the all crash solution. Let us calculate the total cost by adding indirect cost as follows

Duration	30	26	22	16
Direct Cost	60,000	66,000	74,000	98,000
Indirect Cost	90,000	78,000	66,000	48,000
Total Cost	1,50,000	1,44,000	1,40,000	1,46,000

Minimum Cost = Rs. 1,40,000/-
And Optimum Duration = 22 days
Hence the solution of this problem is
(1) Crash activity C by 4 weeks.
(2) Crash activity E by 4 weeks.

3.5 UPDATING

3.5.1 Introduction

The important use of the Network diagram occurs during actual implementation of the project. After the start of the execution, control over the progress is to be exercised. It should be examined at regular interval whether the progress in implementation of the project is as per schedule or otherwise. The actual achievements have to be compared with the planned progress so that any variation may be corrected at that stage only. Thus, during execution of the project, controlling is essential which is complementary to the planning. The control monitor phase is therefore, a continuous phase to see whether the project implementation is as per the schedule and if not, to take corrective steps to bring it back to the planned schedule. This, therefore, requires a flow of information from the persons involved in implementation to the designers and planners through a suitably designed reporting system. This upward flow of information is analysed and the implementation or progress of the project is brought up-to-date with necessary corrective measures.

3.5.2 Necessity of Updating

During the process of implementation of the project according to the network, one may come across one or more of the following situations upon analysing the upward flow informal.
1. Some or all the activities are progressing as per the schedule and the plan is being implemented up-to-date.
2. Some or all the activities are ahead of the planned schedule.
3. Some or all the activities are behind the schedule.

It is seldom that one meets with the situations 1 or 2 above in which case there need no change in the schedule or for updating the network. But in most of the cases the actual implementation is found to be behind the schedule due to the unavoidable difficulties or overestimation in activity duration. If planned network diagram does not conform to the actual progress, the network diagram has to be revised so that the delay is met with. This process is continued till the date is compensated and the project is completed in the planned period or on the date of completion decided at the planning stage. This, therefore, necessitates reconstruction of the network for the remaining part of the work and the complete network diagram has to be revised and redrawn. This process is known as *'updating'*. It may be necessary to reduce the duration of activity wherever possible. This can be done either by logical change or compression of duration of activity period i.e. by crashing the activities which are in progress or which are yet to begin. The critical activities are examined that will reduce the activity duration and later on the period of completion of the project. However, while compressing the activities their cost-time relationship may be taken into consideration so that with the reduction in duration the cost is not increased disproportionately.

3.5.3 When to do Updating

As already stated earlier, CPM has its utility in planning stage as well as in implementation stage. With the preparation of the network and detailed original plan and schedule from the network, about 60 per cent utility may be supposed to be achieved and remaining 40 per cent utility has to be utilised at the implementation stage to see where one stands on a particular date in the progress of the implementation. If this monitoring with the CPM is not done at definite intervals it may result in situation which are

- Early activities take more time than estimated. Late finishing of critical activities may delay the project whereas non-critical activities consume most of the total float available making all the later activities to be critical or near critical.
- Slippage in schedule continues till close to the end of the project and is detected as the tail activities are reached. This provides a situation where few alternatives remain open to the management to make an attempt to exercise any control and to bring the project back to the schedule.

Therefore, it is very necessary that the actual progress achieved during implementation be compared with the planned schedule and if necessary due corrective steps be taken to bring the progress back to schedule if it is lacking. Updating is therefore, a process of incorporating changes that have occurred or are anticipated in the network plan with respect of time and logic so that the delay caused, if any till the date, is compensated in the implementation of the remaining part of the project. It necessitates replanning and rescheduling to suit the changed conditions. This process of replanning and rescheduling is based on the knowledge received during the implementation, the resources available and the information about overall situation and the results obtained till date about the part of the project completed. There are no hard and fast rules regarding the frequency of updating. Depending upon the working period, the progress achieved and overall situation about the difficulties met with, it is upto the person incharge to decide the frequency of updating. For a big work which is running in three shifts updating weekly or even sometimes daily may be required as a large quantity of work is completed during that period whereas there may not be any necessity of updating monthly. In general project updating in later stages may be more frequent than in early stages as changes if any can be easily incorporated at early stages. However, in general the situations which necessitates immediate updating may be given below

- Each time where there is change in the scope of work.
- When non-critical activities have consumed the available float completely.
- If there are non-avoidable difficulties and delays which result in major set back on critical activities.

3.5.4 Procedure of Updating

The information necessary for updating the project at any stage will be as below
- Original network and calculation chart.
- Stage at which updating is done i.e. point in the time of updating.
- Position of execution of the project at that stage i.e. Activities completed and time required for the activities in progress for completion.
- Any new information and knowledge about the activities yet to commence which may affect their duration.
- Change in logic if any.
- New activity in the remaining part of project to be introduced if any and its logic.

The information received may be summarised in a tabular form given below. The duration of time of completion of the activities which are in progress and which are yet to start may be suitably revised in the light of the experience gained and additional information and knowledge received during the execution.

Table for Updating Network

Activity	Position on the Day of Update and Duration for Completion		
	Completed	In Progress	Yet to commence

The information is superimposed on the original network and new network is framed. For the events which have occurred the Earliest event occurrence time is taken as zero and for the activities which are completed the duration is taken as zero. For the activities which are in progress and those which are yet to begin, new estimated duration is entered and on this basis the Earliest Occurrence Time and Latest Occurrence Time of the events are calculated. Thus, the new period of completion of the project or rescheduled date of completion may be decided and the project lying behind the schedule may be brought back to the schedule. The updating cycle is as shown below

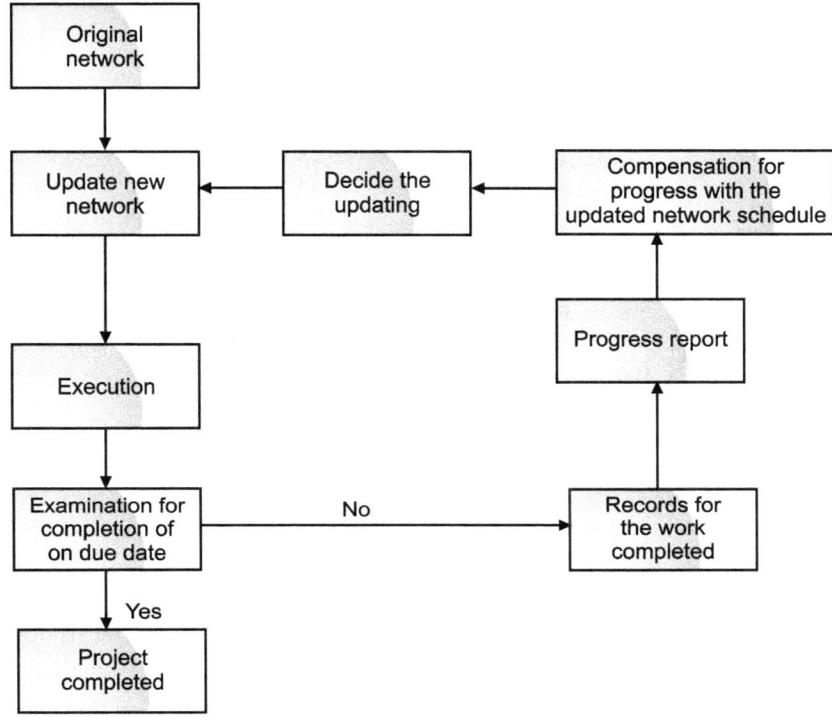

Fig. 3.17

Example 3.3 : The table shows different activities in a project, their duration and the position of the project at the end of 24 days from commencement. Mark the original critical path after drawing the network, update the network and calculate the time of completion.

Activity	Prece-ding Activity	Succee-ding Activity	Duration	Position at the end of 24 days			
				Position	Time taken for activity	Add-itional Time for comple-tion	Dura-tion Needed
A	–	F	10	Completed	20	–	–
B	–	D	16	Not started	–	20	20
C	–	E	20	Completed	16	–	–
D	B	I	12	Not started	–	–	18
E	C	F	6	Completed	6	–	–
F	A, E	G, H, J	14	Incomplete	2	12	–
G	F	I	6	Not started	–	–	6
H	F	K	8	Not started	–	–	8
I	D, G	–	10	Not started	–	–	10
J	F	–	12	Not started	–	–	20
K	H	–	10	Not started	–	–	10

Solution :

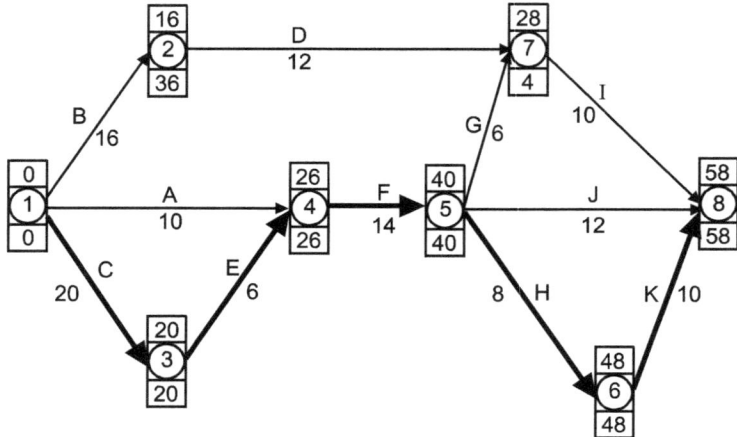

Fig. 3.18

Note that activity J will required more time than scheduled.

Original network and the EST and LFT of different events is as shown above and the critical path is C, E, F, H, K or 1 – 3, 3 – 4, 4 – 5, 5 – 6, 6 – 8. The updated network can now be drawn as shown below

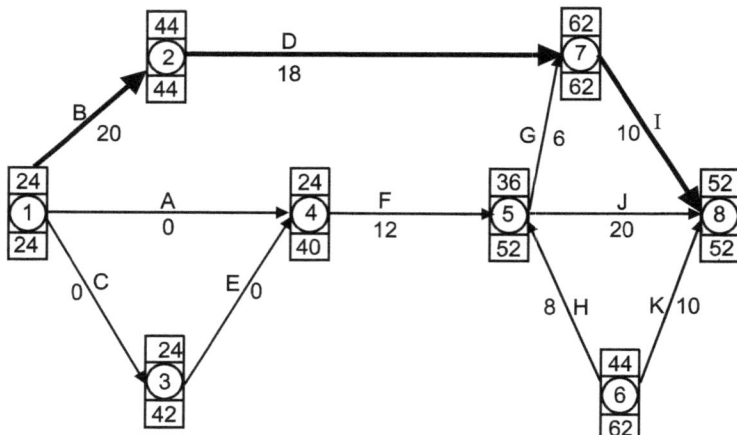

Fig. 3.19

For the events which are yet to occur, the EST is 24 days and for the activities which have been completed the duration is 0. Hence, for event (1) and (3) EST is 24 days and for activities A, C and E duration is zero. The network calculations are completed in usual manner. The critical path is now 1-2-7-8 and now for the updated network the time of completion of project is 72 days in place of 58 days.

3.6 FREQUENCY AND THE TIME OF UPDATING

After the implementation, project starts the actual progress which has to be compared with the planned schedule of progress and when it is found that the actual progress lags behind by considerable period, updating will have to be done. However, the following points will have to be kept in mind while deciding the time of updating.

1. For the project of shorter duration frequent comparison between the actual progress and the planned progress will have to be made and this may lead to frequent updating.
2. For the project of larger duration in the early stages the updating may not be required frequently. However, as the project is progressing towards completion and as the time of completion is continuously decreasing it will be necessary to check the actual progress with the planned one or previously updated network and frequent updating may be necessary compared with the frequency of updating in the early stages of the project. As the project approaches completion it behaves like a project of shorter duration.
3. With the knowledge and information received in the part execution of the project if there is found to be a major change in the duration of any activity then updating will be necessary. If the activity happens to be critical, increase in duration will increase the total duration of the project and hence remedial measures will have to be taken to see that the project will be completed on the date. However, decrease in the duration of critical activity may allow certain changes to be incorporated.

3.7 RESOURCE ALLOCATION

For actual implementation of the project, different resources are required. They include men, material, machines, money and also space without which, implementation of any project cannot commence. 'Men' include planners, designers, specialist personnel, supervisory staff at senior level and at the work site and skilled and unskilled labour. Machinery includes different kinds of equipment for different activities. Out of all above resources except the money and material, all other can be repetitively used. It is presumed that all the resources are available as and when required. Also duration of different activities is derived assuming a particular amount of the resources in the form of men and machinery is available. However, it is not so due to following reasons

- Many activities run concurrently and it may be possible that the total man power needed for concurrently running the activities may not be available.
- There may be limitation of the space available and hence the available resources will have to be used.

- At the planning level, if particular attention is not paid to the availability of manpower, the needed manpower at some level of the project may exceed the demand at other levels which is not desirable.

- Large fluctuations in the demand of resources not only create problems in execution but may delay the project completion and may result in additional cost when the demanded additional resources are not made available as and when needed. It is therefore, necessary that the alternative ways of using the available resources be so decided that the available manpower, machinery and space i.e. limited resources are allocated carefully on the different activities at different phases of implementation and the demand of the different resources is somewhat uniform during the complete duration of the project. This will obtain best outcome and profits from all the resources.

3.7.1 Representing the Resources

The resources, especially incase of manpower, are limited and it is necessary that the person incharge of execution or the manager has to prepare a resource analysis report which may enable him to put to best use at his hand. There will be peaks and valleys in the form of required resources and the manager can try to level out these with the help of resource analysis report. The requirement of a particular type of resource e.g. mason or carpenter or unskilled labour over the complete period has to be known. A graph is plotted for the requirement of resource against the period of requirement and this is known as 'Resource Usage Profile' or in general in the language of statistics a 'histogram'. The histogram will reveal the non-uniform demand over the project duration very clearly. The manager has a definite availability of this resource and he has to plan the requirement of the resource over different periods of execution of the project. He has therefore the following information and alternatives.

- The total requirement of resources over its duration as given by Histogram.
- If the available resources are insufficient, it will result in delay in completion of the project. He has to decide the best allocation of available resources over the entire period of project so that the completion period of the project is extended by minimum duration.
- If the project has to be completed in a fixed period, how best can the available resources be utilised to achieve the goal.

In the above situation it is necessary to have proper resource scheduling to achieve any one of the following objectives

- If project duration is fixed, to level or smoothen the resource demand in such a manner that peaks and valleys in the demand are avoided as far as possible by suitably spacing the different activities and uniform amount/quantity of the resource. Thus, the required uniform resource in the form of manpower or any other is made available. It is presumed that unlimited resource is available. This is 'resource smottening.'

- If the availability of the resources is fixed the same should be so judiciously used so as to complete the project in minimum possible duration. This is 'Resources allocation' and is necessary when a particular type of resource is in scarcity or is limited.

3.7.2 Histogram

Consider the network shown for a project as given below

Example 3.4 :

The Early Start Time (EST) and Latest Start Time (LST) of each event is shown on the network. The critical path 1-2-3-6-10-11-12 is marked. Requirements of skilled labour (mason) and the unskilled labour as envisaged at the time of Network framing comensurating with the duration of the activities are given in the table. The duration of the project is 40 days.

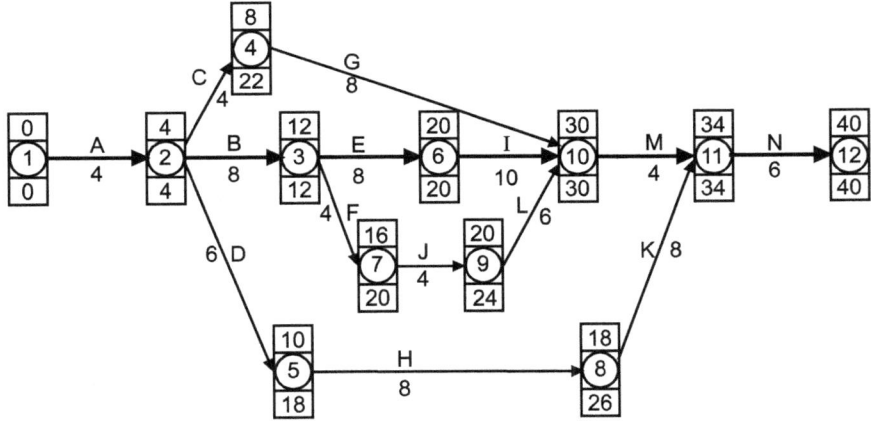

Fig. 3.20

Activity	A	B	C	D	E	F	G	H	I	J	K	L	M	N
Duration (Days)	4	8	4	6	8	4	8	8	10	4	8	6	4	6
Requirement of Mason (M)	2	6	2	4	6	6	10	4	2	2	2	–	2	2
Requirement of Labourers (L)	4	4	6	4	6	4	6	4	6	4	4	8	2	4

The time scaled diagram for the network is as shown below. In plotting this diagram it is planned that all the activities commence its EST. The critical activities will govern the period of completion of the project and hence shown along the horizontal line.

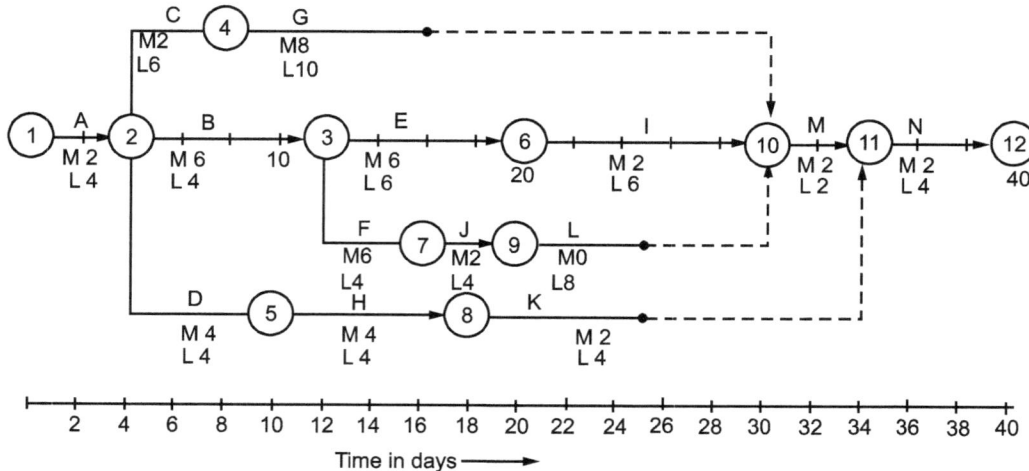

Fig. 3.21

Mason	2	2	12	12	20	20	26	26	12	10	4	4	2	2	2	2	2	2	2
Labour	4	4	14	14	14	14	20	20	14	14	18	18	14	6	6	2	2	4	4	4

The histogram shows wide variations in the requirement of masons and labours over the entire period of the project. The peak requirement is 26 masons and 20 labours and the minimum or valley requirement is 2 masons and 2 labour It is obvious that if 26 masons and 20 labours are employed throughout the project to satisfy the peak demand, they would sit idle during the period of minimum demand and the proposal would be highly uneconomic increasing the project cost enormously and unnecessarily.

The solution may be employing minimum amount of masons and labourers on permanent basis and employing the needed additional masons and labourers as and when required by the peak demand. Practically, however this is risky as not only skilled workers like mason but sometimes even unskilled labourer are also not available on temporary basis without any continuous employment. Hence, proper planning will have to be done so that masons and labourers or any such resource is utilised in a more or less uniform manner and such number be employed on permanent basis till the project is completed. As already indicated this situation is dealt with in two different manners that is either by 'resources smotherning' or by 'resource levelling'. This is employing a set of skilled and unskilled workers for complete period of the project so as to see that the project is completed in its fixed duration. This is also known as *'resource smoothening.'* Other approach is to utilise the available resources uniformly and to reschedule the activities so that the peak demand is reduced to availability.

Here the emphasis is on the proper and uniform use of available resources even at the cost of increase in the duration of the project. This is known as 'resources levelling.'

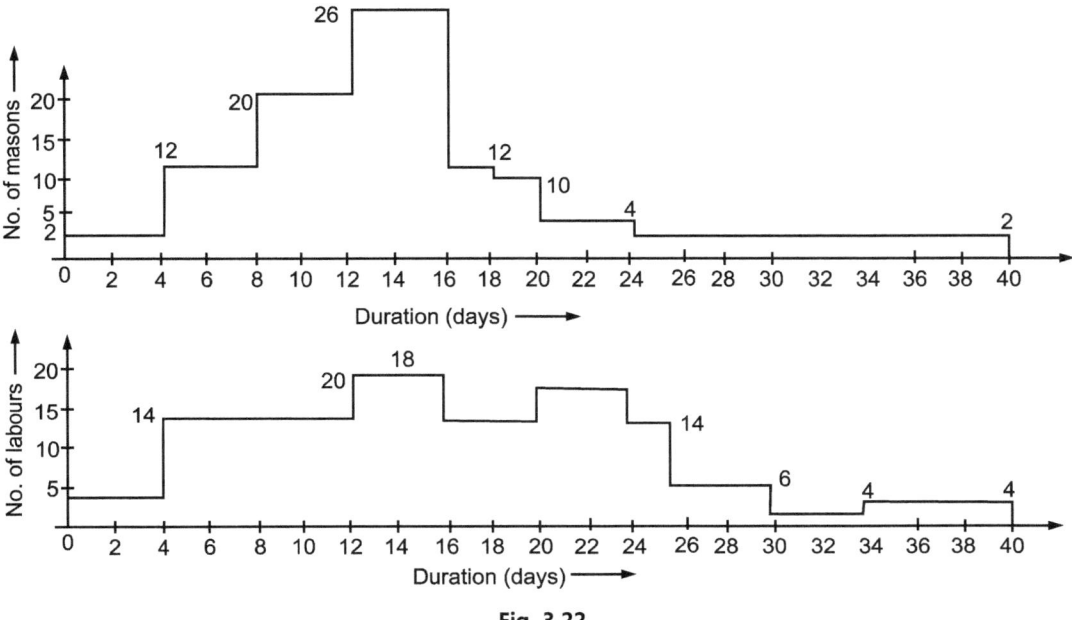

Fig. 3.22

3.7.3 Resources Smoothening

Constrain in this approach is completion period of the project and resources to be uniform as far as possible or for a continuous period of time. Since time period of the project is to be maintained, the critical activities should not be disturbed and the requirement of resources for these activities should be met with.

The additional resources which are needed for the concurrent non-critical activities now can be varied by shifting these activities to the period where requirement of critical activities is reduced.

This can be done by utilising the floats of the non-critical activities by shifting them suitably. This is illustrated by using the data of Example 3.4.

From the network it could be seen that non-critical activities have floats as shown below

Activity	2 – 4	2 – 5	3 – 7	4 – 10	5 – 8	7 – 9	8 – 11	9 – 10
Float (Days)	14	8	4	14	8	4	8	4

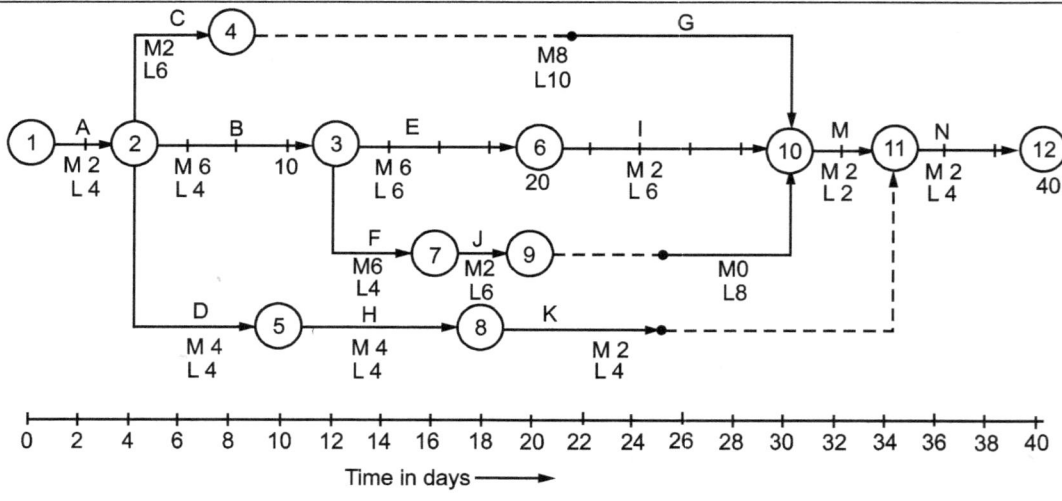

Fig. 3.23

Some of these activities can be suitably shifted utilising the float so that they are concurrent with the critical activities requiring less resources and somewhat uniform requirement is met with.

This will have to be done with two or three trials and the best of the these will have to be adopted. In the above problem it is seen that the requirement of mason between day 12 to day 16 is maximum.

The activity 4 – 10 which is shown in the fig. from 8th day to 16th day be shifted to the period of 23rd day to 30th day so that the requirement of mason is reduced from 20 to 10 and 26 to 16 in the period of 8 to 12 and 12 to 16 days and the requirement of mason from 23rd to 24th day is increased from 4 to 14 and that from 25th to 30th day from 2 to 12. This will also reduce the labour requirement as shown in the Fig. 3.24. Additional labour requirement can further be reduced by shifting the activity 9 – 10 by utilising its float of 4 days. With these changes the time scale diagram, requirement of masons and labours and the histogram is as shown below in Fig. 3.25.

Mason	2	2	12	12	10	10	16	16	10	8	4	14	10	10	10	10	2	2	2	2
Labour	4	4	14	14	8	8	14	14	10	10	10	16	18	14	14	14	2	4	4	4

The below example shows the peak demand for mason is reduced from 26 to 16 and that for the labours are is reduced from 20 to 18 but with more uniform spread over for a long time of the project duration.

Different trials may give still better results and following this procedure it is always possible to smoothen the resources without affecting the duration of the project.

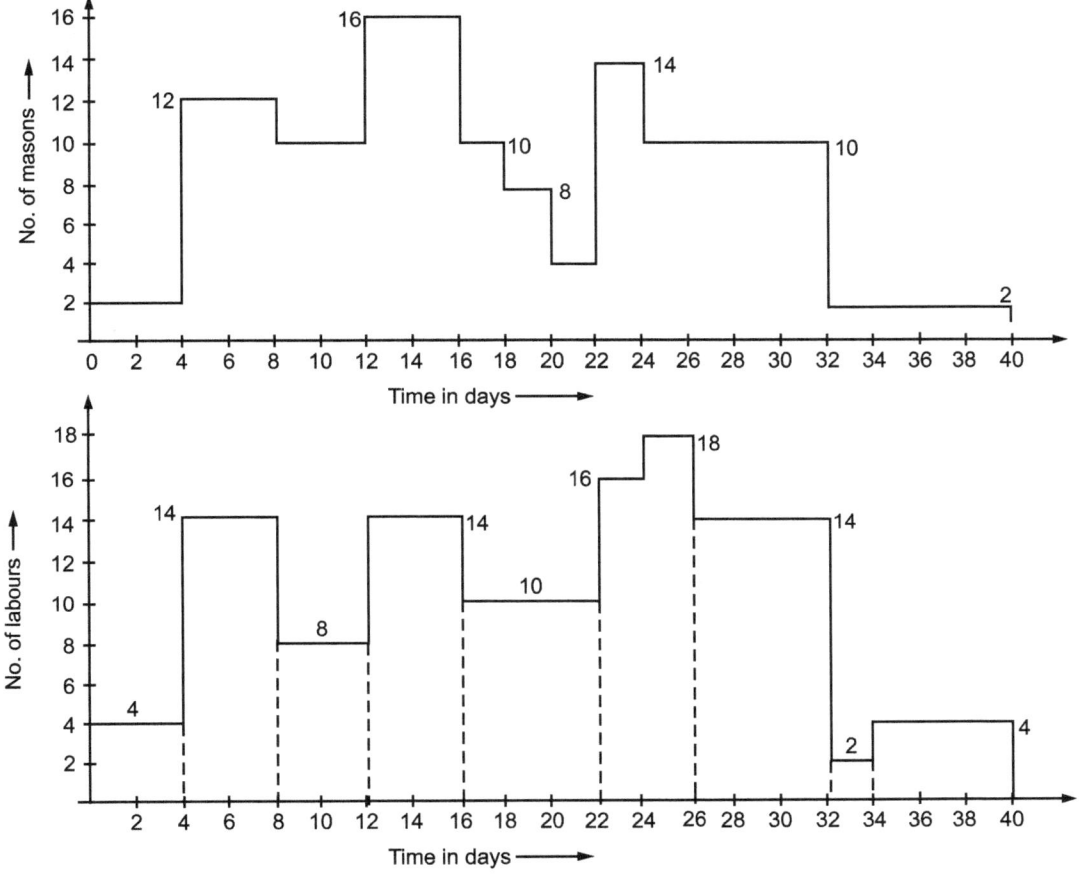

Fig. 3.24

3.7.4 Resource Levelling

In this, there is limited availability of resources. However, normally the available resources should not be less than the maximum number or quantity required for any activity of the project. Therefore, the activity requiring maximum resources dictates the method and along with execution of such activity which ever concurrent activities would be executed, they will be utilising limited resources. Since the requirement of skilled labour, say carpenter, is more and the availability is less, the rescheduling will have to be effected. In this rescheduling, non-critical activities are shifted suitably utilising the available floats. However, even with such shifting the demand for resources may exceed the availability and in that case even the critical activities also cannot be completed in their duration and hence the duration will have to be increased to suit the availability of the resources. This will therefore, result in increase in the duration of the project. But the available resources being the constraint on the project there is no other way than to accept this delay in completion of the project. As such where the completion date is not to be conformed strictly or where there is not likely to be major loss because of some delay in completion of the project and there is availability of limited resources, resource levelling will have to be adopted.

In Example 3.4 the maximum requirement of mason of activity 4 – 10 is 10 masons and maximum requirement of labour of activity 9 – 10 is 8 labour. As such the number of masons and labours available should not be less than 10 and 8 respectively. But even if 10 masons and 8 labours are available as it is seen from the revised histogram that this availability is insufficient even after rescheduling the non-critical activities by using available floats duration of activities to be executed will have to be increased accordingly. Where the requirement of mason is more than 10 and labour more than 8. If the critical activities fall in this process the project duration will be unavoidably increased.

Resource levelling is also a process of trial and mathematical complexity is involved in complex projects having many activities. No technique have been evolved as yet to give a optimum solution to such resource levelling problems and a straight forward solution cannot be obtained. It is only by trial, one can come to a conclusion to the problem of resource levelling. Mathematically, it is not possible to arrive at a unique solution of minimising the maximum required resources for the project. Manager's experience in such problems will only help in bringing out an acceptable and practicable solution for resource levelling.

3.8 COST CONTROL

'Cost control is the process of controlling the expenditure on a construction project at all stages from its inception through its development and design, till the execution and final payment'.

It is a process to maximise the benefits or profit from the limited finance available.

3.8.1 Purpose of Cost Control

1. It provides data of the total expenditure of the work at any instance at a regular time interval. Hence, the contractor can find his profit and loss by comparing the completed work and work ahead and the expenditure involved.

2. In the process of cost control, focus can be made on the area of inefficient functioning and measures can be taken to reduce the cost by controlling the expenses. Cost control data indicates the day-to-day cost incurred on various items of work and gives immediate warning to the site engineers when expenditures exceeds the estimated costs. Also, if two similar jobs constructed by the same method, shows differences in unit costs, it can be result of varying degree of

efficiency of workers or due to mismanagement on the site. Corrective actions can be taken to put the work again at the same speed.

3. Cost control data of a work provides feedback to the estimator for updating the knowledge of output data of men and machines. The unit rates of cost for various items of works can be worked out after the completion of a job and these would help in preparing realistic estimates for other works for which the contractor may like to tender.

3.8.2 Stages At Which Cost Control is Effected

1. **At the Design Stage :** The cost control is dependent to some extent on the design and specifications. Among the various alternatives of designs, only those are considered which are most economical as well as consistent with the requirements. The specifications which add benefits without increasing the cost are chosen. Local materials should be specified as they reduce the cost of transportation.

2. **At the Construction Stage :** Construction cost consists of expenditures on (1) labour, (2) materials, (3) machinery and equipment, and (4) overheads. Out of these four, substantial economy can be achieved in labour and machinery in which the wastage of man-hours can be more. Machinery to be used on site should get fully utilised otherwise its cost/use increases. Also the labour intensive jobs are time consuming and unsuitable for jobs required to be completed within a limited time.

3.8.3 Classification of Cost Control System

The type of cost control system used should not be too costly such that it consumes more expenditure than the cost saved by using it. Hence depending upon the various types and sizes of works, cost control system must be selected. The selection of a cost control system depends on following factors

- Type and nature of work.
- Detailing of the various operations recorded.
- Whether the system is quick and simple ?

Depending on the requirements, following are the types of cost control system

1. **Overall Profit or Loss :** The contractor waits till the work is over and then compares the money he receives for the work with the amount he has spend on it. Such a system is useful only in very small contracts of short duration. In fact, it is hardly a method of control as the information it produces can only be used to avoid similar mistakes in later contracts.

2. **Profit or Loss with Reference to Part Payment :** The contractor is paid for the portion of work completed by him at regular intervals. The costs incurred by

contractor and the payments received can be compared to know the profit and loss position for that part of the work. But this does not take into account all the items of work done and the unused materials on site. It also does not provide break-up of the cost figures and hence does not point to the area needing attention for cost saving.

3. **Unit Costing :** The rate of cost of each item of work is calculated by dividing the expenditure on the item by the quantity of work done. By comparing the rate of cost with the rates in the cost estimates, the efficiency of work can be assessed. It gives the items which need attention. But it does not indicate clearly whether the poor performance of labour, material or machinery which caused the increase in cost.

4. **Comparison with Standard Cost :** In this method, the cost record consists of details of the rate of cost of labour, materials and machinery. These are then compared with the rates of those items known as 'cost standards' as worked out when estimating cost. It is hence possible to pinpoint the area in which there is inefficiency and scope for improvement. This is a costly method as great amount of details are involved.

3.9 PROJECT TIME CONTROL

Project time control is a continuous process starting from the project planning upto project completion. The project is to be controlled in order to complete the job within or before the stipulated time period. Steps in project time control can be given as follows

1. **In the Planning Stage**
   - The scope of the work should be finalised and the requirements of the owner are to be clearly understood by the consultant and the contractor.
   - All the activities are to be planned according to their sequence and requirement of resources. If the sources required for the overlapping activities are the same, more numbers are to be provided so that there will not be idle time left for men and machinery.
   - The quantities for each item of work should be calculated exactly so that at the time of construction, chances of shortage of materials are minimised.
   - Priorities are to be given to the critical activities and no delays are allowed for them. To achieve expected results, the planning for the critical activities is done keeping in mind all the requirements, probable difficulties and provision of finance.
   - Planning for the materials and its orders is to be done carefully keeping in mind the lead time required for each order. The rates of the materials are to be decided with the supplier before the orders are placed and care is to be taken to avoid any kind of misunderstanding.

- Check lists for each item of work is to be made in advance and it is to be followed scrupulously.

2. **In the Execution Stage**
   - Safety stock is to be maintained on the site so that there is no time wasted for want of material.
   - A monitoring cell is to be formed that will look after the progress of the work. Any delays are to be rectified quickly to avoid any increase in the project duration.
   - Techniques such as Crashing of activities are to be used to minimize the project duration.

3.10 LINE OF BALANCE TECHNIQUE

Many construction projects like construction of roads, laying of pipelines or multistorieyed projects contain repetitive activities either horizontally or vertically. E.g. Road construction, involves activities such as preparation of sub-base, preparation of base course, laying of bitumin, compaction etc. These activites span along the length of road. Similarly, for multistoreyed construction, activities like concreting of columns, beams and slab,s brickwork, plastering, tiling, plumbing, painting etc go on repeating at each floor. For such kind of activities an effective technique of 'line of balance' (LOB) is used. It is a 3 dimensional technique of planning i.e. it shows duration, activities and the place of work or length of project or stages of the project.

The LOB technique assumes that the rate of production for an activity is uniform. It is a graphical presentation in which time is plotted on horizontal axis and units or stages of an activity on the vertical axis. The production rate of an activity on the slope of the production line and is expressed in terms of units per time.

3.10.1 How to Draw LOB ?

Let us, take an example of construction of multistoried building in which repetitive activities are involved

Step 1 : The starting step involves plotting of project duration on x-axis and no. of floors on y-axis. The Fig. shows total duration as 32 weeks for 5 floors. It is to be noted that the LOB starts after the plinth level is constructed which is not a repeating activity i.e. a unique activity. (Show Fig. 3.25 for step 1).

Step 2 : The duration of each activity are estimated by normal techniques. E.g. activity 'A' takes 12 weeks to complete for all floors. This means the production rate is 2.4 weeks per floor. It is indicated as shown below. (Show the Fig. 3.26 for step 2).

Step 3 : Now consider activity B with the production rate as one week per floor. It will start when activity 'A' ends on each floor. It is shown as below (Shown in Fig. 3.27 for step 3).

This will be continued for the entire project for other activities. As it is seen from the above Fig. 3.27, there are breaks for activity B at each floor. These breaks or gaps means the crew for 'B' is waiting for some time at each floor and starts as soon as activity A completes on that floor.

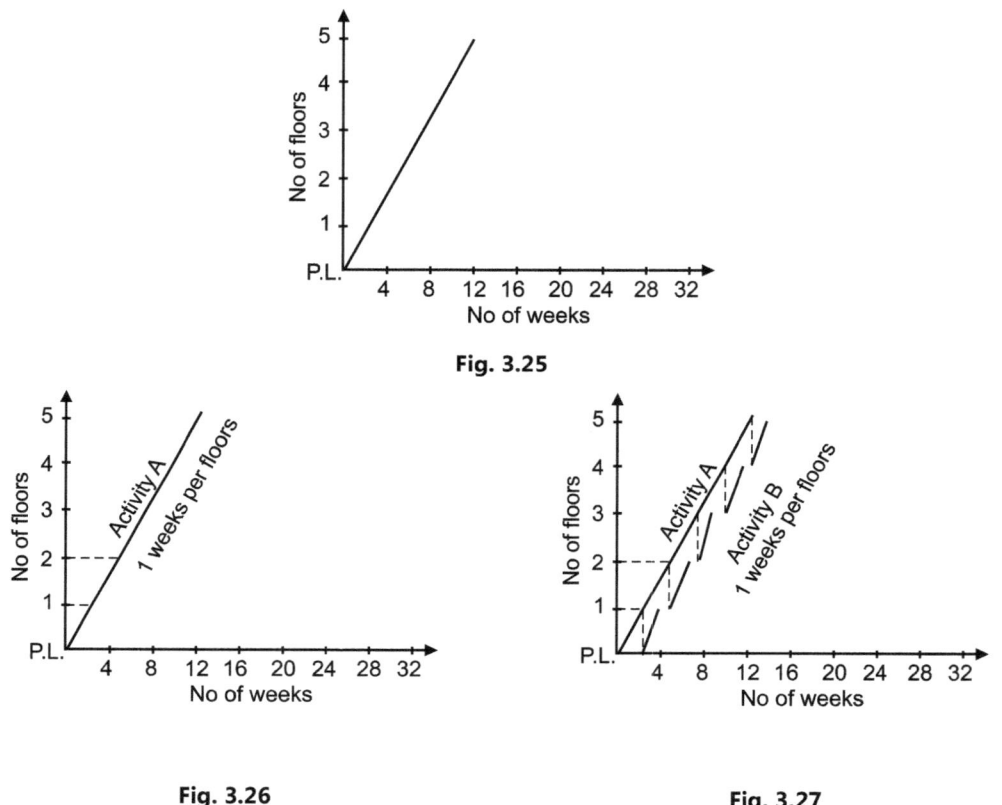

Fig. 3.25

Fig. 3.26

Fig. 3.27

This indicates loss of production and idle manpower for activity B at each floor i.e. avoid this situation, the same activities are represented as below :

The time buffer of week is kept when activity A ends for 5th floor. Working in a reverse way, it activity B has to be completed. 1 week after end of activity A i.e. 13th week, it should start at (13 − 5) = 8th week (rate of production of B is 1 week per floor).

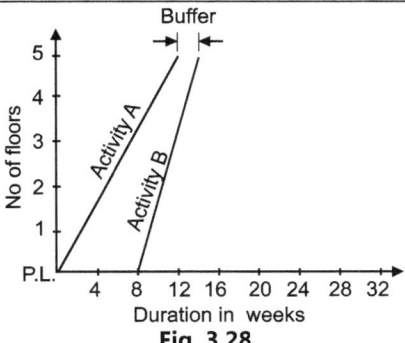

Fig. 3.28

The buffer provides an margin of error and ensures that one activity does not interfere (intersect) with another activity. It is also to be noted that the activities never intersect with each other. The buffer is estimated by the experience of the construction manager and considering the risks, difficulties and probable delays that may occur. The process of drawing LOB is repeated for all activities. The buffers are placed at end or start of activities and are named as 'End Buffer' or 'Start Buffer' respectively. The complete LOB can be shown as adjacent.

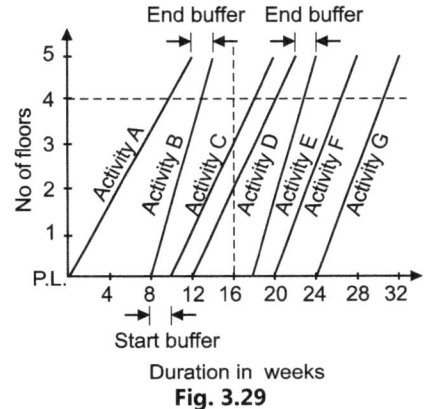

Fig. 3.29

3.10.2 Advantages of LOB Technique

- It's a graphical representation in 3 dimensions i.e. duration, activity and place of work.
- It gives the progress of work at each place of work. E.g. in the above Fig., it indicates the activities which are taking place on 4th floor at different time. Also, on 16th week, it tells us that activities A and B are completed and activities C and D are running. It even gives us the percentage of activity completed.
- It can be effectively used for projects involving repetitive activities.

3.10.3 Limitations of LOB Technique

- It is difficult to recognize the time and space dependencies between the activities.
- It is also difficult to deal with resource and milestone constraints.
- Sometimes, non-linear and discrete activities come across the project which can not be shown on LOB.
- Critical activities can not be shown on LOB.
- Flowless softwares are not available which uses LOB effectively.

QUESTIONS

1. Differentiate between direct cost and indirect cost. What do you understand by outage losses ?
2. What is cost slope and how is it determined ?
3. How is optimum duration and optimum cost of a project determined ?
4. Details of a project consisting of 6 activities are as given below :

Activity	1 – 2	1 – 3	2 – 3	3 – 4	2 – 5	4 – 6
Normal Time weeks	2	7	6	4	2	8
Crash Time weeks	1	5	4	3	1	6
Normal cost ₹	3,000	2,400	4,800	800	8,000	3,000
Crash cost ₹	3,400	4,000	6,000	1,200	8,400	5,000

   (a) Draw the network and identify critical path.
   (b) Calculate the project duration and associated cost if the indirect cost is ₹ 800 per week.
   (c) If the project duration is to be reduced by 1 week how best this could be done and what is the associated cost.
   (d) Calculate the optimum duration and the optimum cost.
5. What do you understand by updating ? Explain its necessity.
6. What information is necessary for updating the project during execution ? How is frequency of updating decided ?
7. Update the network given below after 20 days of execution.

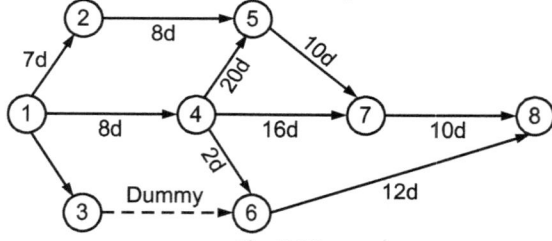

Fig. 3.30

After 20th day of execution the position of activities are as given below

Activity	1 – 2	1 – 3	1 – 4	2 – 5	3 – 6	4 – 5	4 – 6	5 – 7	6 – 7	7 – 8
Position	Completed	Completed	Completed	Not started	In progress	Progress	Not started	Not started	Not started	Not started
Remarks	As per schedule	As per schedule	As per schedule	As per schedule	1	6	As per schedule	To be compressed by 4 days	As per schedule	As per schedule

8. Discuss the problem of resource allocation in brief with different methods of solving.
9. What is resource smoothening and resource levelling ? Differentiate with examples.
10. Illustrate the method of resource smoothening with the help of example.

11. Explain the procedure of controlling the cost is detail.
12. Differentiate various cost control systems and explain each in brief.
13. Manpower requirement for various activities of a project are as follows :

Activity	Duration (Days)	Resource (Men)/Day
1 – 2	5	10
2 – 3	5	5
2 – 4	6	10
3 – 5	5	6
4 – 5	10	4
5 – 6	6	10

    (i) Draw a network and calculate project duration. Show critical path.
    (ii) Draw EST squared network and calculate EFR and IFR for EST solution.
    (iii) Draw LST squared network and calculate EFR and IFR for LST solution.

14. (a) Following data pertains to a small project.

Activity	1 – 2	1 – 3	2 – 3	3 – 5	3 – 4	5 – 6	6 – 7	4 – 7
Duration (Days)	7	9	4	13	10	8	9	16

    (i) Draw a network, calculate project duration and critical path.
    (ii) At the end of 13th day, review was taken which indicates.
       (a) Activity 1 – 2, 1 – 3 and 2 – 3 completed.
       (b) Activity 3 – 4 progressing for 2 days and needs 10 more days.
       (c) Re-assessment of activity 6 – 7, observed that it can be completed within 8 days.
    Draw UPDATED NETWORK and calculate project duration and show critical path.

15. What do you mean by cost control ? Write importance and purpose of cost control.
16. Following table pertains to a small project work, indirect cost of which is ₹ 250 per day.

Activity	Normal Duration (Weeks)	Normal Cost (₹)	Crash Duration (Weeks)	Crash Cost (₹)
1 – 2	7	6,000	5	6,400
2 – 3	9	10,000	5	11,200
2 – 4	8	5,500	4	6,100
3 – 6	10	6,500	7	7,700
4 – 6	4	7,000	3	7,100
6 – 7	0	–	0	–
6 – 8	2	4,000	2	4,000
7 – 8	5	8,000	3	9,000

    (i) Draw network and highlight critical path.

(ii) Calculate Normal project duration and cost of the project.
(iii) Calculate optimum duration and optimum cost of the project by stage by state compression.
(iv) Draw 'optimum duration' squared network of the project.

17. The manpower requirements for the various activities of a project are as given below:

Activity	Duration in days	Restraints	Resource (Men/Day)
A	4	Starting activity	5
B	5	Starting activity	8
C	6	C follows A	3
D	2	D follows B	6
E	2	E follows C & D	9
F	4	F follows C & D	7
G	1	G follows E	5
H	2	H follows F	4
I	4	I follows G & F	2
J	2	J follows I	9

(i) Draw a network and find out project duration and show critical path.
(ii) Draw EST squared network and calculate EFR & IFR for EST solution.
(iii) Draw Histogram for EST solution.

18. What are the objects of Resource allocation?

19. The following table gives the cost duration data for the various activities of a small construction project.

Activity	Normal		Crash	
	Duration (Weeks)	Cost (₹)	Duration (Weeks)	Cost (₹)
1 – 2	6	7000	3	14500
1 – 3	8	4000	5	8500
2 – 3	4	6000	1	9000
2 – 4	5	8000	3	15000
3 – 4	5	5000	3	11000

The Indirect cost of the project is ₹ 3000/- week.
(i) Draw network and find critical path. Calculate normal project duration.
(ii) Draw EST squared network for normal durations.
(iii) Draw EST squared network at optimum stage.
Determine optimum duration of the project and corresponding minimum cost.
(iv) Draw EST squared network at all crash solution stage. Calculate duration and corresponding cost.

20. The following table gives the cost duration data for various activities of construction project.

Activity	Normal		Crash	
	Duration (Weeks)	Cost (₹)	Duration (Weeks)	Cost (₹)
1 – 2	4	2000	3	2600
2 – 3	7	4000	5	7000
2 – 4	6	4500	5	6000
2 – 5	7	1500	6	2300
3 – 6	6	3000	4	4000
4 – 6	4	6000	3	8000
5 – 6	3	1000	2	1150
6 – 7	2	900	1	1600

The Indirect cost is ₹ 1000/week.

(a) Draw network and calculate project duration and show critical path by heavy ruling line.

(b) Draw EST squared network.

(c) Calculate normal project duration and normal project cost.

(d) Calculate optimum project duration and optimum project cost.

(e) Draw EST squared network at optimum stage.

21. (a) Manpower requirement for various activities of a project are as follows

Activity	Duration (Days)	No. of Carpenters
1 – 2	7	12
2 – 3	7	7
2 – 4	8	12
2 – 5	7	8
3 – 5	12	8
4 – 5	8	6
5 – 6	9	6

(i) Draw a network and calculate project duration. Show critical path by heavy ruling line.

(ii) Draw EST squared Network and prepare Resource accumulation table and Calculate EFR and IFR.

(iii) Draw Histogram for EST network.

(b) Explain Resource levelling and Resource smoothing with suitable example.

22. The following are the manpower requirements for each activity in the project.

Activity	Duration (Day)	Manpower Required
1 – 2	4	6
2 – 3	6	6
2 – 4	6	6
3 – 5	0	0
4 – 5	0	0
3 – 6	8	2
5 – 7	10	6
4 – 8	6	4
6 – 9	8	2
7 – 9	10	6
8 – 9	8	4

Draw the squared network and find out EST and LST solution and EFR and IFR.

23. The following table gives the cost duration data for various activities of construction project.

The Indirect cost is ₹ 80/- per day.

(a) Draw network and calculate project duration and show critical path by heavy ruling line.

(b) Draw EST squared network.

(c) Calculate normal project duration and normal project cost.

(d) Calculate optimum project duration and optimum project cost.

(e) Draw EST squared network at optimum stage.

| Activity | Normal | | Crash | |
	Duration (Weeks)	Cost (₹)	Duration (Weeks)	Cost (₹)
1 – 2	2	1000	2	1000
1 – 3	7	500	3	900
2 – 3	6	300	3	420
2 – 4	5	200	4	250
3 – 4	0	0	0	0
3 – 5	9	600	4	900
4 – 6	11	600	6	1000
5 – 6	6	700	3	910

24. Cost and Schedule data for small project are given below. The indirect cost is ₹ 1000/- day.
    (i) Draw normal duration network and calculate project duration.
    (ii) Carryout stage by stage network compression and find out optimum duration and optimum cost.

Activity	Normal		Crash	
	Duration in Days	Cost in ₹	Duration in Days	Cost in ₹
0 – 1	2	500	1	1000
1 – 2	4	400	3	1000
1 – 3	4	250	3	870
1 – 4	3	550	2	1050
2 – 8	4	700	2	2100
3 – 5	7	650	4	1550
3 – 8	2	620	1	1820
4 – 6	5	520	3	2600
5 – 7	2	470	1	1570
6 – 9	5	390	5	390
7 – 8	2	430	1	480
8 – 9	3	530	2	630
9 – 10	2	570	2	570

25. Following table shows the cost-duration data for a small construction project. Indirect cost for the project is ₹ 300 per week.
    (i)   Draw the network, find the normal project duration and the corresponding project cost.
    (ii) If all activities are crashed, what will be the project duration and corresponding cost ?
    (iii) Find the optimum duration and minimum project cost.

Activity i – j	Normal		Crash	
	Duration (Weeks)	Cost (₹)	Duration (Weeks)	Cost (₹)
1 – 2	6	1400	4	1900
1 – 3	8	2000	5	2800
2 – 3	4	1100	2	1500
2 – 4	3	800	2	1400
3 – 4	Dummy	–	–	–
3 – 5	6	900	3	1600
4 – 6	10	2500	6	3500
5 – 6	3	500	2	800

26. Explain the conditions under which updating is carried out.
27. What are the objectives of Resource Levelling ? Explain the procedure of carrying out resource leveling.
28. List factors affecting man-power planning.

29. Find the optimum solution for the following network

Activity	Succeeding Activity	Normal Duration	Crash Duration	Crash Cost (in `)	Normal Cost (in `)
A	B, C	8	8	500	500
B	D, E	4	3	1000	750
C	I	4	3	800	500
D	G	3	3	750	750
E	F	6	4	1500	800
F	H	9	6	2500	1600
G	–	5	4	500	400
H	–	7	5	800	600
I	f	8	5	3000	1500

The indirect cost of each activity is given as ₹ 150/- per day.
(a) Find the duration and normal cost of the project.
(b) Find all crash solution. (c) Find the optimum solution.

30. Explain the steps for quality control for construction of substructure.
31. Explain the terms – Rescheduling and Updating. Also write the procedure for updating of network.
32. Explain Resource Levelling and Resource Smoothening by giving suitable example.
33. Explain the procedure of carrying out Resource Levelling.
34. Discuss the procedure for step by step network compression.
35. Explain the following terms with example : (i) Direct cost of an activity (ii) Indirect cost of an activity (iii) Crash cost of an activity (iv) Normal cost of an activity
36. What are the objectives of Resource Scheduling ?
37. Draw the following network.

Activity	Succeeded by	Duration (Days)	Resources
A	C, D	3	4
B	E	2	6
C	G	1	3
D	E	6	6
E	F, H	4	6
F	G	5	8
G	I, J	3	5
H	K	8	5
I	L	5	4
J	M	6	2
K	M	9	1
L	–	3	2
M	–	3	2

(i) Find the critical path and duration. (ii) Carry out resource smoothening. (iii) Carry out resource leveling. (Solve the example by drawing time scale graph of the network).

38. Explain the concept of line of balance in detail.
39. What are the applications of LOB technique.

UNIT IV
ENGINEERING ECONOMICS AND BANKING

4.1 INTRODUCTION

The term economics touches every field whether it is engineering or day to day working. How many times do we afford to go to a five star hotel for dinner ? How much we can save every year ? Why do petrol prices rise every year ? On what factors do my increments or promotion depend ? Is there any relation exist between price of crude oil to rise in price of gold ? What is the relation between NSE and BSE index ? How the earthquake in Japan may rise the prices of goods in India ? What are the factors that makes the dollar and pound strongest ? Answers to all these questions can be found by studying economics.

In short, Economics is the study of flow of finance right from production to consumption of goods or services. *It is the study of how the society decides what, how and for whom to produce. It is a science that studies human behaviour which aims at meeting maximum objectives of an individual with the help of scarce means.* Economics is also an art as well as science that studies those activities of social, real and normal human beings, which are related to worth.

4.2 IMPORTANCE OF ECONOMY IN CONSTRUCTION INDUSTRY

Construction activities touch every aspect of economy. Following pi chart shows the employment created by construction industry as compared to others. (the Fig. are taken as tentative. It may vary from country to country).

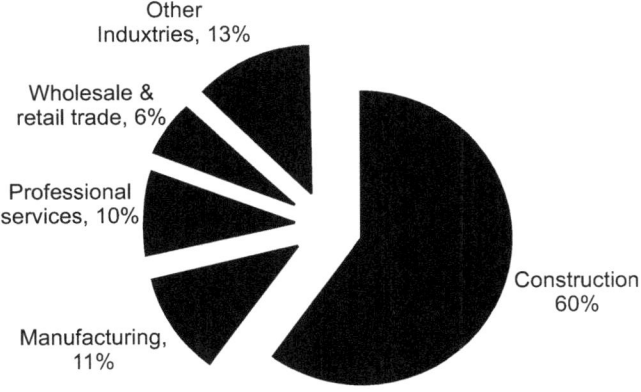

Fig. 4.1 : Contribution of construction industry in economy

With the increasing demand of infrastructure, construction industry is flourishing. Consider any industry may be in service sector or manufacturing unit, one need to invest in construction in one or the other way. The share of construction industry in overall development of economy is as follows

Construction industry gives employment to millions of workers, directly or indirectly. Following Fig. shows, how construction influences other industries and overall economic development directly or indirectly.

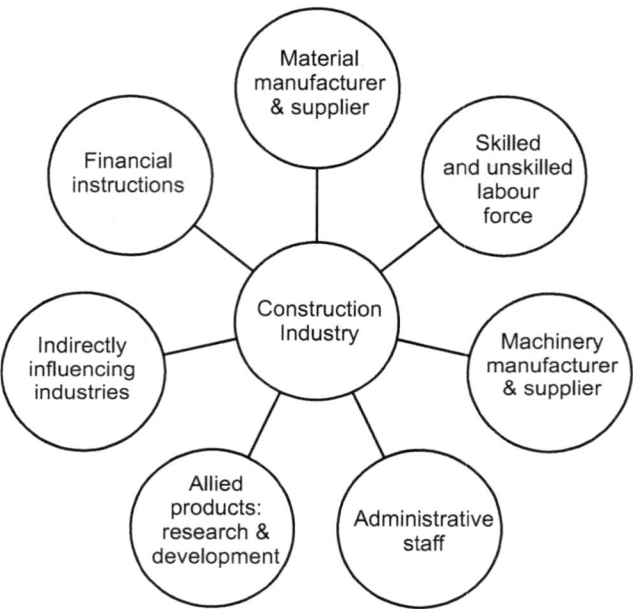

Fig. 4.2

Consider a project, e.g. construction of multistoried buildings. The direct businesses associated with it are

- Material manufacturer and suppliers such as cement, steel, sand, admixtures, tiles, plumbing, electrical, air conditioning, paints, glass, plywood and many more.
- The requirement of skilled and unskilled labours is huge. It attracts large population and provides daily wages to them.
- Machineries like cranes, mixers, transit mixers, vibrators, trolleys, lifts, concrete pumps etc. are required for faster work. So the manufacturing industries get business.
- Large administrative staff is required on site and off site to maintain the organisations. These are indirectly influencing the economy.

- The other allied products such as green building materials, low cost materials, alternate techniques to reduce expenses and increase quality etc. are a need of time. Many nations are investing huge amount in it. The direct and indirect staff required for this also to be counted.

For these large projects, financial backing is given by many institutions on long term basis. This keeps the money circulating and increasing the GDP of nation. Construction also affects the other industries indirectly. Tourism is one of the best example of it. If the infrastructure is good, tourism flourishes in that area. We can also say that for growing tourism, infrastructure development like roads, water supply, hotel industry is a must.

By looking at these reasons and many more, one can say that now-a-days, construction is the vital factor that affects the economy.

4.3 INDIA : CONSTRUCTION INDUSTRY AND ECONOMY

The development of physical infrastructure in India and, consequently, the construction sector has been in focus during the last decade. It is well established that the influence of the construction industry spans across several sub-sectors of the economy as well as the infrastructure development, such as industrial and mining infrastructure, highways, roads, ports, railways, airports, power systems, irrigation and agriculture systems, tele-communication systems, hospitals, schools, townships, offices, houses and other buildings; urban infrastructure, including water supply, sewerage, and drainage, and rural infrastructure. Thus, it becomes the basic input for socioeconomic development.

Today, India is one of the six fastest growing economies of the world and Asia's biggest infrastructure investment opportunity.

Follow some of the facts related to Indian Economy

- More than 140 billion Euros will be invested in energy and infrastructure.
- Construction industry growth rate is higher as compared to overall growth in India.
- In Year 2010-2015, expected annual growth for commercial and industrial construction is almost 10%.
- The speciality of Indian Economy is that it quickly regains the momentum. The recent recession has proved this which witnessed the firm standing of Indian Economy.

India has one of the world's biggest purchasing power and ability to attract large investors from all over the world. In 2010, investments in various infrastructure sectors are expected to be 140 billion euros in which 70% is towards energy sector, 12-15 % for road construction, 4-5% for ports and 7-10% for airports.

The contribution of construction to the GDP at factor cost in 2006-07 was ₹1,96,555 crore, registering an increase of 10.7 per cent from the previous year. This increase in the share of construction sector in GDP has primarily been because of increased government spending on physical infrastructure in the last few years. Programmes such as National Highway Development Programme (NHDP) and PMGSY (Prime Minister Gram Sadak Yojna), Bharat Nirman Programme contribute a lot.

4.3.1 Booming Construction Industry Opportunities in India

India has invested in many infrastructure projects that gained momentum for economic development. Some of them are as follows

Commonwealth Games - 2010 in New Delhi

The Commonwealth Games - 2010 in New Delhi throws mega opportunities for building material companies, construction equipments and technologies companies.

- Commonwealth Games Village project worth $40 million.
- Elevated ring road, widening and redesigning of roads in and around Delhi.
- More subways and 15 to 20 flyovers.
- Sports specialty hospital.
- Setting up of a cultural centre.
- The Delhi Development Authority (DDA) has been asked to earmark eight to nine plots for Five Star Hotels.

Roads

The government has announced four-laning of 48 new projects with an estimated cost of US$ 12 billion. Private sector participation in road projects will grow significantly. "The Golden Quadrilateral Plan" (5850 kilometres) for linking the four metropolitan cities of Delhi, Mumbai, Chennai and Kolkata with an estimated cost of $5.5 billion.

Railways

The railway sector will need an investment of $22 billion for new coaches, tracks and communications and safety equipment over the next 10 years.

A 10-year Corporate Safety Plan of the Indian Railways envisaging an expenditure of $7.24 billion besides development of appropriate technology for higher level of safety in train operation.

Metro Rail Corporation projects worth $12.84 billion in cities like Delhi, Bengaluru, Hyderabad, Chennai, Ahmedabad and many other cities are on target.

Airports

Upgradation and modernization of airports will require $33 billion. This investment is in the next 10 years.

Special Economic Zones (SEZ)

Projects are coming up to develop Special Economic Zones worth $2.5 billion.

Urban Infrastructure - Township, Malls, Office Buildings etc.

India has a large and growing middle class population of 300 million people, out of which a large section need new houses. It is estimated that there is a national housing storage of 41 million units. Retailing is becoming the boom industry with organized retail being a market of $6 billion. NASSCOM-McKinsey surveys have predicted the ITES sector in India will require approximately 100 million sq. ft. of office space, which means a promising opportunity for the construction industry. Water supply and sanitation projects alone offer scope for annual investment of $5.71 billion.

Power

The Ministry of Power has formulated a blueprint to provide reliable, affordable and quality power to all users by 2012.

Sagar Mala

The "Sagar Mala" project for expansion and modernization of ports, inland navigation and maritime transport. This involves an investment of $22 billion within a 10 year period. While the government will take care of 15 per cent of the investment, the rest will come from the private sector. In a report by UNESCO, the Indian Economy will be the third largest in the year 2050 as depicted in the following diagram.

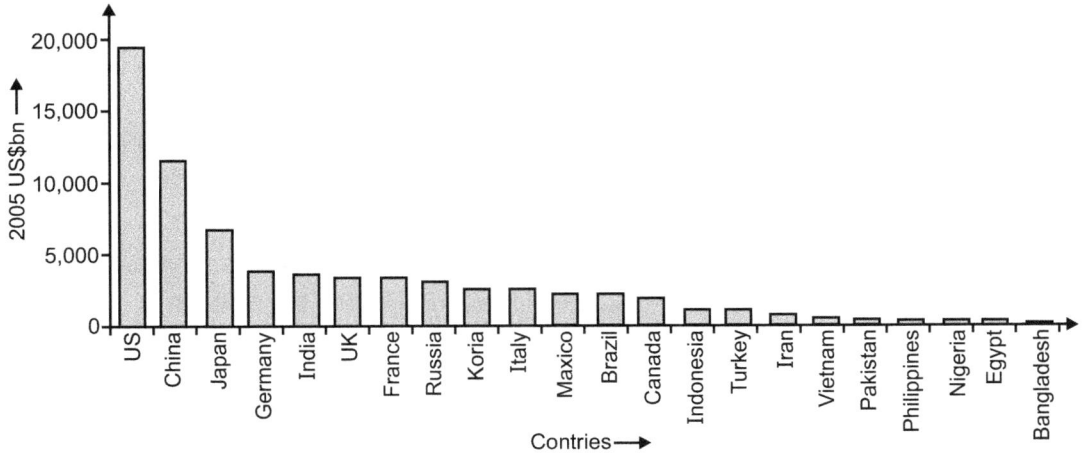

(a) The largest economies in 2025

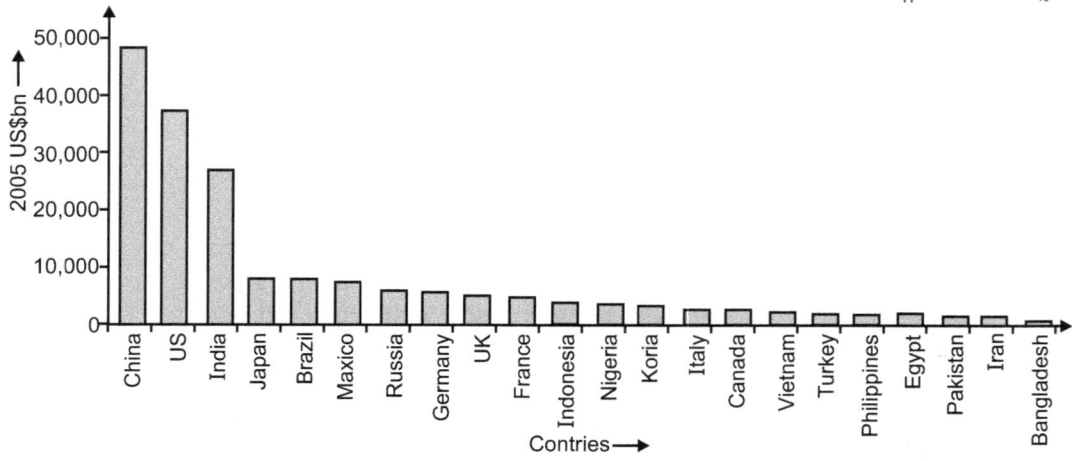

(b) The largest economies in 2050

Fig. 4.3

It shows the prediction that India will be third largest economy of the world. This is a matter of pride for us. But although various steps have been taken to strengthen the construction industry, it is crucial to take necessary measures in order to prepare the industry to meet the challenges of growth.

4.4 DEFINITION OF ECONOMICS

With this introduction to the economy related to construction, let us study Economics further. Let us start with definition of Economics.

- **By A. Marshall :** It is the study of mankind in the ordinary business of life; it examines that part of individual and social action which is most closely connected with the attainment and with the use of material requisites of well being.

- **By L. Robbins :** Economics is a science which studies human behaviour as a relationship between ends and scarce means which have alternative uses.

- **By J. M. Keynes :** It is the study of the administration of scarce resources and of the determinants of income and employment.

In short, Economics can be defined as 'a social science concerned with the proper uses and allocation of resources for the achievement and maintenance of growth with stability'.

4.5 TYPES OF ECONOMY

1. **Micro-Economy :** It offers a detailed treatment of individual decisions about particular commodities. i.e. the study of household's decision whether he prefers bungalow to flat and the developer's decision whether to construct a bungalow scheme or apartment.
2. **Macro-Economy :** It emphasizes the interaction in the economy as a whole. It treats all the goods as 'consumer goods' and study the interaction between household's decision and developer's decision.
3. **Command Economy :** It is a society/market where the government makes all decisions about production and consumption.
4. **Free Economy :** It is a society/market where Government do not intervene.
5. **Mixed Economy :** It is a society/market where Government and private sector interact in solving economic problems. Our country, India is following mixed economy.

4.6 LAWS OF ECONOMICS

1. The consumer gets maximum satisfaction of the goods or services for which he is paying.
2. Man is sensible to balance marginal cost and marginal money gains.
3. All the theories are based on the behaviour of an average man. i.e. their actions cannot be reduced to scientific laws.
4. The theories are based on the things such as taste, price, fashion, price of substitute goods and income of the society. The effect of changes on the demand and supply can be studied by changing any one of these and keeping other things constant.

4.7 DEFINITIONS OF SOME IMPORTANT TERMS

- Market is a set of arrangements by which buyers and sellers are in contact to exchange goods and services.
- Markets in which Government do not intervene is called as Free market.
- When all decisions about the production and consumption are taken by Government, the economy is called as command economy.
- A mixed economy allows the interaction of Government as well as private sectors.

- Gross investment is the money used for production of new capital goods and improvement in existing goods.
- Net investment is the gross investment minus the depreciation of the existing capital stock.
- Assets are what the firm owns.
- Liabilities are what the firms owes.
- Physical capital is the machinery, equipment and buildings used in producing future wealth.
- A firms revenue is the amount it earns by selling goods or services in a given period such as a year.
- Wealth is the addition of capital and land.
- Goods are the physical commodities such as steel, cars, mangoes etc.
- Price is the amount of money given in exchange for a commodity or service.
- Costs are the expenses incurred by the firm in producing goods and services during the period.
- Profits are the excess of revenues over costs.
- Value of a commodity is decided by its utility and one's sentiments and expresses the power of purchasing other goods.
- Money is anything that has general acceptance and passes freely from hand to hand as a medium of exchange.
- Inventory is the goods held in stock by the firm for the production processing to manufacture new goods.
- Want is the desire that can be fulfilled and supported by the ability and willingness to satisfy it.
- Services are the activities such as theatres or teaching which can be consumed or enjoyed at the instant they are produced.
- Utility is the capacity of a commodity to satisfy human wants and depends upon the intensity of the want which it satisfies. It is the amount of satisfaction derived from a commodity or service at a particular time.

4.8 LAW OF DIMINISHING UTILITY

Law of Diminishing Utility

The law is stated by Marshall as 'the additional benefit which a person derives from a given increase in his stock of a thing diminishes with every increase in stock that he already has'.

Definition of Marginal Utility

Marginal utility can be defined as 'the change in the total utility resulting from a one unit change in consumption of a commodity per unit time'.

A person who is purchasing the commodity will constantly weighing it against the price he is giving for it. He will continue till the marginal utility equals the price. E.g. he will buy a mango for ₹ 10. but if he wants to buy two mangoes, he will not pay ₹ 20, but will try to bargain on ₹ 18 only. Thus, the marginal utility for the second mango will be ₹ 8 and not 10. Thus, we can also define marginal utility as the addition made to the total utility by the consumption of last unit considered just worthwhile.

Consider one more example of a person having only one shirt that gives him maximum utilization. As the number of shirts goes on increasing, the utility from each additional shirt goes on decreasing. This can be depicted with the help of following representative Fig.

Table 4.1

Units (Shirts)	Total Utility (Units of Satisfaction)	Marginal Utility (Additional Units of Satisfaction)
1	30	30
2	56	26
3	76	20
4	90	14
5	97	7
6	97	0
7	86	− 11
8	61	− 25

The same can also be applied to the number of bread slices that a man has.

The above table can be represented with the help of histogram as follows,

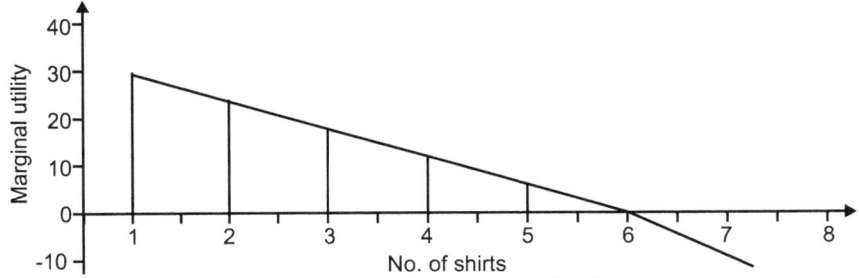

Fig. 4.4 : Diminishing marginal utility

The marginal utility as shown in the above Fig. goes on reducing as shown in Fig. 4.4. The reason for this decrease is that the consumer gets satisfied with the consumption of more and more commodity; his wants get satisfied and does not want further. Another reason is; the same commodities are imperfect substitutes for each other. The utility would have increased by use of another commodity.

Assumptions of the Law
1. The commodity should be taken in suitable units. e.g. The water for drinking for a thirsty man should be measured in glass as the unit and not mere spoonful.
2. The consumption of the commodity should be done at the same time. The foods taken at 10 a.m. and at 2 p.m. have the same utility.
3. The taste of the consumer remains the same.
4. Consumer is an average man without having a strong desire for the commodity and not a miser.
5. Income of the consumer should remain the same.
6. There is no change in fashion.

The law does not hold good for the collection of rare goods and for money but holds good for all types of satisfaction whether good or bad.

4.9 DEMAND AND SUPPLY

Demand and Its Meaning
Consider a poor man who desires to have a piece of bread. Now, consider a clerk working in a bank who wants a TV set in his house. These needs and wants do not make a demand, but when a person is willing to pay for his desire, the desire is changed to Demand.

Definition of Demand
Thus, the demand can be defined as "The various quantities of a given commodity or service which consumers would buy in one market in a given period of time at various incomes or at various prices of related goods" or
"Demand is the quantity of a good, buyers wish to purchase at each conceivable price"

Definition of Supply
"Supply is the quantity of a good; sellers wish to sell at each conceivable price".

Consider an example of chocolates demanded and supplied at varying prices. The demand and supply is changing depending upon price as shown below.

Table 4.2

Unit Price (₹/No.)	Demand (Millions/Year)	Supply (Millions/Year)
0.00	200	0
0.10	160	0
0.20	120	40
0.30	80	80
0.40	40	120
0.50	0	160
0.60	0	200
0.70	0	240

The first column is the different prices of a chocolate and the second column denotes the probable demand of it. Third column indicates the number that the sellers want to supply.

Even if the chocolates are free of cost, there is a limited demand depending upon the age and taste of the consumers. Also they become bore for eating the chocolates. As the price increases, demand starts decreasing and it becomes zero when the price exceeds ₹ 0.4/-. This is also because the consumers may think its marginal utility as zero for more price. Similarly, the seller does not wish to sell them free of cost or with a very low price such as ₹ 0.1/- which is not going to add to his profit. The quantity supplied goes on increasing with the increase in the price.

Also, as the demand is more than the supply, the seller will quickly run out of stock, realizing that he should have charged more price. At some intermediate price, the quantity demanded just equals the quantity supplied which is called as *equilibrium price*. So, ₹ 0.3/-is the equilibrium price. If the price of the chocolate is more than ₹ 0.3/-, there is excess supply and the sellers get frustrated. Similarly, for higher prices i.e. for price of ₹ 0.5/-per chocolate, nobody wish to buy the chocolate.

To recoup the money spent on the production, the seller will cut down the price to clear the stock. The process of cutting the prices will continue until price is ₹ 0.3/- per chocolate which is called as *Equilibrium price* and the quantity is called as *equilibrium quantity*.

At any particular instant, the market price may not be the equilibrium price. If not, there will be excess demand or excess supply, depending upon the price. But these forces themselves provide the incentive to change prices towards the equilibrium price. In this sense, markets are self correcting.

4.10 DETERMINATION OF MARKET PRICE

Market prices are decided depending upon the demand and supply curve as seen above and also on the type of good, whether it is perishable or durable.

Price Determination of Perishable Goods

In case of perishable goods, like fish, milk etc., the supply is limited to the quantity available or the stock in hand for the day. Consider the demand curve DD for a given supply as shown in Fig. 4.5.

E is the point of equilibrium for the given supply and demand. If the demand increases to D'D', the equilibrium price will increase to E' as the supply remains the same. On the other hand, for a decrease of demand to D"D", the price falls to E". The quantity sold remaining the same for both the conditions.

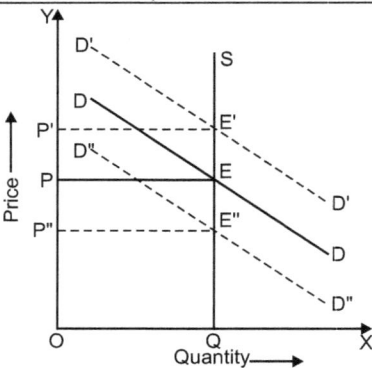

Fig. 4.5 : Market price of perishable goods

Price Determination of Durable Goods

The supply curve is as shown in Fig. 4.6. After a certain limit the quantity remains the same as represented by QR. SQ is the stock available with the firm.

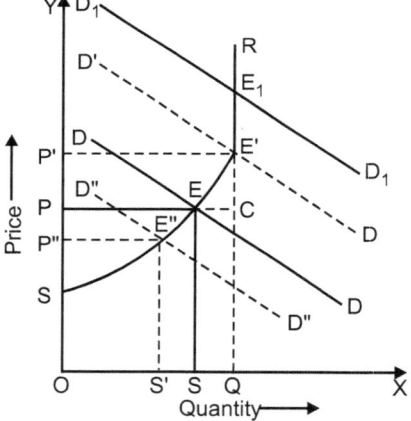

Fig. 4.6 : Market price of durable commodity

For the given price P, supply and the demand curve is DD, the equilibrium point is E. For the increase of the demand from DD to D'D', the price increase is from P to P' and the equilibrium point shifts to E' utilising all the available stock.

If the demand increase still further to D_1D_1, but the supply remaining the same, only price will increase at a faster rate and the equilibrium will be point E_1 which is much higher. However, if the demand is decreased to D"D", the price will fall to OP" and the equilibrium at E".

4.11 TYPES OF DEMAND

There are Three Types of Demand

1. Price demand
2. Income Demand
3. Cross Demand

1. **Price Demand :** It refers to the various quantities of a commodity or service that a consumer would purchase at a given time in a market at various hypothetical prices with other things constant. Demand of an individual consumer is called as **consumer demand** while the total demand of all consumers is called as **industry demand**. Total demand for the product of an individual firm at various prices is known as individual seller's demand.

2. **Income Demand :** Various quantities of goods and services which would be purchased by the consumer at his various levels of income is called as income demand, with other things such as taste and price remaining constant. When income of an individual increases, his purchase of high priced goods also increases and vice versa.

3. **Cross Demand :** The cross demand means the quantities of goods or services which will be purchased with reference to change in price of substitutes or complimentary goods. E.g. change in the price of tea is going to affect demand for coffee.

Of all these three demands, price demand is the most commonly used. Let us study the demand curve, i.e. price demand curve in detail.

4.12 DEMAND CURVE

Consider a demand curve for an imaginary consumer.

From the Fig. it is clear that as the price decreases, the demand increases and vice versa. The demand curve slopes downwards in accordance with the law of diminishing marginal utility. When the price falls, more suppliers enter into the market and old purchasers may purchase more. The reasons why the people buy more when the price falls is :

- A consumer can afford to buy more because other things being cheaper, his real income increases. This is called as *income effect*.
- As the good becomes cheap, it can be substituted wholly or partly by another. This is called as *substitution effect*.

  The income effect and substitution effect combines to increase the ability and willingness of the consumer to buy more.

- As the price decreases, the commodity is put to more uses and for less important works.
- By the fall in price there is a divergence between the marginal utility and price. This is rectified by buying more commodities bringing its marginal utility to the level of the price.

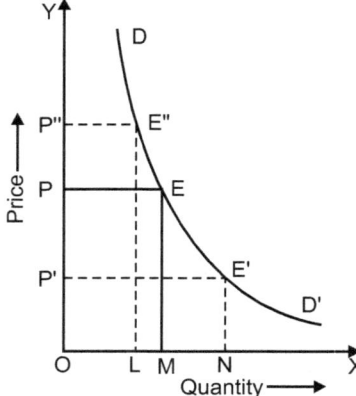

Fig. 4.7 : Demand curve

Exceptions to the Demand Curves

Following are the circumstances when the demand curve shows increase in demand for the price rise and vice versa.

1. When a serious shortage is anticipated, the people get panic and buy more quantity even if the rates are high.
2. To prove the dignity, the people try to buy goods of higher price to be included in the list of distinguished personages.
3. Sometimes, people buy more at a higher price in sheer ignorance.

4.12.1 Law of Demand

The law of demand which is based on the law of diminishing marginal utility, states the relationship between increase in price and its effect on demand. It states as "A rise in the price of a commodity or service is followed by a reduction in demand, and a fall in price is followed by an increase in demand, if conditions of demand remain constant".

In other words, it can be stated as "The greater the amount to be sold, the smaller must be the price at which it is offered in order that it may find purchasers; or the amount demanded increases with a fall in price and diminishes with a rise in price".

Exceptions to the Law

1. With the change in taste or fashion, the demand may decrease though there is decrease in price.

2. If consumer's income increases, the demand for some commodities may increase though there is increase in price.

3. If the price of the substitute good decreases more than the commodity, the demand decreases. E.g. if the price of coffee decreases more heavily than that of tea, people may wish to drink coffee more than tea.

4. With the discovery of substitute items, the demand may decrease inspite of decrease in the price.

4.13 SUPPLY CURVE

Supply Curve

Again considering the example of chocolates, (refer table no. 4.2), plot the demand curve DD and supply curve SS as shown in Fig. 4.8.

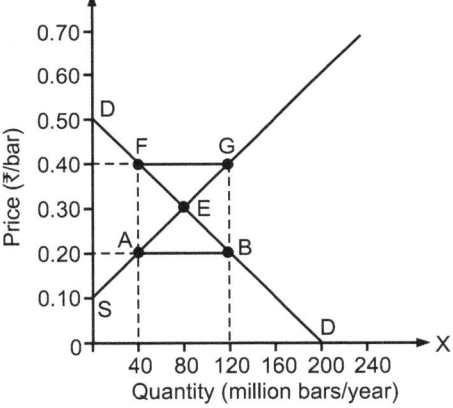

Fig. 4.8

E is the equilibrium point. At a point below E, the horizontal distance between supply curve and the demand curve at this height shows the excess demand at this price.

For E.g. at ₹ 0.2/chocolate, the quantity supplied is 40 millions per year, the quantity demanded 120 millions per year and the distance AB represents the excess demand of 80 millions per year.

Conversely at a price above the equilibrium price, there is excess supply.

At ₹ 0.4/chocolate, 40 millions chocolates per year are demanded, 120 millions per year are supplied and the horizontal distance FG measures the excess supply of 80 millions chocolates per year. Hence, any quantity larger than 40 millions per year at a price of ₹ 0.40/chocolate would involve buyers in forced purchases. Similarly, when the price is ₹ 0.20, any quantity larger than 40 millions per year would involve sellers in forced sale.

Supply is the amount of the goods offered by a seller to sale at a given price. Meyer defines supply as "A schedule of the amount of good that would be offered for sale at all possible prices at any one instant of time, or during any one period of time such as a day or a week and so on, in which the conditions of supply remains the same".

4.13.1 Law of Supply

Supply depends upon the price of the commodity. Thus, the Law of Supply is given as, "Other things remaining the same, as the price of a commodity rises, its supply is extended and as the price falls, its supply is contracted".

The law of supply can be again elaborated with the help of previous example. For reference, the table is given below again.

Table 4.3

Unit price (₹/no.)	Demand (Millions/Year)	Supply (Millions/Year)
0.00	200	0
0.10	160	0
0.20	120	40
0.30	80	80
0.40	40	120
0.50	0	160
0.60	0	200
0.70	0	240

At the price ₹ 0.7 per chocolates, as many as 240 million chocolates were offered to sale. But at the low price of ₹ 0.2 per chocolate, the quantity offered for sale was only 40 millions. This shows the law of supply.

The curve (in this example a straight line) is as shown below

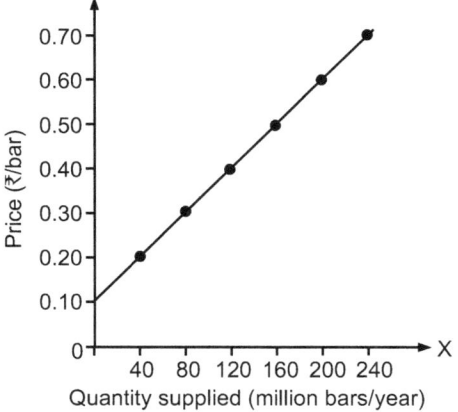

Fig. 4.9

In this diagram, the quantity supplied is shown on X-axis whereas the price is given on Y-axis. Conversely with the demand curve, the supply curve slopes upward from left to right. The price below which the seller refuses to sell is called as the reserve price. If the price falls too much, supply may dry up altogether.

4.14 ELASTICITY OF SUPPLY

'If small rise or fall in the price leads to a large decrease or increase in supply respectively, the supply is called as *elastic supply*'. On the other hand, 'if a large change, in price brings only a small change in the supply, it is called as *inelastic supply*'.

If a slight increase in price is followed by the entry of many new firms having minimum average cost equal to price and the marginal cost does not rise, the supply is said to be perfectly elastic. However, in case the increased output can be obtained only by an infinite increase in price and no new firm is attracted to the industry, the supply is inelastic. Between these two extremities, lies various degrees of Elasticity.

Measurement of Elasticity of Supply

$$\text{Price Elasticity of Supply} = \frac{\text{Proportionate change in amount supplied}}{\text{Proportionate change in price}}$$

$$E = \frac{\text{Change in amount supplied}}{\text{Amount supplied}} \div \frac{\text{Change in price}}{\text{Price}} \qquad \ldots (4.1)$$

Following Fig. gives the method used to calculate the elasticity of supply.

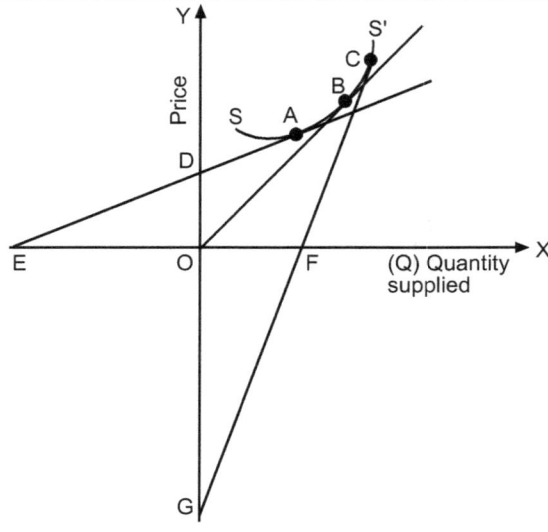

Fig. 4.10

SS' is the supply curve. Consider three points on it A, B and C and draw tangents to the curve through these points. The tangents touches the X-axis at points E and F whereas touches the Y-axis at points D and G. The tangent through point B passes through the origin. The price elasticity of supply at a given point is measured by the distance along a tangent to the horizontal axis divided by the distance along it on the vertical axis.

Thus,

E_s at A is $\dfrac{AE}{AD}$ which is greater than unity since AE is greater than AD.

E_s at B is $\dfrac{BO}{OB}$ which is unity equal to one.

E_s at C is $\dfrac{CF}{CG}$ which is less than unity since CF is greater than CG.

4.15 PRICE DETERMINATION

Market equilibrium is shown by the intersection of the demand curve DD and supply curve SS, at a price ₹ 0.3, at which 80 million chocolates per year are supplied. The Fig. 4.8 shows that there is excess supply at all prices above the equilibrium price of ₹ 0.3. Sellers react to unsold stocks by cutting prices. Only when prices are reduced to the equilibrium price, excess supply will be eliminated.

The equilibrium position is shown by the point E. Conversely at prices below ₹ 0.3, there is excess demand, which bids up the price of chocolate, gradually eliminating excess demand until the equilibrium point E is reached. In equilibrium, buyers and sellers can trade as much as they wish at the equilibrium price and there is no incentive for any further price changes.

Factors Affecting the Supply Curve

1. **Technology :** A supply curve is drawn for given technology. An improvement in technology will shift the supply curve to the right since producers will be willing to supply a larger quantity than previously at each price.

2. A particular supply curve is drawn for a given level of input prices. A reduction in input prices like, lower wages, lower fuel cost etc., will induce firms to supply more output at each price, shifting the supply curve to the right. Higher input prices make production less attractive and shift the supply curve to the left.

3. **Government Regulations :** Government regulations like stringent safety regulations may increase the cost of production and thereby increase in the prices. This will shift the supply curve to the left, reducing quantity supplied at each price.

Shifts in Supply Curve

Given the above constants, a supply curve SS is drawn. (Fig. 4.11). The equilibrium is at point E for the supply quantity Q. Consider that due to the technological advancements, the goods can be produced more for the same input cost.

The supply curve get shifted from SS to S'S' as shown in Fig. 4.11. Due to this shift, the equilibrium point also shifted to the left. But note that, though the equilibrium price has increased, the quantity supplied is decreased.

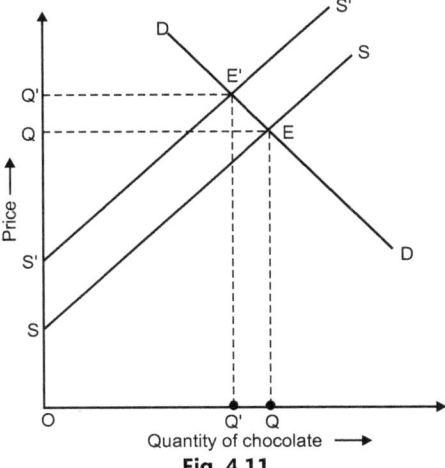

Fig. 4.11

If the supply curve shifts to the right, then the equilibrium points also shifts to the right leading to the increase in quantity supplied but decreasing the equilibrium price. In case of free markets, the prices respond quickly to the changes in demand and supply, whereas, in case of command economy, Government intervenes for the control of the effective prices. Prices are of two types, one is the floor price (minimum price) and other is the ceiling price (maximum price). Ceiling prices are advantageous in case of goods with scarce supply, especially for the necessary food items. Otherwise the poor people suffer due to hike in price.

Consider the demand and supply curves as shown in Fig. 4.12. In normal circumstances, the equilibrium is at point E with the initial price as P_0. But due to the effect of ceiling price P_1, the equilibrium point has to be A which is below the point E. This decreases the supply of the commodity from Q_0 to Q_1.

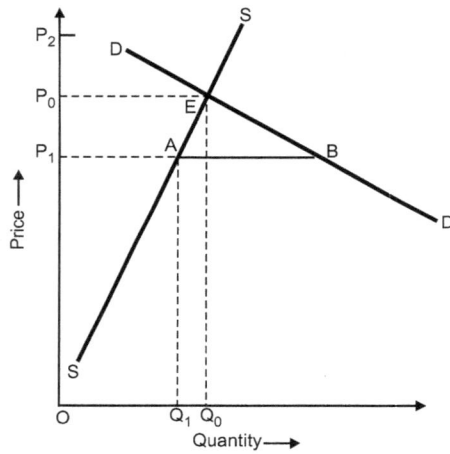

Fig. 4.12

But in this case, the excess demand is available as AB which will create a tendency among the suppliers to reserve this supply for their friends or to take bribes from the society who can afford to buy this supply. This develops the black market. Thus, price ceiling may not help the poor people. To control the black market, the ceiling prices are to be accompanied with rationing by quota organized by Government.

But, now consider another example where the Government decides some minimum wages to help the poor. (Fig. 4.13). In the normal circumstances, the equilibrium point is at E for the Q_0 hours of employment with W_0 wage rate. If Government forces the wage rate to be minimum W_1, the hours of employment reduces from Q_0 to Q_1 that leads the excess supply CB. The effect of this is as some of the workers get benefited from the increase in wages but some will be unemployed.

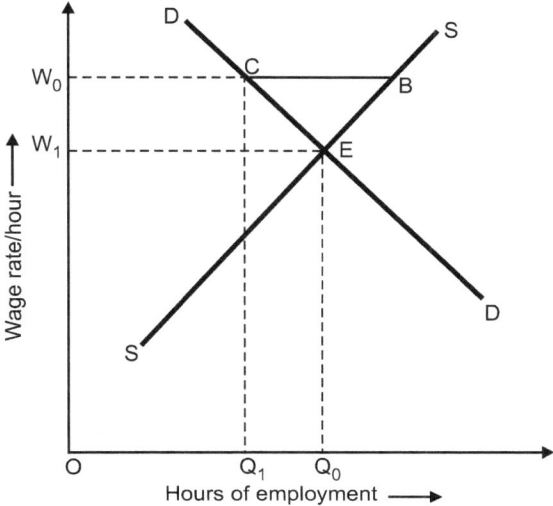

Fig. 4.13

4.16 INDIFFERENCE CURVE ANALYSIS

The various commodities required by the consumer are not on the same scale of preference. Some of them are urgent or important where others may not find that much necessity. The consumer ranks his desire and builds the scale of preference which is guided by the scarcity of the goods, urgency, his taste and the utility. All the time, the consumer is trying to reach the equilibrium, i.e. a position in which he gets maximum satisfaction from the money at his disposal. All the objects of his desire find place on the scale of preference depending upon the equivalence. The consumers scale of references is independent of the prices ruling in the market. He builds up scale of references from the commodities he consumes. On its basis, he knows that one combination of the goods yields him the same satisfaction as another.

On the basis of the scale of preference, we can draw the indifference curves. An indifference curve represents satisfaction of a consumer from two commodities. It is drawn on the assumption that for all possible points on an indifference curve, the total satisfaction or utility remains the same. Hence, the consumer is indifferent as to the combinations lying on an indifference curve. It is also called as *Iso-utility curve*.

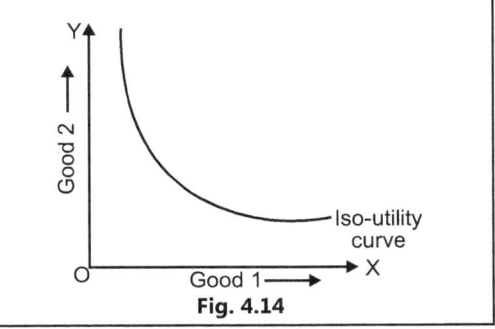

Fig. 4.14

Consider a consumer having ₹ 50/- with him and wants to buy apples and mangoes. He can have various combinations of apples and mangoes that give him the same amount of satisfaction. Thus, the indifference schedule for apples and mangoes are as follows

Table 4.4

Combination	Apples	Mangoes
1	15	1
2	11	2
3	8	3
4	6	4
5	5	5

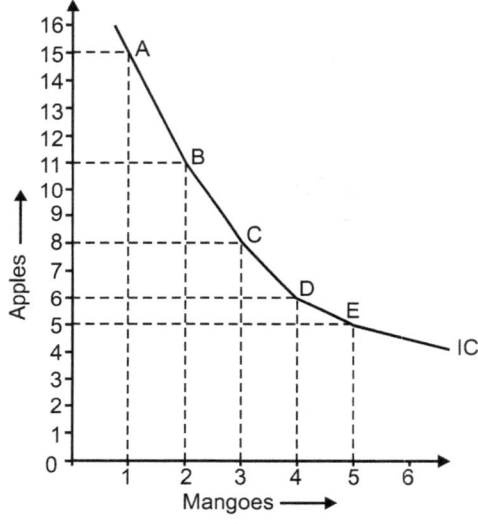

Fig. 4.15

Mangoes are measured along X-axis while apples are measured along Y-axis. For the various combinations of apples and mangoes, points are plotted as A, B, C, D and E. If we join all the points, we get the indifference curve, each point on it showing the same satisfaction or the indifference of the consumer towards the various combinations. We can draw similar indifference curves showing various combinations of apples and mangoes for various amounts to spend, which represent greater and lesser satisfaction as shown below.

In this figure, all the points on IC_5 and IC_4 are preferred to all the points on IC_3 or IC_2 or IC_1. Indifference curve IC_1 represents a lower level of satisfaction than IC_2, IC_3, IC_4 and IC_5. It is to be noted that, we cannot say how much more utility the higher indifference curve represents. That is the aggregate utilities are rankable but not measurable.

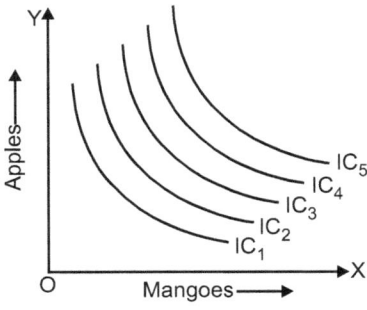

Fig. 4.16

Properties of Indifference Curve

1. **It Slopes Downwards to the Right :** It is because when the consumer decides to have more units of one of the two goods, he will have to reduce the number of the other goods, if he has to remain on the same indifference curve, i.e. if level of satisfaction is to remain the same. Looking at the Fig. 4.14, we find that when the consumer moves from point A to B, he has more mangoes than before, but the number of apples with him falls.

2. **The Curves are Non-Intersecting :** The indifference curves shows higher and higher levels of satisfaction. If these are intersecting, it means that at the point of intersection of the two curves, the consumer gets equal satisfaction which is absurd.

3. **The Curves are Convex at Origin :** This is because, the marginal rates of substitution are different for different goods. If the indifference curve happened to be straight, it indirectly means that the marginal rate of substitution is equal for both the goods which is incorrect. Again, if the curve is concave at origin, it means that the marginal rate of substitution is increasing which is against the normal behaviour of the curve which has to be diminishing.

4.17 CONSUMERS EQUILIBRIUM OR MAXIMUM SATISFACITON

In order to explain the consumer's equilibrium, following assumptions are made

1. The consumer has indifference curves showing his scale of preferences.
2. His income does not change.
3. Prices of goods are fixed.
4. Each unit of commodity is homogeneous and divisible.
5. The consumer tries to maximize his satisfaction.

Earlier we have seen the indifference curve and the price line AM which shows all possible combinations of the two goods that are open to this consumer. Any point not lying on this price line cannot be a possible equilibrium point.

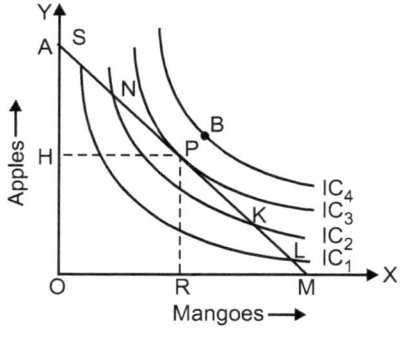

The consumer will be in equilibrium at point P maximizing his satisfaction. This is the point where the price line is tangent to the indifference curve. So he will be buying OR mangoes and OH apples. Any combination other than point P, gives less satisfaction to the consumer.

Fig. 4.17

If the consumer chooses a point say S on the curve IC_1, it gives him less satisfaction than point P. Similarly, points N, K and L gives him less satisfaction which lie on the lower indifference curves. In equilibrium at the point P, the marginal rate of substitution (MRS) of mangoes for apples is equal to the price ratio between the two goods.

MRS of mango and apple = Price ratio

$$= \frac{\text{Price of mango}}{\text{Price of apple}}$$

Now, consider a point B which is on the indifference curve IC_4. As the price line cannot touch this curve, the consumer cannot go for this level of satisfaction though he desires the same.

4.18 INCOME EFFECT

Now, let us study the effect of a change in consumer's income on consumer's equilibrium, relative prices of commodities remaining the same. Obviously, as a result of change a change in income, his satisfaction will either increase or decrease, for he has larger or smaller income to spend.

Now, if the income of the consumer increases, the price line shifts to L_2M_2 and the new point of equilibrium is P_2. This will continue for various indifference curves and price lines and we will get various equilibrium points such as P_1, P_2, P_3 etc. If all these points are joined together, we get a line passing through all these points which is called as Income Consumption Curve (ICC). It shows how the consumption of two goods get affected by the change in income when prices of both goods are given and constant. Most of the goods represent the shape of ICC as shown in the Fig. 4.18.

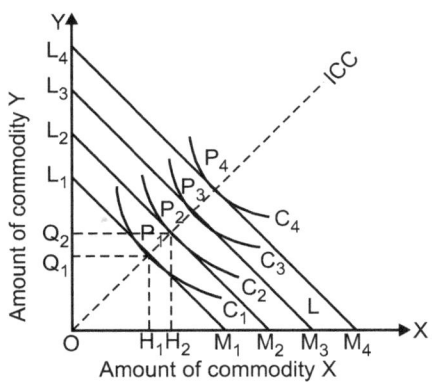

The income effect can be explained as shown in Fig. 4.18. Consider the initial indifference curve C_1 with the budget or price line as L_1M_1. Thus, the equilibrium point is P_1 with OH_1 quantity of commodity X and OQ_1 quantity of commodity Y.

Fig. 4.18 : Income effect

However, when the income of the consumer increases, he tries to purchase better substitute goods. As a result, the ICC tends to bend towards X or Y axis depending upon availability of the substitute goods. This is most commonly seen in case of inferior goods.

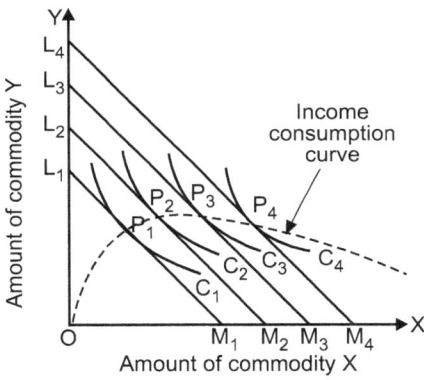

Fig. 4.19 : Income effect : inferior good Y

4.19 SUBSTITUTION EFFECT

Keeping the income of the consumer the same, if the relative prices of the commodities are changed, the effect on the economy is called *as substitution effect*.

It means the change in quantity of a good purchased which is due to the change in relative prices, money income remaining the same.

The substitution effect can be explained very easily with the help of following example.

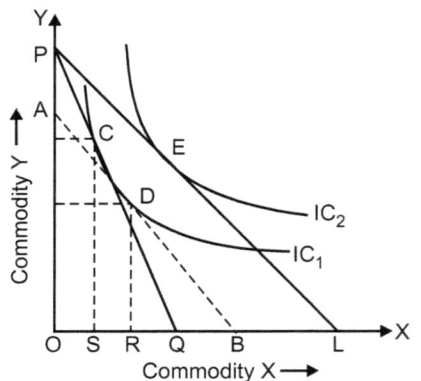

The consumer is in equilibrium at point C where the given price line PQ is tangent to indifference curve IC_1. When the price of X falls, while that of Y remaining the same, the price line will shift to PL. The consumer will now in equilibrium at point E as the line PL is tangent to IC_2. But as IC_2 is for the increase in budget, we have to find out the point of satisfaction on the curve IC_1.

Fig. 4.20 : Substitution effect

This can be done by taking a line AB parallel to PL and tangent to IC_1 as shown in Fig. 4.20. The tangent point D is now the new point of equilibrium giving the same level of satisfaction to the consumer. This shift of the equilibrium point from C to D can be explained as : When the price of good say X, falls, real income of the consumer would increase. In order to find out the change in the quantity of X purchased, due to the change in the relative price of X, the consumer's money income must be reduced by an amount so as to cancel out the gain in real income that results from price decrease.

Referring the above diagram, BL or AP is the amount of money income that should be taken away from the consumer so that the gain in real income which results from the fall in the price of X is decreased. Movement from C to D on the same indifference curve IC_1 is due only to the relative fall in the price of X. At point D, the consumer buys SR more of X than at C as X is now relatively cheaper. This SR is the substitution effect which involves movement from C to D.

4.20 PRICE EFFECT

It studies how a consumer's equilibrium shifts as a result of a change in the price of one of the goods, while his income and the price of other goods remaining the same.

Suppose with a certain fixed income and given market prices of the two goods X and Y represented by the price-income line ML_1, the consumer is in equilibrium at point P_1 in the diagram. Suppose the price of X falls, price of Y remaining the same, new price line becomes ML_2 and the equilibrium point shifts to P_2. If this is continued, we get various points of equilibrium such as P_3, P_4 etc. When all these points are joined together, we get Price Consumption Curve of the consumer for the good X.

This shows the price effect. It shows how the consumption of commodity X changes, as its price changes, the consumer's income and price of Y remaining the same.

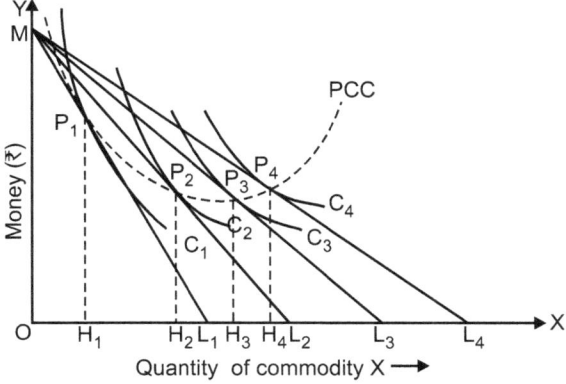

Fig. 4.21 : Price effect

4.21 ELASTICITY OF DEMAND

As per the law of demand, as the price of the commodity changes, the demand also changes. For some commodities, the rate of change of demand is rapid while for others it is slow. A small change in price may lead to a great change in demand (elastic demand) while for others it is unaffected, e.g. though the price of salt increases, the quantity demanded remains the same (inelastic demand). The rate at which the demand for a commodity changes, when its price changes, is known as the Elasticity of Demand.

Thus,

$$\text{Elasticity of demand} = \frac{\text{Proportionate change in amount demanded}}{\text{Proportionate change in price}}$$

$$E = \frac{\text{Change in amount demanded}}{\text{Amount demanded}} \div \frac{\text{Change in price}}{\text{Price}} \qquad \ldots (4.2)$$

The above method of finding the elasticity of demand is called as proportional method. The elasticity of demand can also be described as "The elasticity of demand in market is great or small according to the amount demanded increases much or little for a given fall in price and diminishes much or little for a given rise in price".

The elasticity of demand will be elastic, inelastic (less elastic) or having unit elasticity. There are five cases that describe the elasticity.

1. Perfectly elastic (infinite elasticity)
2. Perfectly inelastic (zero elasticity)

3. Relatively elastic
4. Relatively inelastic
5. Unit elasticity

These can be shown with the help of following graphs :

Perfectly Elastic

This is a horizontal line parallel to the X-axis. It shows that even a small decrease in price can bring unlimited extension of demand.

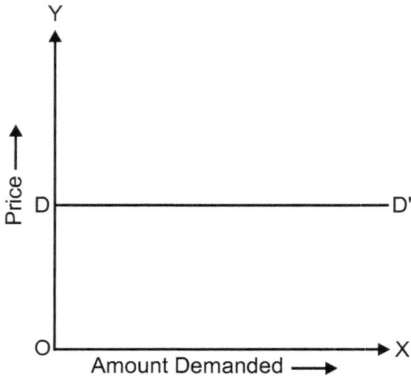

Fig. 4.22 : Infinite elasticity

Perfectly Inelastic

This is a horizontal line parallel to Y-axis indicating that even for large increase in the price, the quantity demanded remains the same. E.g. though the price of salt is increased, it affects a little on the demand or consumption.

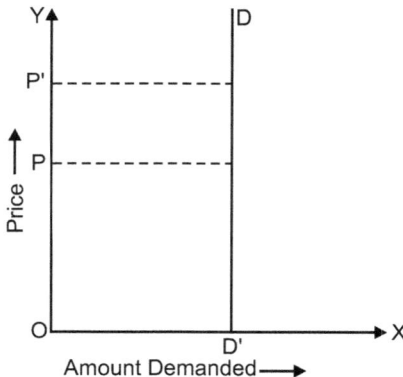

Fig. 4.23 : Zero elasticity

However it can be seen that the perfectly elastic or perfectly inelastic demands are two extremes that are seldomly seen in real life.

Following two Fig. shows the relatively elastic and relatively inelastic demand respectively. In Fig. 4.24, the area OM'P'N', indicating the total revenue earned by the seller is less than OMPN, i.e. the total revenue earned the seller before the price change.

Thus putting the values in equation 4.2, we get the elasticity less than 1 and called as inelastic demand. In Fig. 4.25, OM'P'N' is greater than area OMPN, the elasticity is greater than 1.

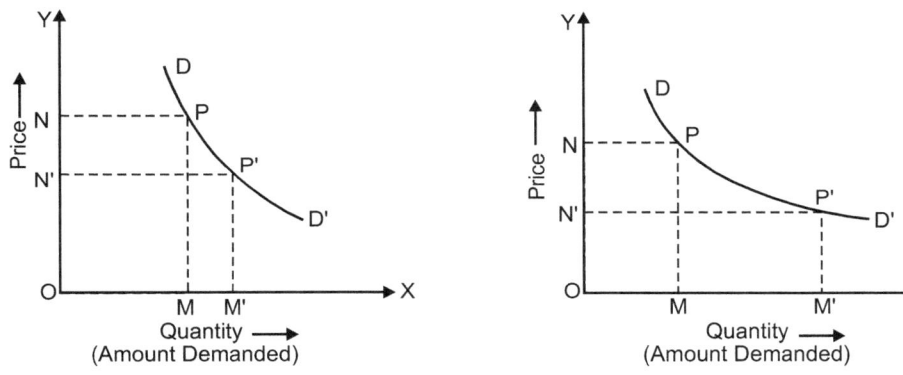

Fig. 4.24 : Low elasticity   Fig. 4.25 : High elasticity

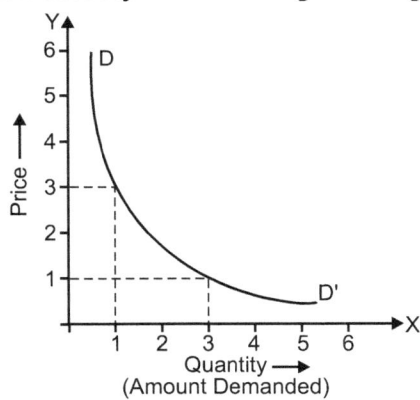

Fig. 4.26 : Unit elasticity

Now, study the graph as shown in Fig. 4.26, where it can be seen that the area of rectangles are equal and hence the elasticity is unity. Such a curve is called an equilateral or rectangular hyperbola. The demand is inelastic when the marginal utility falls rapidly, and elastic when it falls slowly.

4.22 TYPES OF ELASTICITY

1. **Price Elasticity :** It measures responsiveness of potential buyers to changes in price. It is the ratio of per centage change in quantity demanded in response to a per centage change in price. Normally, when we talk about the elasticity, we mean the price elasticity.

2. **Income Elasticity :** It is a measure of responsiveness of potential buyers to change in income. It shows how the quantity demanded will change when the income of the purchaser changes, the price of the commodity remaining the same. Thus, it can be defined as, 'the ratio of the per centage change in the amount spent on the commodity to a per centage change in the consumers income, price of commodity remaining constant'.

   Thus,

   $$\text{Income Elasticity} = \frac{\text{Proportionate change in the quantity purchased}}{\text{Proportionate change in income}}$$

   It is equal to unity when the proportion of income spent on a good remains the same even though income has increased. It will be greater than one when the proportion of income spent on a good increases as income increases while less than one when the proportion of income spent on a good decreases as income increases. Generally speaking, our tendency is to purchase more when the income increases unless it is an inferior good. Normally, since the income effect is positive, income elasticity of demand is also positive. It is zero when there is no change in purchase with the increase in income and it is negative when with the increase in income we purchase less as in case of inferior goods.

3. **Cross Elasticity :** Here, a change in the price of one good causes change in the demand for the another.

   Cross Elasticity of demand for X and Y is =

   $$\frac{\text{Proportionate change in purchases of commodity X}}{\text{Proportionate change in purchases of commodity Y}}$$

   This type of the elasticity arises in case of substitute goods or complimentary goods. In case of complimentary goods decrease in price of X increases the demand for Y and vice versa giving positive cross elasticity while in case of substitute goods (or rival goods), increase in price of X (e.g. tea) increases the demand for Y (e.g. coffee).

Factors Determining the Price Elasticity of Demand

1. Type of good whether it is a conventional and necessary good – inelastic.
2. For luxury items – elastic.

3. The proportion of the expenditure spent on the good with the total expenditure. If it is very small, the demand is inelastic and for more proportion, it is elastic.
4. Availability of the substitutes or the complimentary goods.
5. If the good has various uses, the demand for such a commodity is elastic because when it is cheap it can be used lavishly for many purposes. But when the price becomes high, its use is restricted only to the important purposes.
6. For very cheap or very expensive goods, the demand is inelastic.
7. The demand on the part of poor people is more sensitive to price changes as they have to fit the daily budget within very restricted income.

Measurement of Elasticity

The elasticity of demand can be found by various methods.

1. **Proportional Method**

$$\text{Elasticity of demand} = \frac{\text{Proportionate change in amount demanded}}{\text{Proportionate change in price}}$$

$$E = \frac{\text{Change in amount demanded}}{\text{Amount demanded}} \div \frac{\text{Change in price}}{\text{Price}}$$

2. **Total Outlay Method**

This method was first used by Marshall and it is known as Marshallian method. In this method, the total expenditure on the commodity is calculated with the change in price. If with the decrease in price, the total expenditure (or total outlay) increases, the elasticity of demand is highly elastic. If with the decrease in price, the total expenditure remains the same, the elasticity of demand is unity and when the decrease in price decreases the total expenditure, the elasticity of demand is inelastic. It can be represented with the help of following table.

Table 4.5

Price	Units of Commodity Demanded	Total Expenditure	Elasticity
₹ 10	300	₹ 3000	E > 1
₹ 9	400	₹ 3600	Highly elastic
₹ 8	500	₹ 4000	
₹ 7	600	₹ 4200	E = 1
₹ 6	700	₹ 4200	Elasticity is one
₹ 5	800	₹ 4000	E < 1
₹ 4	900	₹ 3600	Low elasticity or inelastic
₹ 3	1000	₹ 3000	

3. Geometrical Method

This method can be used to find the elasticity of any point on demand curve. Consider a straight demand curve DD' as shown in following Fig. 4.27.

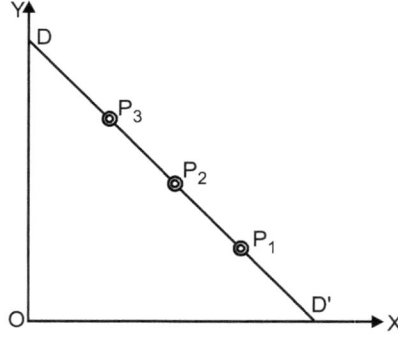

Fig. 4.27

Elasticity is represented by the fraction of distance from D to a point on the curve divided by the distance from the other end to the point. Thus elasticity for the points P_1, P_2 and P_3 are given as, (D'P_1/DP_1), (D'P_2/DP_2) and (D'P_3/DP_3) respectively. If P is the point in the middle of the curve, its elasticity will be one. The elasticity at a lower point of the curve will be less than one and for higher point it is greater than one. This can be depicted with the help of following diagrams.

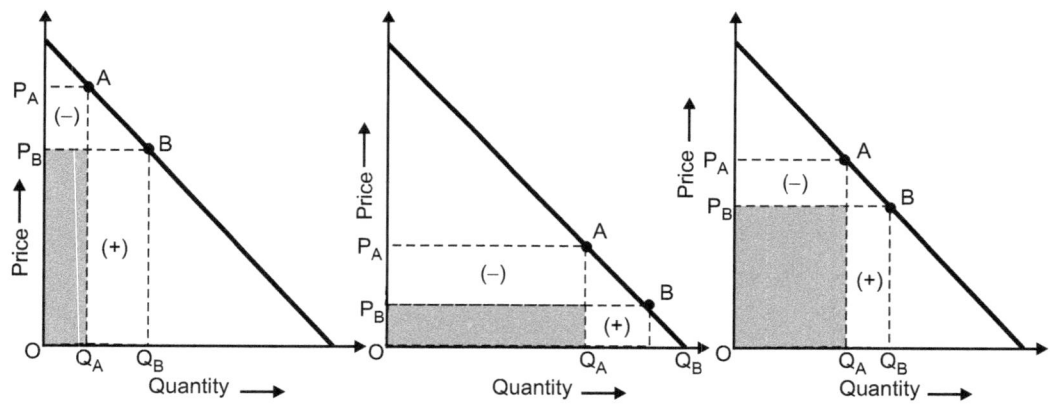

| Case A : Demand is elastic and expenditure increases when price falls | Case B : Demand is inelastic and expenditure falls when price falls | Case C : Demand is unit-elastic and expenditure is unchanged when price falls |

Fig. 4.28

When the price is reduced from P_A to P_B, expenditure changes from OP_AAQ_A to OP_BBQ_B. Thus, expenditure rises when demand is elastic (Case A), falls when demand is inelastic (Case B) and remains unchanged when demand is unit-elastic (Case C). Even if the demand curve is not a straight line, the above formula can be used. A tangent will, however, have to be drawn at the point on the curve where elasticity is to be measured.

4.23 BANK

Bank is a financial intermediary that accepts deposits and channels those deposits into lending activities, directly or indirectly by loan or capital market respectively. A bank links customers having surplus money and having deficit of money.

The history of banking dates back from 9000 BC when Barter system started. It consisted of exchange of goods for goods. Money in the form of grains, cattle, food etc. were used earlier. In 12,500 BC there are evidences which showed use of stone-age obsidian as an exchange media. A more popular banking system was originated by the merchants of the ancient world, who made grain loans to farmers and traders. This began in 2000 BC in Assyria and Babylonia.

Later on, temple was considered the safest place to keep previous belongings. Temple was a solid building constantly attended by sacred characters which may deter thieves. But the fact was, all these remained idle there while others in the trading or in Government needed it. In Babylon at the time of Hammurabi, in 18th century B.C., there are records of loans made by the priests of the temple which was the starting of Banking.

Prior to 17th century, gold and silver were used on commodity money. In the period of Song Dynasty, (between 960 to 1279 AD), bank notes or true paper money was issued nationally.

4.23.1 Banking in India

Banking in India originated by two banks, "Bank of Hindustan" (1770 – 1829) and the General Bank of India (1786) the State Bank of India which is the oldest and largest of all, was originated from Bank of Calcutta in 1806.

Bank of Bengal, Bank of Bombay and Bank of Madras were the three presidency banks which were established under charters from British East India Company. The three banks merged in 1921 to form the 'Imperial Bank of India' which upon India's independence become the State Bank of India in 1955. It acted as quasi-central bank for many years until Reserve Bank of India was established in 1935.

In 1969, the Indian Government nationalized all the major banks to remain under Government ownership. They are run under a structure known as 'Profit Making Public Sector Undertaking' (PSU) and are allowed to compete and operate as commercial banks.

4.23.2 Functions of Bank

Broadly, functions of a bank can be described as Primary functions and secondary functions. These can be shown by following diagram

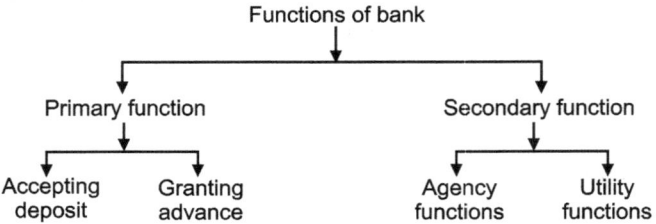

Fig. 4.29

These can be explained briefly as follows

Primary Functions

(a) Accepting deposits in the form of

- **Saving Deposits**
  - To encourage saving habits.
  - Low rate on interest.
  - Withdrawals are allowed subject to certain conditions.
  - Account can be operated singly or jointly.
  - Suitable for salary and wage earned.

- **Fixed Deposits**
  - Lumpsum amount deposited at one time for certain period.
  - Interest rate varies with period of deposit.
  - Withdrawals are not allowed before maturity date.
  - Short term loans can be taken against deposits.

- **Current Deposits**
  - Used for businesses.
  - Withdrawals are freely allowed.
  - No interest is paid.
  - Service charges are charged.
  - Benefit of overdraft facility for account holder.

- **Receiving Deposits**
    - Certain amount is deposited periodically.
    - Withdrawals are permitted after maturity.
    - Higher rate of interest.

(b) Granting Loans and Advances

Bank gives loans or advances to business or any other member of society. The rate charged is higher than that of deposits. The difference in these interest rates is its profit.

The types of loans and advances are

- **Overdraft**
    - Gives conditional sanctioning over and above the deposits in current account against collateral security.
    - Certain amount is sanctioned as overdraft which can be withdrawn within a certain period of time.
    - Interest is charged on actual amount withdrawn.
    - Sanctioned to businessman and firms.

- **Cash Credits**
    - The client is allowed cash credit upto a specific limit fixed in advance.
    - Given to current account holders as well as to others who do not have account in bank against tangible assets and / or guarantees.
    - Separate cash-credit account is maintained.
    - Interest is charged on amount withdrawn in excess of limit.
    - Crash credits have longer period and larger amount of loans than that of overdraft.

- **Loans**
    - Short term or medium term.
    - Repayments of loan is in the form of installments spread over a period of time.
    - Interest is charged on the actual amount sanctioned.
    - Rate is interest are slightly lower than that of overdrafts and cash credits.
    - Loans are secured against tangible assets of company.

- **Discounting of Bill of Exchange**
    - Bank can advance money by discounting or by purchasing bills of exchange (cheques) both domestic and foreign bills.

- Bank pays the bill amount to the drawer or the beneficiary of the bill by deducting usual discount charges.

- On maturity, the bill is presented to the drawee or acceptor of the bill and the amount is collected.

Secondary Functions

These are called as non-banking functions which are further divided into agency functions (when bank acts as an agent of its customers) and utility functions. All these functions are described as follows

(a) Agency Functions

- **Transfer of Funds**

    - Bank transfers funds from one branch to another or from one place to another.

- **Collection of Cheques**

    - To collect the money of cheques of its customers through clearing section.

- **Periodic Payment**

    - Bank makes periodic payments on standing instructions of the client. E.g. electricity bills, rent, corporation taxes etc.

- **Portfolio Management**

    - Purchase and sell of shares and debentures on behalf of clients and accordingly debits or credits the account.

- **Periodic Collection**

    - Collection of salary, pension, divided etc on behalf of client.

- **Other Agency Functions**

    - To act as executors, advisors, trustees and administrators for their clients.
    - To act as representatives of clients to deal with other banks and institutions.

(b) General Utility Functions

- **Issue of Drafts and Letter of Credits**

    - To issue drafts for transferring money from one place to another.
    - To issue letter of credit and travelers cheques.

- **Locker Facility**

    - To provide locker facility for the safe custody of clients valuables.
    - Extra charges are deducted from clients accounts.

- **Underwriting of Shares**
    - The bank underwrites shares and debentures through its merchant banking division.
- **Dealing in Foreign Exchange**
- **Project Reports**
    - To prepare project reports on behalf of its clients.
- **Social Welfare Programmes**
    - To undertake social welfare programmes such as adult literacy programmes, public welfare campaigns etc.
- **Other Utility Functions**
    - To act as referee to financial standing of customers.
    - To collect information of credit-worthiness about clients of its customers.
    - To provide travelers cheque facility.

4.23.3 Reserve Bank of India

Each country has a central Bank to maintain its monetary and financial stability. E.g. European Central Bank (ECB) and Federal Reserve of USA. It is an institution that manages nations currency, money supply and interest rates. This central bank possesses a monopoly on increasing the 'amount of money' and prints nations currency.

In India, Reserve Bank of India (RBI) serves on the Central Bank. Major functions of RBI are as follows

(a) Issue of Bank Notes

RBI has the sole right to issue currency notes except one Rupee notes which are issued by Ministry of Finance. Currency notes issued by the Reserve Bank are declared unlimited legal tender throughout the country. This brings uniformity in notes issue, makes effective state supervision, easier to control and regulate credit in accordance with the requirements in the economy.

(b) Banker to Government

As banker to the Government, RBI manages the banking needs of the Government. It has to maintain and operate the Government's deposit accounts. It collects receipts of funds and makes payment on behalf of the Government. It also represents the Government of India as the member of the International Monetary Fund and the World Bank.

(c) Custodian of Cash Reserves of Commercial Banks

RBI has the custody of the country's reserves of international currency and this enables the RBI to deal with crisis connected with adverse balance of payments position.

(d) Lender of Last Report

RBI takes the commercial banks out of financial difficulties though it might charge a highe rate of interest.

(e) Central Clearance and Accounts Settlement

This is an essential function of the reserve bank. Commercial banks keep their surplus cash reserves deposited with RBI. It is used to settle the claims of each on the other through book keeping entries in the books of the RBI.

(f) Controller of Credit

Credit is controlled by the RBI in accordance with the economic priorities of the Government. It is a key element of nations economic stability.

4.24 TYPES OF BANKS

The banking sector has witnessed a rapid growth in India in the past few decades and has come a long way. The Reserve Bank of India functions as the Central bank and has a control over all the nationalized banks of India.

The various types of banks in India are as follows:

Savings Banks

The savings banks are especially for those who belong to the low income groups or those who are salaried. The savings banks function with the intention to help people culminate the saving habits. The post office is also in a way a saving bank, where people can open recurring accounts to save money.

Commercial Banks

The main function of these types of banks is to give financial services to the entrepreneurs and businesses. It gives financial to the businessmen like providing them with debit cards, banks accounts, short term deposits, etc. with the money deposited by people in such banks. The commercial banks also lend money to these businessmen in the form of secured loans, unsecured loans, credit cards, overdrafts and mortgage loans. It got the tag of a nationalized bank in the year 1969 and hence the various policies regarding the loans, rates of interest, etc are controlled by the Reserve Banks of India.

The further classifications of the commercial banks are private sector banks, public sector banks, regional banks and foreign banks.

Private Sector Banks

These banks are owned and operated by the private institutes and are controlled by the market forces. The greater share of the private sector banks is held by private players and not the government. Some good example of Private sector banks are Kotak Mahindra bank, ICICI Bank, HDFC Bank, Axis Bank, etc.

Public Sector Banks

These type of banks are operated by the Government. Their main focus is to serve the people rather earn profits. State bank of India, Punjab National bank, State bank of Patiala, Allahabad Bank, etc. are the some of the important examples of Public sector bank.

Regional Banks

The regional banks are those banks which can only operate in the areas specified by government of India. These banks are owned by sponsor bank and Sate Government. They came into operation with the objective of providing credit to the agricultural and rural regions and were brought into effect in 1975 by the Reserve Bank of India (RRB) Act . Prathama Bank located in Moradabad, UP is one such example of regional rural bank.

Co-operative Banks

- The co-operative sector is very much useful for rural people and provide finance to farmers, salaried people, small scale industries, etc. These banks are controlled, owned, managed and operated by the cooperative societies and came into existence under Cooperative Societies Act in 1912.

The co-operative banking sector is divided into the following categories

- State co-operative Banks
- Central co-operative banks
- Primary Agriculture Credit Societies

Investment Banks

Investment banks are financial institutions which provide financial assistance to its customers. Their clients include government organizations, individuals or businesses. When there is an acquisition or merger, these customers are provided with necessary support like foreign exchange, foreign trading, marketing, sale of equities, fixed income instruments, etc. These banks, apart from capital raising, also render valuable financial advise to their various kinds of businesses and customers. Banks like the Bank of America, Deutsche Bank, Citi Bank, etc. are some examples of Investment Bank.

Specialized Banks

The main function of specialized banks is to provide unique services to their customers. Some examples of specialized banks are foreign exchange banks, industrial banks, development banks, export import banks, etc. Specialized banks also provide financial support to various kinds of projects and businesses who have to export or import their services or goods.

Central Bank

It is called the banker's bank in our country. The Reserve Bank of India is the central Bank that is fully owned by the Government. It is governed by a central board (headed by a Governor) appointed by the Central Government. It issues guidelines for the functioning of all banks operating within the country. The monetary control is the primary function of a central bank and is also considered as the lender to various commercial banks.

Development Banks/Financial Institutions

There are various banks established to cater the needs of large number of sectors in India. A brief description of some of them is as follows

The Industrial Finance Corporation of India (IFCI) is the first Development Financial Institution in the country to cater to the long-term finance needs of the industrial sector. , IFCI remained solely responsible for implementation of the Government's industrial policy initiatives Until the establishment of ICICI and IDBI. It made a significant contribution to the modernization of Indian industry, export promotion, import substitution, pollution control, energy conservation and generation through commercially viable and market-friendly initiatives. IFCI benefited following sectors

- Agro-based industry (textiles, paper, sugar)
- Service industry (hotels, hospitals)
- Basic industry (iron & steel, fertilizers, basic chemicals, cement)
- Capital & intermediate goods industry (electronics, synthetic fibres, synthetic plastics, miscellaneous chemicals) and Infrastructure (power generation, telecom services)

Industrial Development Bank of India (IDBI) is a Universal that offers personalized banking and financial solutions to its clients in the retail and corporate banking arena through its large network of Branches spread across India and abroad. IDBI Bank is the youngest, new generation, public sector universal bank that rides on a cutting edge core banking Information Technology platform. This enables the Bank to offer personalized banking and financial solutions to its clients

ICICI Bank is India's largest private sector bank that was originally promoted in 1994 by ICICI Limited, an Indian financial institution, and was its wholly-owned subsidiary. ICICI Bank offers a wide range of banking products and financial services to corporate and retail customers through a variety of delivery channels and through its group companies.

National Bank of Agriculture and Rural Development (NABARD) : At the instance of Government of India Reserve Bank of India (RBI), constituted a committee to review the arrangements for institutional credit for agriculture and rural development (CRAFICARD). The Committee felt the need for a new organisational device for providing undivided attention, forceful direction and pointed focus to the credit problems arising out of integrated rural development and recommended the formation of National Bank for Agriculture and Rural Development (NABARD). The Parliament, through Act,61 of 1981, approved the setting up of NABARD. The bank came into existence on 12 July 1982 by transferring the agricultural credit functions of RBI and refinance functions of the then Agricultural Refinance and Development Corporation (ARDC). NABARD runs on the motto to Promote sustainable and equitable agriculture and rural prosperity through effective credit support, related services, institution development and other innovative initiatives. NABARD provides Short, Medium and long Term loans for Eligible schemes for refinance under NFS. It also helps in Institutional Development of Farm Sector and Non Farm Sector, Financial Inclusion, giving Micro Credit , Research and Development. It also provides Core Banking Solution to Co-operative Banks.

Export-Import Bank of India (EXIM Bank) is the premier export finance institution of the country which acts as a catalyst to enhance exports from India, to integrate the country's foreign trade and investment with the overall economic growth. Exim Bank of India is a key player in the promotion of cross border trade and investment. Exim Bank of India has evolved into an institution that plays a major role in partnering Indian industries, particularly the Small and Medium Enterprises through a wide range of products and services offered at all stages of the business cycle, starting from import of technology and export product development to export production, export marketing, pre-shipment and post-shipment and overseas investment.

National Housing Bank is an apex level institution for housing finance. NHB is wholly owned by Reserve Bank of India, which contributes the entire paid-up capital. NHB has been established to achieve following objectives –
- To promote a sound, healthy, viable and cost effective housing finance system to cater to all segments of the population and to integrate the housing finance system with the overall financial system.
- To promote a network of dedicated housing finance institutions to adequately serve various regions and different income groups.
- To augment resources for the sector and channelise them for housing.
- To make housing credit more affordable.
- To regulate the activities of housing finance companies based on regulatory and supervisory authority derived under the Act.
- To encourage augmentation of supply of buildable land and also building materials for housing and to upgrade the housing stock in the country.
- To encourage public agencies to emerge as facilitators and suppliers of serviced land, for housing.

Small Industries Development Bank of India (SIDBI), is the Principal Financial Institution for the Promotion, Financing and Development of the Micro, Small and Medium Enterprise (MSME) sector and for Co-ordination of the functions of the institutions engaged in the promotion and financing or developing industry in the small scale sector and for matters connected therewith or incidental thereto. These MSMEs contribute significantly to the national economy in terms of production, employment and exports and are important pillars of Indian economy as it contributes greatly to the growth of Indian economy.

The **North Eastern Development Finance Corporation Ltd (NEDFi)** is a Public Limited Company that provides financial assistance to micro, small, medium and large enterprises for setting up industrial, infrastructure and agri-allied projects in the North Eastern Region of India and also Microfinance through MFI/NGOs. Besides financing, the Corporation offers Consultancy & Advisory services to the state Governments, private sectors and other agencies.

4.25 BANKING SYSTEM
4.25.1 Working of Banks

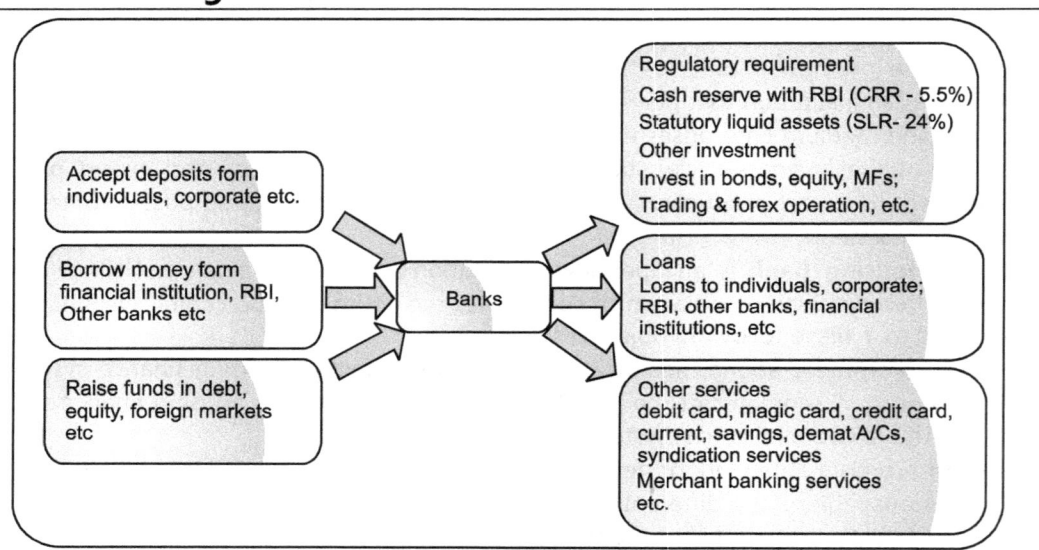

Fig. 4.30

Bank works on the simple principle as under
1. Accept the money in the form of deposits, money borrow, fund raising and savings from its customers and pay an interest of x% on it.
2. Give the money to those who need (e.g. industries, individuals) and charge an interest y% on it.
3. Profit of the bank is (y-x) times the total collections in the bank after deducting the administrative expenses.

This can be depicted with the help of following Fig. 4.30. The core operating income of a bank is interest income (comprises 75-85% in the total income of almost all Indian Banks). Besides interest income, a bank also generates fee-based income in the form of commissions and exchange, income from treasury operations and other income from other banking activities. As banks were assigned a special role in the economic development of the country, RBI has stipulated that a portion of bank lending should be for the development of under-banked and under-privileged sections, which is called the priority sector. Current rules stipulate that domestic banks should lend 40% and the foreign banks should lend 32% of their net credit to the priority sector. On the cost sides, the major items for a bank are interest paid on different types of deposits, bonds issued and borrowings, and provisioning cost for Non-performing Assets (NPAs).

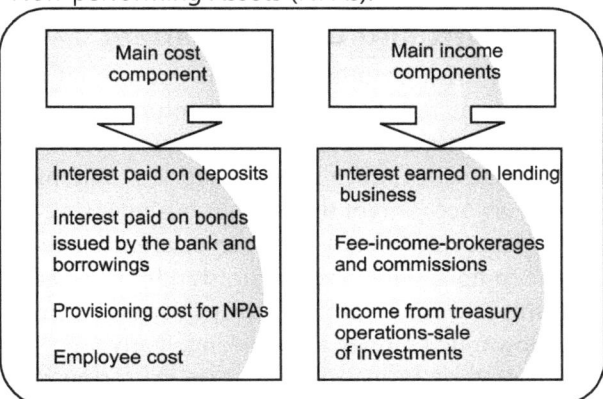

Fig. 4.31

4.25.2 Banking Regulations

The banking industry in India is highly regulated. Few important regulations are mentioned as below

1. A bank has to set aside a certain percentage of total funds to meet regulatory requirements. The primary regulatory ratios are **Cash Reserve Ratio (CRR) and Statutory Liquidity Ratio (SLR).** RBI uses both these instruments to regulate money supply in the economy.
2. **CRR** is the percentage of net total of deposits a bank required to maintain in form of cash with RBI. This is used to control the liquidity in the economy. Higher the CRR, lower is the amount that banks will be able to use for lending activities and vice versa.
3. **SLR** is the minimum percentage of deposits that the bank has to maintain in form of gold, cash and/or other approved securities. This is used to regulate the credit growth in Economy. Higher the SLR, lower is the amount that banks will be able to inject in the economy and vice versa.

4.26 PROFIT AND LOSS ACCOUNT

4.26.1 Definition

It is an account in the books of an organization to which incomes and gains are credited and expenses and losses debited, so as to show the net profit or loss over a given period. In short, it is a financial statement showing a company's net profit or loss in a given period.

Thus, it is a financial statement that summarizes the revenues, costs and expenses incurred during a specific period of time usually a fiscal quarter or year. These records provide information that shows the ability of a company to generate profit by increasing revenue and reducing costs. The P&L statement is also known as a "statement of profit and loss", an "income statement" or an "income and expense statement".

4.26.2 Necessity of Profit and Loss Statement

Sole traders, partnerships and small proprietary companies are not required to prepare and lodge a profit and loss statement with their annual tax return. However, they are very useful in helping you to objectively determine the financial performance of your business. Most accounting software packages will produce a profit and loss statement, but you may need the help of a bookkeeper or an accountant unless your business is very small.

All public companies and large proprietary companies are required by law to prepare a formal financial report that complies with accounting standards for each financial year.

Producing regular profit and loss statements (at least quarterly or monthly) will enable you to Answer the question, "How much money am I making, if any?"

- Compare your projected performance with actual performance;
- Compare your performance against industry benchmarks;
- Use past performance trends to form reasonable forecasts for the future;
- Show your business growth and financial health over time;
- Detect any problems regarding sales, margins and expenses within a reasonable time so adjustments may be made to recoup losses or decrease expenses;
- Provide proof of income if you need a loan or mortgage; and
- Calculate income and expenses when completing and submitting your tax return.

4.26.3 Example of P & L Statement

A **single-step income statement** is one of two commonly used formats for the income statement or profit and loss statement. The single-step format uses only one subtraction to arrive at net income. It is shown as below

Net Income = (Revenue + gains) − (Expenses + Losses)

An extremely condensed income statement in the single-step format would look like this

```
Sample Products Co.
Statement of Profit and Loss
For Three Months Ended June 30, 2014

    Revenues & Gains       Rs. 108,000
    Expenses and Losses    Rs.  90,000
    Net Income             Rs.  18,000
```

The points to be noted are

1. The heading of the income statement conveys critical information. The name of the company appears first, followed by the title "Income Statement."
2. The third line tells the reader the time interval reported on the profit and loss statement. Since income statements can be prepared for any period of time, you must inform the reader of the precise period of time being covered.

The more complex **Multi-Step income statement** takes several steps to find the bottom line as follows

1. Initially the gross profit is calculated.
2. It then calculates operating and, when deducted from the gross profit, yields income from operations.
3. Adding to income from operations is the difference of other revenues and other expenses.
4. When combined with income from operations, this yields income before taxes.
5. The final step is to deduct taxes, which finally produces the net income for the period measured.

A sample income statement in the multi-step format would look like this.

Sample Products Co.
Statement of Profit and Loss
For Three Months Ended June 30, 2014

Revenue and Gains
Sales Revenue	Rs 100,000
Interest revenues	Rs 5,000
Gain on sales of assets	Rs. 3,000
Total revenue & Gains	Rs 108,000

Expenses & Losses
Cost of Goods sold	Rs. 75,000
Commissions office	Rs. 5,000
Office supplies expense	Rs. 3,500
Advertising expense	Rs. 2,000
Interest expense	Rs. 500
Loss from lawsuit	Rs. 1,500
Total expenses & losses	Rs. 90,000

Net Income   Rs. 18,000

4.27 APPRECIATION AND DEPRECIATION OF MONEY

Currency depreciation is the loss of value of a country's currency with respect to one or more foreign reference currencies, typically in a floating exchange rate system.

It is most often used for the unofficial increase of the exchange rate due to market forces, though sometimes it appears interchangeably with devaluation. Its opposite, an increase of value of a currency, is currency appreciation. The **appreciation** of a country's currency refers to an increase in the value of that country's currency.

4.27.1 Some Important Points to Understand

- Exchange rate is the price of foreign currency (USD, Yen, Euro, Pound etc) in terms of domestic currency (rupee) i.e. amount of domestic currency needed to buy one unit of foreign currency.

- Currently price of 1$ = Rs. 61.33, which means 1$ can be purchased in exchange of Rs. 61.33

- Exchange rate tells us the value of domestic currency in relation to one unit of foreign currency. 1$ is worth Rs. 61.33.

- Rupee prices keep fluctuating all the time. Sometimes we need more rupees to buy one unit of foreign currency and sometimes we need fewer rupees to buy one unit of foreign currency.

- This change in rupee price is known as rupee appreciation or depreciation.

- Rupee appreciation is when value of rupee increases (becomes expensive) and fewer rupees can buy one unit of foreign currency. This is also known as strengthening of rupee as now INR is worth more than foreign currency.

- Suppose exchange rate changes to 1$ = Rs. 58, we say rupee has appreciated as 1$ can buy fewer INR.

- Rupee depreciation is when rupee value decreases (becomes less expensive) and more rupees can buy one unit of foreign currency. This is also known as weakening of rupee as now INR worth is less than foreign currency.

- If exchange rate changes to 1$ = Rs. 63, we say rupee has depreciated as 1$ can buy more INR.

- Currency price is always stated in relation to another currency. So when one currency appreciates the other currency depreciates

4.27.2 How Currency Appreciates?

A currency appreciates as a result of increased demand for that currency on world markets its value in the world market increases. This increase in demand can occur for several reasons: When a country's exports are high, the buyers of these exports need its currency to pay for those exports. When the country's central bank increases interest rates, people will want that currency to deposit in the banks to earn that higher interest rate. When employment and per capital income in a country increase, the demand for its goods and services increases, along with demand for that country's currency in the local market. When the demand of the currency is high in foreign exchange market Due to Government borrowing or loosening of fiscal policy.

4.27.3 Causes of Nation's Currency Appreciation or Depreciation

Factors that can cause a nation's currency to appreciate or depreciate include:

1. **Relative Product Prices :** If a country's goods are relatively cheap, foreigners will want to buy those goods. In order to buy those goods, they will need to buy the nation's currency. Countries with the lowest price levels will tend to have the strongest currencies (those currencies will be appreciating).

2. **Monetary Policy :** Countries with expansionary (easy) monetary policies will be increasing the supply of their currencies, which will cause the currency to depreciate. Those countries with restrictive (hard) monetary policies will be decreasing the supply of their currency and the currency should appreciate. Note that exchange rates involve the currencies of two countries. If a nation's central bank is pursuing an expansionary monetary policy while its trading partners are pursuing monetary policies that are even more expansionary, the currency of that nation is expected to appreciate relative to the currencies of its trading partners.

3. **Inflation Rate Differences :** Inflation (deflation) is associated with currency depreciation (appreciation). Suppose the price level increases by 40% in India, while the price levels of its trading partners remain relatively stable, Indian goods will seem very expensive to foreigners, while Indian citizens will increase their purchase of relatively cheap foreign goods. The Indian rupee will depreciate as a result. If the Indian inflation rate is lower than that of its trading partners, Indian rupee is expected to appreciate. Note that exchange rate adjustments permit nations with relatively high inflation rates to maintain trade relations with countries that have low inflation rates.

4. **Income Changes :** Suppose that the income of a major trading partner with the U.S., such as Great Britain, greatly increases, greater domestic income is associated with an increased consumption of imported goods. As British consumers purchase more U.S. goods, the quantity of U.S. dollars demanded will exceed the quantity supplied and the U.S. dollar will appreciate.

4.27.4 Calculating Currency Appreciation or Depreciation

Given 2 exchange rates in terms of a Base Currency and a Quote Currency we can calculate appreciation and depreciation between them using the percentage change calculation. Letting e_1 be the starting rate and e_2 the final rate. The percentage change of the Quote Currency relative to the Base Currency is $((e_1 - e_2)/e_2) * 100$. The percentage change of the Base Currency relative to the Quote Currency is $((e_2 - e_1)/e_1) * 100$. A positive change is appreciation and a negative change is depreciation.

4.27.5 Example Calculation

For example, calculating between USD and INR; if a year ago 1 USD = 42.553 INR and today 1 USD = 54.054 INR we have e1 = 42.553 and e2 = 54.054.

The percentage change of INR relative to USD is $((e1 - e2)/e2) * 100 = ((42.553 - 54.054)/54.054) * 100 = -21.277\%$; Relative to USD, INR Depreciated 21.277%.

The percentage change of USD relative to INR is $((e2 - e1)/e1) * 100 = ((54.054 - 42.553)/42.553) * 100 = 27.027\%$; Relative to INR, USD Appreciated 27.027%.

(USD = U. S. Dollar)

QUESTIONS

1. What is the importance of Economics in case of Civil Engineering field.
2. Define the term Economics and its relevance to the Engineering by giving suitable examples.
3. What are the demand and supply curves ? Explain how the price equilibrium takes place.
4. What are the types of demand ? Explain each of these by giving examples.
5. What is the elasticity of demand ? Describe each one in detail.
6. What is the indifference curve analysis ?

7. Explain the methods of determining the elasticity of demands. What are the elasticity of demand for necessary good and luxury goods ?

8. What are the income effect, price effect and substitution effect ?

9. Give the definitions of Demand and Supply. Also explain the 'Law of Demand'.

10. Draw the supply curve and explain it. Also describe the elasticity of supply.

11. Explain with one example, the 'Law of Diminishing Marginal Utility'.

12. What are the factors that decide the price of a commodity ?

13. What is the importance of Economics in Civil Engineering Construction Field.

14. Give definitions of the following : Cost, Price, Value, Goods, Wants.

15. What are the different law of returns ? Explain any one in brief.

16. Explain demand and supply with suitable example.

17. Discuss the indifference curve technique.

18. What is meant by equilibrium price and equilibrium quantity ? Explain equilibrium price and equilibrium quantity in relation to demand and supply with example.

19. State the factors that decide the price of a commodity. Discuss any three factors in detail.

20. Discuss the following in brief :

    (i) Equilibrium price

    (ii) Equilibrium amount.

21. Explain with suitable example, the law of diminishing marginal utility.

22. What are demand and supply curves ? Describe the elasticity of supply.

23. Define Engineering Economics and explain the importance of it in Civil Engineering.

24. State and explain the Law of Returns.

25. State and explain law of Diminishing Marginal Utility.

26. Explain in brief the different types of tools for Engineering Economics.

27. Define Price and explain its relevance to marketing utility.

28. Explain law of increasing returns. State the factors affecting it.

29. State and explain Law of Supply.
30. Explain in brief Elasticity of Demand.
31. Define :

    (i) Wealth, (ii) Goods, (iii) Wants, (iv) Cost, (v) Price, (vi) Value, (vii) Demand
32. Discuss Applications of Economics to Civil Engineering.
33. What are the function of a Bank ?
34. Give the list of Banks and explain its importance in brief.
35. What is Profit and Loss Account ?
36. Explain Profit and Loss Account by suitable example.
37. What is appreciation and depreciation of money ?
38. Explain appreciation and depreciation with the help of suitable examples.

Unit - V
EXCAVATING AND HAULING EQUIPMENTS

5.1 INTRODUCTION

Excavation is a very preliminary activity of a construction site. We have to excavate earth for many reasons, viz. laying of pipelines, casting of footings, road work, bridge construction, construction of dams, driving tunnels and many more. Also, the site conditions vary widely that decides the type of equipment to be used, e.g. excavation near an existing wall, working in unapproachable areas, etc. To move this excavated soil and place it at a distant place, hauling equipments are required. We come across different kinds of soil and hence, various kinds of excavating and hauling equipments are used. These equipments are parts of 'Earth Moving Equipment' which can be classified as follows

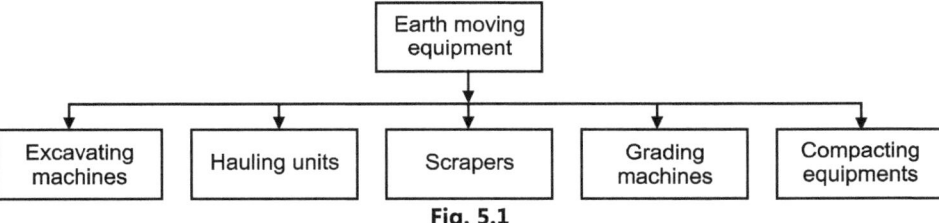

Fig. 5.1

We will study the types of excavating and hauling equipments in this section.

5.2 TYPES OF EXCAVATORS

Excavator is a general term used for the category of equipments, commonly known as 'Shovel family' consists of power shovel, backhoe, dragline and clam shell. Each one performs differently and each one is having different applications. They are available in a wide variety of sizes and capacities and choice is to be made according to the requirement.

5.2.1 Basic Shovel

The structure of basic shovel is as follows

The parts of the basic shovel are explained as below

- **Mounting** It indicates either the crawler mounted or truck mounted shovel. The points of differences between truck mounted and crawler mounted equipments are
    - Crawler mounted equipments are used for the rough terrain as it makes its own path. Truck mounted equipments are used for plain terrain.
    - Crawler mounted excavators are more stable and can be of greater capacity whereas truck mounted excavators are less stable as compared to crawler mounted.

- Travel speed of crawlers is very less as compared to trucks. This point is crucial when the equipments are to be moved from one site to another after finishing the job. It can be improved by keeping the crawlers on trucks and transporting from one place to another.
- Crawlers damage the roads on which it is moving.

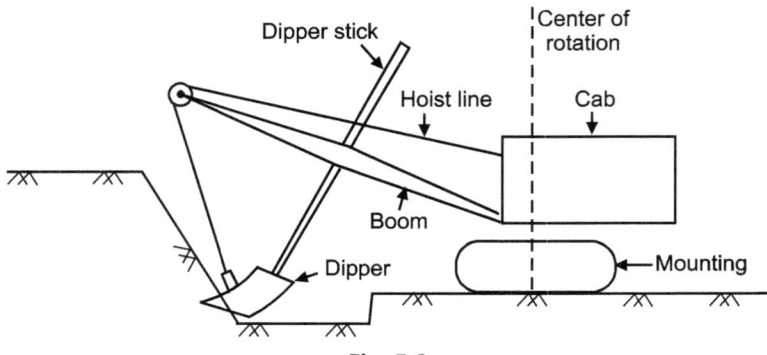

Fig. 5.2

- **Cab :** It is the controlling cabinet where the operator sits and controls the machine
- **Center of Rotation :** The shovel revolves around this imaginary line.
- **Dipper or Bucket :** The excavated soil is collected in the dipper. It has sharp teeth which penetrates in the soil and excavates by loosening the soil.
- **Dipper Stick :** It acts as a spoon which is attached to the dipper.
- **Hoist Line and Boom :** These two controls the movement of dipper and dipper stick

The choice between truck mounted and crawler mounted depend upon the above mentioned facts.

5.2.2 Attachments to Basic Shovel

As discussed in the previous section, following are the attachments to use the basic shovel as power shovel, backhoe, dragline and clamshell.

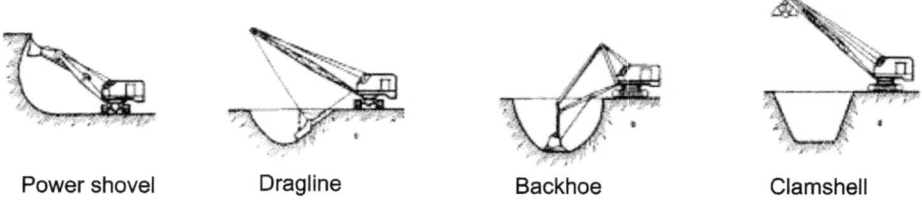

Power shovel   Dragline   Backhoe   Clamshell

Fig. 5.3

As seen in the above Fig. 5.3 keeping the basic shovel as it is, we can convert it as power shovel, dragline, backhoe or clamshell.

5.2.3 Basic Operations of Shovel

The four basic operations that the shovel has to perform are as follows
- **Walking :** It is the movement of machine along the work. It involves travelling of the machine upto the actual site where excavation is to be performed.
- **Swinging :** It is the revolving action of the superstructure of the shovel.
- **Rigging :** This is the working of actual attachment to get the desired effect such as digging, hoisting, etc.
- **Dumping :** This involves dumping of excavated material in the hauling unit such as trucks, wagons etc.

Thus one complete cycle of the shovel involves following activities
1. Loading the bucket with muck by penetrating the teeth in the soil and stripping the surface
2. Swing with the load and adjust over the hauling unit
3. Dump the load in the hauling unit
4. Return to original position for cutting

With normal working conditions where the shovel does not have to 'walk', the time required for each of the above activity is as follows
- Load bucket   :   7-9 sec
- Swing the load :   4-6 sec
- Dump load   :   2-4 sec
- Return swing   :   4-5 sec
- Thus, one cycle time is between 17-24 sec

5.2.4 Shovel Production or Output

The shovel family is basically meant for excavation of earth. Hence, the production of shovel relates to the total volume excavated per hour. It is represented by the following formula

$$\text{Production or Output} = \frac{3600 \times Q \: F \times (AS:D) \times E}{t \times 60 \times \text{volume correction}}$$

Where,
Q = bucket capacity
F = bucket fill factor
AS:D = angle of swing and depth of cut correction
t = cycle time in seconds
E = Efficiency (minutes per hour)
Let us study each factor in detail
- **Bucket Capacity :** The factors that decides the bucket capacity are as follows
  - Depending upon the type of soil used, the bucket capacity can be classified as 'heaped' capacity and 'struck' capacity. The struck capacity is simply a theoretical

capacity based on an envelope covered by the dump body. It can be explained with the help of a load of sand in the bucket which will be at the level of the top. That's the struck capacity and it only really exists in theory as a mathematical calculation. It is shown with the help of following Fig. 5.4.

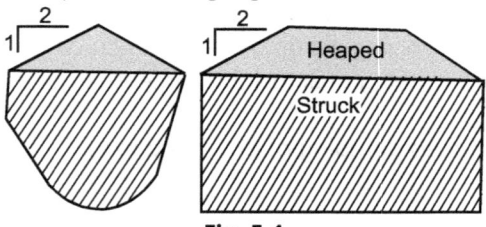

Fig. 5.4

Thus, heaped capacity is basically the struck capacity plus a heaped load at a 2:1 angle (or as per the type of soil) on top up to a point in the centre. As a rule of thumb heaped capacity is generally about 1/3 more than struck. However, the actual heaped load can depend significantly on the material being used and bucket teeth length/configuration, and additionally vary with moisture content/stickiness of the material. This indicated that the capacity of the bucket is typically site and machine specific.

• The size of the bucket decides the capacity of the shovel to excavate. There can be small, medium and large sizes of the buckets that are available in market. Correct size of the bucket is to be chosen as per the requirement and to match the capacity of the loader or truck. If the capacity of the truck is small, then using bucket of big capacity will spill the excavated earth over the trucks. On the other hand, if the truck capacity is large and bucket capacity is very small, more number of cycles are required to fill the truck. In both the cases, production decreases. Ideally, the truck should be filled completely within 3-4 cycles of the shovel.

- **Bucket Fill Factor :** When the operator is excavating the earth, the activities involved are

  Forcing the teeth of buckets in the soils

  Striping the surface of the earth and filling the bucket.

  • To fill the bucket completely, the operator has to repeat this procedure twice or thrice so that the buckets gets filled completely by earth. Still, this may not ensure that the bucket is completely filled with earth. If the capacity (heaped or struck) of the bucket is 'x' cu.m., the actual collection of earth is less than 'x' by some percentage. Thus, the bucket fill factor will be always less than or equal to 1.

- **Depth of Cut :** While filling the bucket with loosened earth, the operator requires striping the soil surface along the face. It can be done under the following conditions

  • If the depth is shallow, the operator requires more than one pass to fill the bucket thus increasing the cycle time. This reduces the production of the shovel.

- If the depth of cut is large, then operator may reduce the teeth penetration in the soil to ensure that the bucket will get filled by earth when it comes up. He can also excavate in two parts: initially, top portion will be excavated and then the remaining bottom portion or the bucket can also be run up the full height allowing excess earth to spill over. In all these options, the cycle time is increased, reducing the production. Thus the optimum depth of cut is that depth which allows the bucket to fill completely while striping the soil surface from bottom to the cut to the top. Optimum depth of cut ranges from 30 to 50% of maximum digging height. Lower percentage is for easy-to-load material such as sand, gravel or loam. Sticky clay or blasted rock which is hard-to-load, requires a greater optimum height in the range of 50% of the maximum digging height value. Common earth would require around 40% of the maximum height.
- The percent of optimum depth of cut can be calculated by dividing the actual depth of cut by the optimum depth for the given material and bucket, then multiplying the result by 100. Thus if the actual depth of cut is 2.5 m and the optimum depth is 3.5 m, the percentage of optimum depth of cut is

$$\frac{2.5}{3.5} \times 100 = 71\%$$

- **Angle of Swing :** It is the angle expressed in degrees between the position of the bucket when it is excavating and the position where it discharges the load. The cycle time includes digging, swinging to the dumping position, dumping and returning back. If the angle of swing increases, the cycle time also increases thus reducing production. Ideal production is based on operating at 90° swing and optimum depth of cut. The conversion factors for different depth of cut and angle of swing are depicted in the following table. It is used to calculate the production by multiplying with the conversion factor.

Percentage of Optimum Depth	Angle of Swing (in Degrees)						
	45	60	75	90	120	150	180
40	0.93	0.89	0.85	0.80	0.72	0.65	0.59
60	1.10	1.03	0.96	0.91	0.81	0.73	0.66
80	1.22	1.12	1.04	0.98	0.86	0.77	0.69
100	1.26	1.16	1.07	1.00	0.88	0.79	0.71
120	1.20	1.11	1.03	0.97	0.86	0.77	0.70
140	1.12	1.04	0.97	0.91	0.81	0.73	0.66
160	1.03	0.96	0.90	0.85	0.75	0.67	0.62

- **Production Efficiency :** As no two projects are alike, the site conditions vary place to place. The efficiency will be optimum if the excavation site is large and open with firm well-drained floor where trucks may be located on either side of the excavator. Also, the ground is uniformly level, the depth of cut is optimum and the haul roads

are not affected by climatic conditions. But actually, the site conditions are not ideal and it affects the production. Thus the factors that affects production efficiency are as follows
- Loading area layout
- Maintenance of equipment
- Haul road conditions
- Haul unit size and number
- Operators efficiency
- Competency of field management

Studies have proved that the actual production time is only 50 to 75% of the available working time. This gives the production efficiency as only 30 to 45 minutes.

- **Swell Factor :** It is the ratio of the weight or volume of loose excavation material to the weight or volume of the same material in place. It can be explained with the help of following Fig. 5.5.

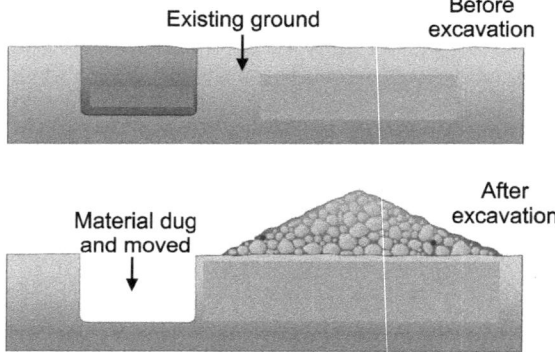

Fig. 5.5

If the marking of 1 m x 1 m is made on the plain ground, and then excavated for 1 m depth, the total volume on ground will be 1 cu.m.

This is the naturally occurring soil and the volume is called as **Bank Measure Volume (BMV)**. When excavated and kept in a heap, the volume becomes 1.25 cu.m. because of loosening of the soil particles which occurs due to swelling. This volume is called as **Loose Measure volume (LMV)** which is swell factor x Bank Measure Volume.

Now, when this soil is used for compaction, the volume decreases which many times becomes less than the BMV. The volume is called as **Compacted Volume** and it depends upon the extent of compaction.

Thus

BMV is less than LMV; LMV = BMV x swell factor

This relation can be depicted with the help of following Fig. 5.6.

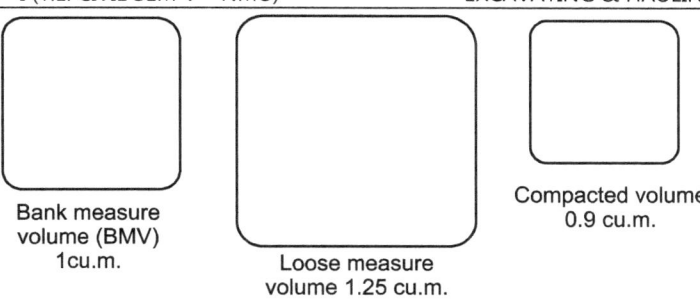

Fig. 5.6

5.3 BACKHOE

This is a very common and popular attachment to the shovel to excavate below natural surface of the ground. It is more commonly used for excavating trenches and pits for basement. One of its advantages over the power shovel is that it can operate in close range work. i.e. it can excavate a trench very near to the compound wall. The basic parts are as shown below.

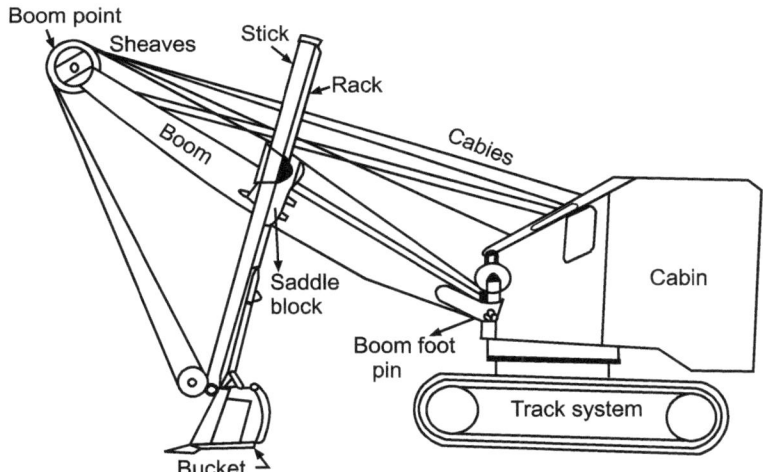

Fig. 5.7 : (Show the Arrows)

The cycle time and factors affecting output of the backhoe are same as that for shovel. Except that it excavates below the ground level, all the other factors are same as power shovel.

5.4 DRAGLINE

The machine is so named because of its digging operation by dragging the bucket. The basic parts are as shown in the Fig. 5.8.

Fig. 5.8

The salient features of the dragline bucket are as follows

- Dragline has a very long boom so that it can reach upto desired distance.
- Because of the long boom crane and the bucket which is the digging tool is loosely attached to the boom through cables, a dragline can dig and dump over longer distances. Hence, it is not necessary to stand near the pit for operation.
- Dragline is used for digging wet materials or underwater construction, river dredging operations, digging trenches and ditches, in quarries and stripping the overburden.

5.4.1 Dragline Operations

- Bucket is lowered in fully dumped position till it rests the ground
- Bucket is dropped using the momentum beyond the radius of the boom
- Hoist cable is slackened slightly and drag pull is applied. This action fills in the earth and bucket takes a horizontal position
- Bucket is hoisted with the help of pull between hoist and drag cable such that bucket has no tendency to spill during the hoist and swing.
- Boom is swung to the position of dumping.
- The load is dumped off.
- Boom is swung back to digging position.

5.5 CLAMSHELL

Another very useful attachment in the shovel family is the clamshell bucket which is attached to a crane boom. The bucket consists of two halves with or without teeth.

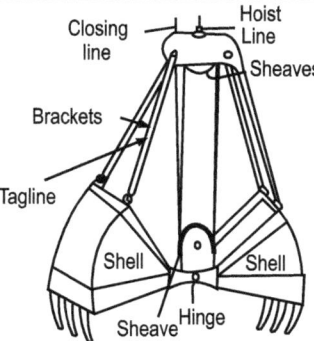

Fig. 5.9

5.5.1 Operations of Clamshell

The operations or cycle of clamshell are as follows
1. Bucket is dropped from a height to required place.
2. The teeth penetrate the soil because of its own weight.
3. While lifting and using the hoist line and tagline, the shells are closed, grabbing soil in it.
4. The exact position of dumping is located by swing action
5. Shell is opened and the soil is dumped in the hauling unit.

5.5.2 Application of Clamshell

- Applied for handling or digging of loose or soft and medium hard material only.
- Also, it is useful when operation is required in a vertical range and placement needs precision. E.g. charging of bins, loading a carrier, building stock piles, etc.
- It has a wide application in removing the wet soil in the trenches by constructing sheet piles on both sides.

5.6 COMPARISION BETWEEN VARIOUS EXCAVATING EQUIPMENTS

After learning different types of excavating equipments, the points of comparison are as follows

Point of Comparison	Shovel	Backhoe	Dragline	Clamshell
Operation in Hard Soil	Good	Good	Average	Poor

Operation in Wet Soil	Poor	Poor	Good	Good
Distance between Footing and Digging	Small	Small	Long	Long
Efficiency in Loading Carrier	Very good	Very good	Moderately good	Precise but slow
Digging Level	At or above foot level	Below footing level	Below footing level	At, above or below footing level
Cycle Time	Shortest	More than shovel	More than backhoe	Longest
Excavation near Existing Structure	Moderately useful	Useful	Not useful	Not useful
Excavation below Footing	Very little	Possible	Possible	possible
Ease of Operation	Easy	easy	Difficult	Difficult

5.7 BULLDOZER

This equipment is used to push or doze the excavated soil. Over a short distance upto 100 m, bulldozer is the cheapest way of moving spoil from one place to another on site. The commonly used bulldozer is as follows

Fig. 5.10

The salient features of bulldozer are as follows
- The earth is pushed in front of blades
- Two or three bulldozers are used in parallel to move the soil and clear the ground.
- Generally bulldozers are crawler mounted.
- Dozers are used for the operations such as
  - Moving earth or rocks for short distances
  - Spreading earth or rock fills
  - Backfilling trenches
  - Making pilot roads through mountains and rocky terrain
  - Clearing the floors, land of timber
- Various types of blades are used for different applications such as stripping, sidehill cuts, ditching, backfilling and spreading operations.

QUESTIONS

1. What are the basic parts of shovel? Draw neatly and name different part. Also, explain the working of each.
2. State the formula for calculating the output of an excavator.
3. What are the factors on which production of power shovel depend upon?
4. What are the factors on which production of backhoe depend upon?
5. How can the output for following projects be improved?
    (a) Highway project
    (b) Dam project
    (c) Projects in hilly area
6. Draw the sketch of following equipments and name its different parts
    (a) Backhoe
    (b) Clamshell
    (c) Dragline
7. List the applications of dragline and clamshell.
8. Compare between dragline and clamshell.
9. What is the swell factor? Explain with suitable example.
10. Explain following term
    (a) Depth of cut
    (b) Angle of swing
    (c) Efficiency
    (d) Bucket Fill Factor

11. Explain the working of Bulldozers.
12. What are the limitations of dozers?
13. Differentiate between power shovel and backhoe.
14. What is the cycle time for following?
    (a) Backhoe
    (b) Clamshell
    (c) Dragline
    (d) Dozer
15. Explain classification of earth moving equipment.

UNIVERSITY QUESTION PAPERS
Construction Management - I
May 2015

Time : 3 Hours **Total Marks : 80**

Attempt any Two out of a, b, c in each Questions.

UNIT - I

1. (a) Explain construction industry and construction team in detail. [8]
   (b) Explain concept of job layout with example. [8]
   (c) State forms of organizations, explain any one in detail. [8]

UNIT - II

2. (a) State comparison between CPM and PERT with examples. [8]
   (b) Explain Bar charts with examples. [8]
   (c) Find the EST, EFT, LST, LFT and total float (TF) for all activities of the network shown in Fig. 1, Also indicate the critical path in the network and determine the earliest project completion time. [8]

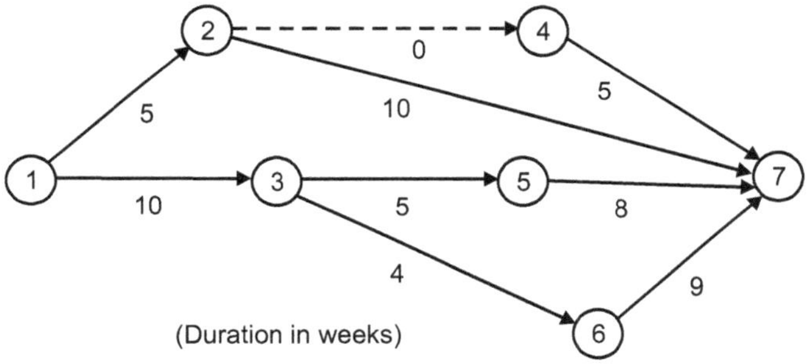

(Duration in weeks)

Fig. 1

UNIT - III

3. (a) Explain cost analysis and cost curve in detail. [8]
   (b) Explain line of balance – concept and uses in detail. [8]
   (c) Explain Updating of network during monitoring in detail. [8]

UNIT - IV

4. (a) Explain bank, its type and functions in detail. [8]
   (b) State concept of Engineering economics and its importance in detail. [8]
   (c) Explain profit and loss account in detail. [8]

UNIT - V

5. (a) State types of Draglines and explain any one with figure. [8]
   (b) Explain power shovels in detail. [8]
   (c) Explain Bulldozers, its types for constructions works. [8]

www.ingramcontent.com/pod-product-compliance
Lightning Source LLC
Chambersburg PA
CBHW062129160426
43191CB00013B/2242

9789351641193